Bite Yu Finga!

Bite Yu Finga!

INNOVATING BELIZEAN CUISINE

Lyra H. Spang

The University of the West Indies Press
Jamaica • Barbados • Trinidad and Tobago

The University of the West Indies Press
7A Gibraltar Hall Road, Mona
Kingston 7, Jamaica
www.uwipress.com

© 2019 by Lyra H. Spang
All rights reserved. Published 2019

A catalogue record of this book is available from the
National Library of Jamaica.

ISBN: 978-976-640-714-8 (paper)
 978-976-640-715-5 (Kindle)
 978-976-640-716-2 (ePub)

Cover photograph (centre): Ms Juanita Teck, member of the Indian Creek Mayan Arts Women's Group, with bowls of callaloo leaves and jippy jappa palm heart. The Indian Creek Mayan Arts Women's Group strives to preserve and teach about the heritage foods of Belizean Maya communities.

Book and cover design by Robert Harris
Set in Scala 10.5/14.5 x 24

The University of the West Indies Press has no responsibility for the persistence or accuracy of URLs for external or third-party Internet websites referred to in this publication and does not guarantee that any content on such websites is, or will remain, accurate or appropriate.

Printed in the United States of America

*This book is dedicated to the memory of my
amazing grandmothers: Laura Gaul Spang,
for showing me with every meal that food is love,
and Nanelle Davis Russ, who gave me unconditional love
and support and taught me to never give up on myself.*

CONTENTS

List of Illustrations / viii

List of Tables / ix

Preface / xi

Acknowledgements / xiii

1 Coconuts and Sauerkraut / 1

2 Pirate, Fisherman, Tour Guide / 12

3 Tourists and the Placencia Foodscape / 47

4 "Foreigners" and "Aliens": Immigration and the Placencia Foodscape / 89

5 Cosmopolitanism, Cultural Capital and Code-Switching / 114

6 Who Is a "Real" Belizean? The Cultural Politics of Gastronationalism / 134

7 Building a Belizean Cuisine / 171

8 The Quest for Cuisine / 214

Afterword by Chef Sean Kuylen / 226

A Short Culinary Glossary / 231

Notes / 237

References / 247

Index / 259

ILLUSTRATIONS

Figure 1. Map of Belize / **2**
Figure 2. Map of Placencia Peninsula and the mainland to the west / **13**
Figure 3. Venn diagram of overlapping cultural and Belizean food categories / **163**
Figure 4. A typical Kriol home in Placencia Village / **175**
Figure 5. Ms Buela's grand-niece grating coconuts to make coconut oil / **177**
Figure 6. Ms Radiance's blackboard, listing her daily lunch specials / **180**
Figure 7. Evening specials board at a Placencia restaurant owned by graduates of the Culinary Institute of America / **194**

TABLES

Table 1.   Population by Cultural Group, Placencia Peninsula / **33**
Table 2.   Terms Commonly Employed by Tourists in Food Interviews / **73**
Table 3.   Food Venues in Placencia Village and on Placencia Peninsula, June 2014 / **81**

PREFACE

IT SEEMED MOMENTOUS THAT AS I WAS COMPLETING final edits on this book, news arrived of Anthony Bourdain's passing. Academia and popular media increasingly overlap in the arena of food, which, like death, is integral to life. Many of my fellow food researchers considered Tony to have matured into a sort of honorary culinary anthropologist as he used his fame to tackle big social and political questions through the lens of food. This is the great power of our daily bread. Through the material substance of our meals we can discover and explore so much about our individual and collective lives on this little planet. This was news a few decades ago, but no longer. Now scores of researchers and culinary professionals from all walks of life embrace the power of food to guide us to a deeper understanding of humanity.

I was incredibly fortunate to grow up on a farm, where not only can you see, touch and taste the food-supply chain right in front of you, but you might even take it in your own hands and wring its neck for supper. No wonder so many cultures ask that we thank the animals and plants that give us our sustenance. There is something inherently sacred about food, the mana without which our bodies fall apart and return to the earth, transformed into nourishment for someone else. Ashes to ashes, dust to dust, food to food. When I die, I want a mango tree planted over my grave. I am sure those mangoes will taste sweet!

The world of food exploration (of which scientific research forms only a small part) is vast, chaotic and as complexly intertwined as the neural pathways of Albert Einstein. I owe a great debt to everyone who has cooked with me, talked food with me, shared a drink or meal, discussed ideas, given suggestions and lent their time to the process that led to this book. I have been inspired by many fellow researchers, friends and family, cooks and chefs, authors and food enthusiasts. To my fellow participants in culinary madness, this book is not big enough to include everyone who is contributing to the project of Belizean and global culinary innovation, but I thank you and invite future conversations, meals and collaborations. Please get in touch!

It was suggested that I call my work an ethnography, not a tale. But this book is not just a collection of intensively gathered and analysed data but also a story, a story of food and its symbolic significance. In the Caribbean and Central America, where this culinary narrative unfolds, food is magical, incredibly powerful and laden with great meaning that goes far beyond calorie count, probiotic levels and micronutrient content. I discovered this as a young child, when my grandmother Laura wrote letters to my brother and me about missing our morning ritual of pouring honey over our cereal.

Food is love. Food is power. Food is identity. Food can heal or harm. Food can feed the soul even more than the body. As you read this book about tourism and cosmopolitanism, globalization and cultural politics, innovation and tradition, identity and cuisine, think about your own culinary narrative. What do you eat? What does it say about who you are? Does your food feed your soul as well as your body? We all have a food tale to tell. I hope you will find this one intriguing.

ACKNOWLEDGEMENTS

THERE ARE SO MANY PEOPLE WITHOUT WHOM THIS book would never have been completed. Many thanks, especially for the wonderful memories of my childhood, to mentors Uncle (and Dr) Michael Steffy and Dr Heather McKillop, who introduced my brother and me to the wonders of anthropology and archaeology at an early age.

A heartfelt thank you to my parents, Tanya Russ and John Spang; my brother (and best friend for life), Nathaniel Spang; my brother-from-another-mother Said Lopez; and my grandparents, aunts, uncles, cousins and entire extended family on both sides, for your unconditional love and support. I would never have reached so high without you. I am one of the fortunate ones. I love you.

Thank you to my friends; *gracias a tod@s mis amig@s*. You have blessed me with a world of love, open doors and comfortable couches. I know ten thousand miles or twenty years will make no difference to you. Without you all, why even bother to write?

Many thanks to my research participants (too many to name individually) in Placencia and across Belize. Many of you are now my friends and colleagues in the tourism industry. Without you this research would never have been possible. You took hours out of your days to answer questions, sort pictures of food and discuss the important points of our delicious and diverse culinary heritage. Thank you for all your wisdom and guidance. *I no di fihget unu!*

A special thank you to Dan Baucco for a wonderful sabbatical in Indiana while finishing my dissertation. Peter Dacoff, your unconditional love and support make every day better and motivated me to get my editing done!

Thank you to my mentor Dr Rick Wilk. You kept me on track and quelled my concerns whenever I started to worry. Thanks for looking out for me! Thanks to Dr Catherine Tucker and Dr Eduardo Brondizio for excellent feedback on my work, and to Dr Anne Pyburn for her inspiring advice both on and off the academic court. To my colleagues who studied with me at Indiana University's Department of Anthropology, thanks for all the good conversations and ideas. Thanks, Dr Lauren Miller Griffith for taking time to read and reread my manuscript; this book is much better for it. Many thanks to Dr Barbara Miller, whose wonderful intro course convinced me to major in anthropology, and all the staff and faculty in the Department of Anthropology at George Washington University.

Many thanks also to the Department of Anthropology at Indiana University, to the Institute of International Education and the Fulbright Foundation for funding my research, and to the National Institute of Culture and History and Institute of Social and Cultural Research in Belize for making my fieldwork possible.

Thanks to Mark Leslie. At the beginning of my research you introduced me to important people I needed to talk to and shared your love of food and Placencia. You departed this world suddenly in November 2017, but your love of good food lives on. Two other research participants have passed away since my work started. Lorraine Cabral and Adrian Vernon, thank you for our conversations and your insights, advice, friendship and warmth. You are sorely missed by me and many others. May you rest in peace.

Last but not least, a sincere thanks to Keith Morrison and the Above Grounds coffee shop, my unofficial Placencia office, where I collected, analysed and wrote up mountains of data over the past six years. Go there for the best coffee in Belize!

1
COCONUTS AND SAUERKRAUT

BELIZE, A SMALL ENGLISH-SPEAKING COUNTRY ON THE CARIBBEAN coast of Central America, is, the advertisements say, "only a two-hour flight" from the continental United States. Not only is it, according to the Belize Tourism Board (BTB), "mother nature's best kept secret"; it is my home and dear to my heart. There are just under four hundred thousand inhabitants in this lightly populated nation. Garifuna, Kriol,[1] Maya, Mestizo and East Indian people mingle with more recent Mennonite, Chinese, North American and Spanish-speaking immigrants, populating six districts from the pine-dotted Maya Mountains plateau and hilly green rainforests to sandy coastal communities such as Placencia Village.

"The Jewel", our green and blue land, is a culturally and ecologically diverse corner of the planet that is experiencing dramatic post-colonial development. Rapidly growing involvement in international tourism, the leap in some areas from zero connectivity to widespread use of communications technology, and a relative lack of industrialization have led anthropologist Anne Sutherland to label Belize "postmodern" (1998). Today controversies over mass cruise-ship tourism, the effects of climate change and a tourism-driven real-estate boom further complicate Belize's path thirty-seven years after independence.

In this book I explore the evolving culinary identities of our country via an ethnography of tourism development and good eating in the small coastal village of Placencia. These pages document the culinary development of a young, culturally diverse nation recently emerged from the grip of European colonialism. The real question at hand is how cuisines have developed and evolved in a country initially created as a colonial logging camp.

Figure 1. Map of Belize – Placencia Peninsula is on the southern coast (http://www.orangesmile.com)

MY POSITIONALITY

Anthropology has progressed from its dubious origins as a discipline centred on "white" people from industrialized countries "objectively" studying the "exotic other" of the far-flung colonies. Since the Burg Wartenstein conference on indigenous anthropology in 1978, "the practice of anthropology in one's native country, society and/or ethnic group" has become commonplace (Fahim and Helmer 1980, 644). Today many post-colonial nations have their own anthropologists who examine issues in their own backyards. In the United States there is even an Association of Indigenous Anthropologists (AAA 2018). As my small part in this effort to bring anthropology home, I felt it was important to investigate food in the tourism context, linking the two biggest sectors in the Belizean economy. Through this research I have been able to explore important questions about culinary development in the post-colonial world.

I cannot claim to be a dispassionate, impartial or disinterested observer. My personal interests in identity and food shaped my questions about how migration and tourism have affected foodways and the development of cuisine in Placencia Village, the fishing-turned-tourism community that was my primary field site. In fact, how we define indigenous anthropology touches directly upon some of the questions in this book as we examine how we Belizeans describe "Belizeanness". How do we decide whether a given individual or group can claim to belong to a certain country, society or ethnic group? A second-generation child of immigrants, a holder of dual citizenship with a Belizean childhood and American relatives, some question my identity and, therefore, whether my work can be labelled as indigenous anthropology. This is not a work of auto-ethnography; my conclusions are drawn from an extensive body of data collected from a wide range of research participants, but I feel it is important for scientists[2] to share their positionality with those who follow their research. These questions of Belizean identity and belonging are fundamental to defining Belizean cuisine, and my personal experiences drive my interest in understanding how we humans categorize ourselves and others through food.

I grew up on an organic cacao farm in Toledo, the southernmost region of Belize, once known as the "forgotten district". My father, a cynical former employee of a US government environmental office, and my mother, a fresh-faced consular officer for the US Consulate General, met in Belize City in the late 1970s. After marriage and a year of disillusioning experiences with the diplomatic service outside Belize, my mother and father returned to the remote coastal property where my father had lived since 1971 and started homesteading. Thanks to this turn of events, I grew up in an intellectually stimulating jungle environment where my parents introduced my brother and me to the joys of organic food, holistic farming systems, moderate socialism and hard work.

Because of my second-generation immigrant status, I occupy the somewhat uncomfortable position of a fence-sitter. As a food researcher this turned out to be an advantage. Growing up exposed to food in different countries and cultures, I gained a heightened awareness of difference and similarity among ingredients, preparation, seasoning and dining etiquette. As a very light-skinned Belizean with blue eyes, I am often taken for a tourist by other Belizeans and by visitors. My identity is regularly questioned by those who doubt that someone of my complexion can really belong. My child-of-immigrants status denies me the full-fledged roots and helpful connections of long-established Belizean families, though my experiences growing up in the jungle and my fluency in our lingua franca, Belizean Kriol, give me credibility with some.

Food was always an important part of my life. For my Pennsylvania German grandmother it equalled love and I picked up on that message quickly. As a child of immigrants, I noticed that my parents did not cook the same food that other people seemed to be eating. While we were chowing down on spaghetti with vegetarian tomato sauce or potato and onion soup, my friends were devouring spicy crab soup and corn tortillas, cassava bread, fish stew made with coconut milk, and other treats. We regularly ate the Belizean staples of beans and rice at home, but our stewed beans did not have salted pigtail in them and my mother's rice never came out Belizean style, with each grain perky as a soldier fresh back from R&R. We did not use coconut oil or milk – essential in many Belizean recipes – because they upset my father's stomach. My father, a natural cook who never measured, would regularly prepare Pennsylvania German dishes such as milk and vinegar–based cucumber salad or pepper cabbage. Served next to a plate of rice and stewed beans, they made a strange *mélange* that reflected the diversity of my food experiences growing up. We visited my grandma in Pennsylvania every year, indulging in homemade pie, scrapple,[3] bratwurst and sauerkraut, then returned to Belize for habanero sauce and serre,[4] tamales and tacos, rice and beans. I became an expert at living the culinary double life, downing pizza and soft pretzels, scrapple and frozen yogurt in the United States, and digging into freshly made flour tortillas, rice cooked in coconut milk, boiled land crabs and sugar cane in Belize.

As a tour guide and founder of Belize's first culinary tour company, I experience first-hand the balancing act between visitor expectations and

Belizean self-representation through food, which I call "culinary code-switching". As Bruner puts it in *Culture on Tour: Ethnographies of Travel*, "Whatever else may be said of my tour guide role, it had the one overwhelming advantage of allowing me to be the closest I could come to studying tourism from an ethnographic perspective, by actually being there on tour" (Bruner 2004, 2). This personal experience with self-commodification and the complex interplay between the "tourist gaze" and the "host gaze" sparked my interest in the way that food is used to maintain, demarcate, replicate and express identity and belonging.

How do culture and country relate through the medium of food? Belize is a young nation arbitrarily created by the forces of colonialism, a culturally heterogeneous society experiencing substantial migration and attuned to the needs of its tourism industry. In this fluid context, who is a real Belizean? Is there such a thing as Belizean cuisine? In 1999 anthropologist Richard Wilk wrote a seminal article on the anthropology of food that asks this question. Titled "Real Belizean Food", it shares his observations on how the concept of Belizean food as a national category has appeared and evolved since Belize's independence in 1981 and the role of external forces in driving its creation and shaping its form and content (Wilk 1999). In this book I build on his initial foray with a detailed ethnographic study that examines the roles of cultural politics, models of national identity, migration and Belize's tourism industry in culinary demarcation, exploration, innovation and change in the former colony. This story of post-colonial culinary development is based on an in-depth case study of Placencia Village, a beautiful beachside community at the tip of Placencia Peninsula, in Stann Creek District, southern Belize. My research reflects the qualities of that particular locale, but its broad message should be familiar and valuable to readers from other countries. It is an ethnography of modern culinary innovation that will intrigue any traveller, food lover or tourism-industry professional. The view is not bad, either.

RESEARCH METHODS

To learn more about our culinary practices I conducted research with tourists, immigrants from both industrialized and developing countries, and born Belizeans.[5] My field research spanned a thirteen-month period from February 2012 to March 2013. My main tools were multiple food-focused pile sorts conducted with Belizean participants of different cultural backgrounds, food-centred oral life histories, interviews with food-business owners, interviews with tourists, and participant observation in a broad range of food-oriented activities, events and venues.

The pile sorts were fundamental to gaining a detailed understanding of how Belizeans think about and categorize the foods available to them within the country, driving many of the conclusions presented in chapter 6. Textual analysis of the interviews allowed deeper understanding of how visitors and Belizeans think and talk about Belizean cultural cuisines and the nationalized category of Belizean food. Data from the interviews explained how tourism both enables and drives culinary experimentation and change in Belize.

Conclusions drawn from analysing the forty gigabytes of data obtained through these methods of inquiry form the backbone of this book, providing substantial on-the-ground investigation and application of the concepts and hypotheses presented by Wilk (1999) and Appadurai (1988) in their seminal articles on national cuisine development. With this book I contribute to the exciting task of answering the questions of how tourism, nationalism, culture and agriculture combine to create new national cuisines in countries that are emerging from the shadows of colonial domination. I join other intrepid culinary researchers such as Clare Sammells (2017), Steffan Igor Iyora-Diaz (2012), Jeffrey Pilcher (1996) and Jane Fajans (2012), some of whom are working in their own countries.

WHAT IS CUISINE, ANYHOW?

Defining cuisine is an essential first step in this research as some descriptions of the term are narrow in focus, rendering them relatively useless in comparative research. I use Farb and Armelagos's approach, which states that there are four components to any cuisine (Farb and Armelagos 1980): (1) the foods that are actually eaten, selected from the wide range of possible edibles in the environment (what is considered edible in one culture might not be in another); (2) the manner of preparing the food (all forms of cooking, preserving, slicing and dicing); (3) the flavour principles (herbs, spices, condiments and so on) used to give often bland staples appeal and character; and finally (4) the rules and regulations governing food distribution and consumption, including etiquette.

A given cuisine is more than just those technical parts, however. Cuisines, whether affiliated with an entire nation (as in French cuisine), a specific geographic region (Southern cuisine) or a culture (Garifuna cuisine), are all cultural products; hence they are dynamic and change over time through the many small choices, decisions and experiments made by human beings in the kitchen. Famed food anthropologist Sidney Mintz (1996, 96) argues that

> a cuisine is not a set of recipes aggregated in a book or a series of particular foods associated with a particular setting ... I think a cuisine requires a population that eats that cuisine with sufficient frequency to consider themselves experts on it. They all believe and care that they believe, that they know what it consists of, how it is made, and how it should taste. In short, a genuine cuisine has common social roots; it is the food of a community – albeit often a very large community.

In other words, cuisine requires consensus. In order for a cuisine to exist, there must be a certain level of social agreement and a sense of passion and expertise regarding the ingredients used, the manner of preparation, the flavour principles and etiquette.

At one time the study of food (except in the form of agricultural production) was considered frivolous and superficial, a topic too mundane for a real scientist or academic to pursue. Today we realize that, to the contrary, its ubiquity makes it of the greatest importance. Food is fundamental. Without it, we die. It is a daily necessity, a material good that (in times of plenty) we consume every day. It is not surprising that as a species we have experimented, innovated, explored and developed coherent systems of food preparation and consumption – that is, cuisines – in every corner of the planet. Through cuisine, we express ourselves, our culture, our religion, our ecosystem, our agricultural practices, our likes and dislikes. Cuisines reflect, create and transcend cultural, religious and political boundaries. Through cuisine we share ourselves with the rest of the world in a real, material and essential manner.

Many studies have been done on cuisine in places such as France that are famous for their food, but few researchers have investigated the evolution of a national cuisine in the countries arbitrarily created through European colonialism. Given that many nations in Africa, South America, Central America, North America, the Caribbean, the Pacific and parts of Asia were invented in this manner, this is no small oversight. Gastronationalism is not the exclusive purview of the developed world.

TOURISM

It is essential to investigate the role of tourism, the world's second-largest industry, in the evolution of these post-colonial cuisines. Tourism both highlights and forms one of the global linkages that tie culinary systems together in a dynamic dance, one with important implications for the future of food. Understanding the response of the host gaze to visitor expectations will go a long way towards explaining the dynamics of culinary landscapes in tourism zones and the evolution of cuisines in countries with important tourism sectors (Moufakkir and Reisinger 2013).

The international tourism industry is a catalyst for the production, maintenance and transformation of identity, fostering cross-cultural comparison, adoption and exchange not only of money and material goods but also of ideas and identities. This peculiar form of global encounter challenges anthropologists to reconsider the nature of the international forces shaping identity, culture, economic development and inequality. Unlike the flows of goods, information and money commonly associated with globalization, the movement of tourists typically involves a high degree of face-to-face interaction. Tourism creates a distinct intercultural space where disparate groups temporarily observe and interact with one another in what is often a carefully structured and power-saturated environment.

What happens to cuisine in this atmosphere? Tourism and tourism-driven training and migration influence food marketing, menu contents and local foodscapes. It changes how people think about their own food. It leads to culinary cosmopolitanism and culinary code-switching as tourism professionals engage with people from different culinary backgrounds. Many studies have been conducted on the expression of cultural and national identity through food, but relatively few have examined the role of tourism in shaping those expressions. This is surprising, as culinary tourism is one of the fastest-growing segments of a booming international tourism market that generates more income than any other global industry (UNWTO 2012).

Those of us interested in how foodways change over time desperately need a better understanding of how tourism drives culinary change and development. Does the scrutiny of the tourist gaze push Belize towards one simple, homogenized cuisine or promote diversity and a proliferation of culinary categories? Is something more happening? Traditions, cultural heritage and self-representation are often strategically deployed in the tourism context. As Ronda Brulotte and Michael Di Giovine eloquently argue in the book *Edible Identities*, food is a powerful arena for the invention of tradition and, as a form of cultural heritage, is particularly evocative and tangible, creating a gustatory link with past generations and eras (Brulotte and Giovine 2014). Together with models of nationalism, moral codes and culinary code-switching, these identity practices play a role in how and to what degree the tourism industry affects the culinary field in Belize.

What is often ignored is the role of the host gaze in interpreting and creating meaning – culinary, cultural and economic – within the tourism environment. Tourism studies are now attempting to redress this wrong by examining how hosts in tourism destinations deploy their own gaze and actively mediate, deflect and appropriate the tourist gaze. As Yuk Wah Chan states in one of the first articles to discuss this important topic, hosts, "rather than being passive objects of the tourist gaze, are in fact active agents casting fierce gazes on the tourists" (Chan 2006, 187).

Examining the way food, identity and tourism interact is particularly exciting in Belize because we are a young nation with a growing international tourism industry, an important agricultural sector, an evolving sense of nationalism in an increasingly cosmopolitan world and a culturally diverse population that is undergoing profound demographic changes. Because of its fast-growing involvement in the industry over the past forty years, Placencia Village offers an ideal spot to observe the workings of national, cultural and local food politics and how tourism and tourism-driven migration influence the foodscape of a tourism zone.

This book expands on discussions of the post-colonial evolution of "national cuisine", initiated by famed Indian anthropologist Arjun Appadurai, by examining in detail the development of national and cultural cuisines in Belize. Appadurai had this to say about his early investigation of the development of a national cuisine in a culturally diverse post-colonial country:

> In the Indian case the cuisine that is emerging today is a national cuisine in which regional cuisines play an important role and the national cuisine does not seek to hide its regional or ethnic roots. . . . The Indian pattern may well provide an early model of what might be expected to occur with increasing frequency and intensity in other societies having complex regional (or cultural) cuisines and recently acquired nationhood, and in which a postindustrial and postcolonial middle class is constructing a particular sort of polyglot culture. (Appadurai 1988, 4)

According to Appadurai, the development of signature "national dishes" and "national cuisines" reflects the power-laden hierarchy of multiple cultural groups coexisting in a heterogeneous society. These power hierarchies affect the development and visibility (both nationally and internationally) of cultural culinary categories as well. In this book I document the processes by which individuals, businesses and institutions select and use food as expressions of cultural and national identity in Belize. I explain how cultural politics and competing models of nationalism determine what foods and whose foods are deemed representative of this young nation, and how economic considerations, moral codes, host gaze and tourist likes and dislikes shape which of those representative ingredients, flavours and dishes appear on restaurant menus.

GASTRONATIONALISM

The interaction between cuisine, culture, citizenship and what makes someone a "real" Belizean is a major theme in this book. Any work on national cuisine development must acknowledge the concept of *gastronationalism*. The term, coined by Michaela DeSoucey, describes the way food is harnessed to express national pride and identity in response to the homogenizing pressures of neo-globalization (2010).[6] Gastronationalism refers to processes of food-based national expression, such as increased awareness and appreciation of local foods, and incites place-based forms of culinary identity expression in response to the global presence of brands such as McDonald's (Wilk 2006). It is a strategic deployment of culinary heritage as national identity on the international stage. Instead of cultural, regional and local foodways being destroyed, they are appropriated as important symbols of national identity.

The Eurocentric Slow Food Movement and Denomination of Origin laws protecting and promoting certain foods across Europe and North America (and, to a much lesser extent, elsewhere) are popular examples of culinary heritage being deployed as a national display of identity and loyalty to a country's farmers and producers.

But what power struggles lie behind the decisions to select this or that aspect of a nation's cultural and culinary heritage and project it to the world through gastronationalism? Brulotte and Di Giovine remind us that ethnic boundaries and cultural heritage are created and constantly being modified through highly contextual dialectic discourses (2014). Cuisines are a product of these processes. Gastronationalism is shaped by the dynamic discourse that guides the expression of cultural heritage in the national culinary arena, and as such its evolution is a messy process, particularly in culturally diverse nations.

To broaden the scope of gastronational research I apply the concept to a non-European, post-colonial context, investigating how cuisine development relates to the construction and evolution of national and ethnic identity in Belize. What is the role of cultural identity and cultural capital in Belizean gastronationalism? Whose foodways are chosen to represent the nation? What do the various framings of food in Belize say about local models of nationalism and Belizean citizenship and their role in cuisine development and identity-based marketing? What place do home cooking and professional cooking practices have in the development of a cuisine? To answer these questions, let us take a trip to a little Belizean beachfront village called Placencia.

2

PIRATE, FISHERMAN, TOUR GUIDE

NOT JUST ANOTHER PARADISE LOST

WHERE TO GO TO ANSWER THESE BURNING QUESTIONS? I needed to be in a Belizean tourism zone, and after ten years of living in landlocked places, the Caribbean Sea of my childhood was calling my name. Placencia Village was perfect for this culinary adventure. Its young and growing tourism industry, its relatively small size and the high number of food businesses catering to locals, visitors and immigrants[1] made it an ideal site for researching cuisine development. Gazing out at the many shades of blue gently lapping the shore, I knew I had come home to the right place. Placencia is nearing the end of an economic transition from fishing to tourism. It has uneven distribution of wealth (a situation which preceded but has been exacerbated by tourism), an influx of wealthier outsiders and tourists, a sometimes controversial real-estate boom, and socio-economic and cultural frictions resulting from its rapid change and growth.

Placencia Village is located in southern Belize at the southernmost tip of a fifteen-mile-long peninsula running parallel to the coast of Stann Creek District, about an hour's drive south of the district capital, Dangriga Town. The communities of Seine Bight, Maya Beach and Riversdale share the peninsula with Placencia Village. Kriol, Garifuna, Mestizo, Maya and Euro–North American people jostle shoulders on this narrow strip of sand. The Kriol people, a product of the British colonial enterprise, claim a mix of European and African ancestries (often accented with a dash of Asian, East Indian or Maya); they founded Placencia Village. The Garifuna, descended from West African and Carib

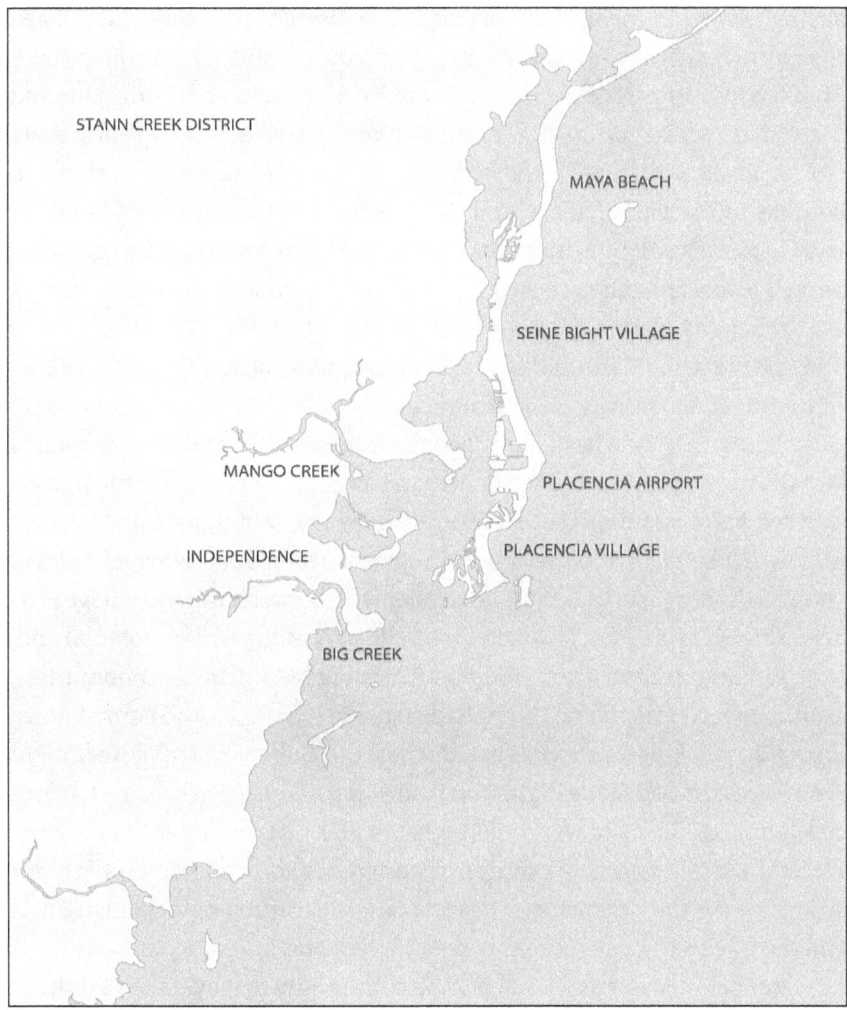

Figure 2. Map of Placencia Peninsula and the mainland to the west (adapted from a map at http://www.chabilmarvillas.com)

people (the original settlers of the Caribbean), founded Seine Bight Village, which is five miles north of Placencia Village on the peninsula. Descendants of the ancient Maya migrate from southern and western Belize to seek work here, alongside recent immigrants from Guatemala and Honduras, many of whom are Mestizo blends whose ancestors were Maya and Spanish conquerors.

North American immigrants and retirees, of whom I will speak in depth in later chapters, are also relative newcomers to the peninsula, most having arrived in the past thirty years. Maya Beach is a recently developed community that arose from a 1960s Canadian real-estate development. Even today, over half of the residents are North American immigrants and part-timers who come down over the winter. Riversdale, a village of around five hundred inhabitants, hosts fisherfolk, some of whom are related to families in Placencia Village and others who immigrated from Honduras and Guatemala, along with a small group of North American immigrants, a small resort and other, mostly Mestizo, residents, some of whom work in nearby banana plantations.

Seine Bight, the Garifuna[2] community five miles north of Placencia Village, was founded in the early nineteenth century; it has a strained relationship with Placencia. In the past, many people from Seine Bight worked at menial jobs in landscaping and construction and as house servants for the lighter-skinned Kriol population of Placencia. Today many of those same jobs are performed by Spanish-speaking immigrants from Guatemala, Honduras and El Salvador (Spang 2013). The relationship between the two villages has been shaped by racism; favouritism on the part of the British colonial and, later, Belizean central governments; and strong but unequal economic ties, leading to resentment and intervillage tension (Carne 2010; Shoman 2010; Spang 2013). This was exacerbated when the Belize central government initially passed over Seine Bight when providing assistance with early tourism development. Some of those old tensions and racism linger today; some Placencia locals and new immigrants are quick to blame Seine Bight for any crime on the peninsula. I discuss Kriol–Garifuna cultural dynamics and the effects of racism in more detail in chapter 6.

Placencia Village was a Kriol fishing community that over the past thirty years has shifted to a more tourism-based economy. This change has had far-reaching effects, causing rampant real-estate speculation, driving up the prices of goods and services and bringing new jobs and wealth into the community, which attracts both Belizeans and immigrants looking for work. The village population, according to the 2010 census, was 1,512 persons, but this number likely fails to account for the many part-time residents who come to work during the high season or who own a vacation home in Placencia (SIB 2013). These changes have also led to an incredible growth of the food-services industry: more than thirty-eight sit-down restaurants, bars, "cool spots"[3] and snack shacks in downtown Placencia Village alone.

The peninsula and Placencia Village were not always so well endowed with dining locations.

I spent months learning the fascinating backstory of this community, which many claim was founded by pirates. The descriptions of day-to-day life found in this chapter are derived from in-depth interviews with dozens of Placencia villagers, including village elders. I have shared only information that was corroborated by many of the interviewees. Where possible I have supported their stories with verifiable historical sources, but much of this daily life was never captured by any newspaper or journal article.

THE EARLY DAYS

The history of Placencia Peninsula is so rich that whole books could be devoted to the pre-European period alone. Prior to European contact, Placencia Peninsula, like the rest of Belize, was inhabited by the Maya, as evidenced by multiple sites where pottery and other artefacts have been found (MacKinnon 1989). When the Spanish arrived, bringing disease and war with them, the Maya peoples abandoned their coastal sites. The ensuing post-contact era is still being explored by archaeologists hoping to learn more.[4] In the seventeenth and eighteenth centuries, English Puritans from Nova Scotia and the Colombian island of Providencia (then a British-controlled area) fished and logged on the peninsula, but those settlements had died out by the 1820s (Belize Specialists 2013; Carne 2010). In the 1850s a Spaniard, Manuel Rodriguez, purportedly named Placencia after his hometown (Carne 2010). The name stuck, rendering the peninsula forever unpronounceable for many a visitor.

Over the past 150 years Placencia Village has been dominated by a Belizean Kriol population of mixed Old World origins that claims ancestry from England, Portugal, Germany, Spain and France, often ignoring or downplaying the African, East Indian, Maya and Miskito Indian contributions. In the late 1800s the village area was resettled by the Garbutt[5] family from Monkey River, then a thriving town of about twenty-five hundred people[6] (Belize Specialists 2013). They were soon followed by Abner Westby (in 1894) and John Eiley, half-brothers from the Crooked Tree Village area in Belize District, about 140 miles north of Placencia (Belize Specialists 2013; Carne 2010). They were the founding patriarchs of what are today two of

Placencia's principal families. Later the Cabrals, a Portuguese family, arrived in the Placencia area from São Paolo, Brazil, and the Leslies, a large family with branches across Belize, moved there from the then British-controlled Honduran island of Roatan (Carne 2010; Spang 2013). Some of these families, including the Leslies, the Cabrals and the Fauxes, established homes on islands near fishing grounds on the barrier reef (Spang 2013). Others were more involved in mainland logging and coastal trading activities.

For more than a hundred years Placencia remained a tiny sleepy fishing village of several hundred people, mostly descendants of the five "founding families" and several other early arrivals. According to members of the families whom I interviewed, in the early 1900s several families living in the village were given a grant from the governor for ten acres "from beach to lagoon", thus obtaining title to significant pieces of property. Some fishing families obtained ninety-nine-year leases from the government for cayes (islands) off the coast and made their permanent homes there. There they were close to the barrier reef, an easy sail to prime fishing grounds and across the Bay of Honduras to the towns of Puerto Cortez, Honduras, and Puerto Barrios, Guatemala, where salt fish and turtle meat could be traded for rice, salt, flour, onions and garlic, canned milk, salted meat, cloth, tools, kerosene for lamps, and other necessary goods. Few people lived full-time on Placencia Peninsula itself. Those who did were involved in coastal trading and the nearby logging industry, which was located chiefly near Monkey River in the pine savannah on the mainland, south, west and north of the peninsula.

FOOD SYSTEMS

During the early days of the Placencia community, the main source of income and food for many was the sea. Conch, lobster, shrimp, a wide variety of fin fish and the prized "sea meat" – turtle and manatee – were protein staples and valued trade items (Spang 2013). Until the early 1970s, fishing boats were almost all locally made dugout canoes called dories, or larger sloops powered by sail. The first outboard motor arrived in Placencia in 1959 and had become ubiquitous by the mid-1970s (Carne 2010).

Until the early 1970s, when the first ice plant was established on the peninsula, surplus fish was salted and dried, and sea-turtle meat was brined in buckets (Carne 2010). Villagers made trips to the nearest town, Monkey

River, and the Stann Creek District capital, Dangriga, to sell and trade goods. These products were also sailed over to Puerto Cortez, Honduras, or Puerto Barrios, Guatemala. Those who lived on the peninsula sent coconut oil, preserved craboo,[7] salt fish and other sea products to Belize City on the passenger boats *Heron H.*, *Maya Prince* and *Chulistro*, and later the *Honduran* (Spang 2013). These freight, mail and passenger craft served as the main transportation for coastal Belize in an era of non-existent or horrendous roads (Hyde 2017). Their routes ran along the coast from Puerto Barrios, Guatemala, in the south all the way to Belize City, from around 1940 into the 1970s, when the *Honduran* sank. By then road access to the south had improved, rendering coastal boat transport obsolete (Carne 2010; Spang 2013).

Apart from the sale of seafood outside the community, sea products had value within the village itself. Even before the arrival of tourism, Placencia always had some degree of class division. More prosperous families with "good names" would make loans to or help out their poorer neighbours. In return, the recipient of aid might provide seafood, free labour or other services to the household as a way of paying back the loan (Spang 2013). Into the 1960s, according to village elders, particularly large catches were sometimes shared among villagers without any exchange of cash. In those circumstances word would go out around the village and people would head down to the harbour with a wash pan to get their portion.

Most of the fishers were male, although exceptions existed (Key 2002; Spang 2013). Women typically kept house, cooked, did laundry, made coconut oil, tended to any livestock (pigs and chicken were common) and raised their children while the men fished. Before the 1970s there was no electricity; cooking took place over an open hearth in the yard next to the house. These gendered work roles were flexible if necessity demanded. Women would go out fishing with their partners if childcare demands did not keep them at home and men would help make coconut oil and participate in other activities around the home and yard when the weather was bad or their help was essential (Key 2002; Spang 2013). Children typically assisted their parents according to gender. Boys were usually tasked with fishing and outdoor chores while girls were expected to help their mothers around the house and with childcare, but those roles were flexible to a degree, particularly if no one of the "right" gender was around to help out.

Most families ate some type of seafood on a daily basis, including the much-prized turtle known locally as "sea meat". Manatee was hunted by harpoon and eaten into the 1950s and later. Older informants describe the animal as containing "four meats" in different parts of its body that were likened to beef, pork, lamb and chicken. Hunting was another way of obtaining animal protein. Iguana, gibnut,[8] armadillo and even the wild peccary[9] could be found in the dense littoral forest of the peninsula of that time. Turtle, iguana and seabird eggs, as well as the roe of some fish, were also prized finds. Local inhabitants boated up the creeks that feed Placencia Lagoon into the heart of the pine savannah to camp and hunt white-tailed and red brocket deer and other game animals (Spang 2013).

Most families kept a few chickens and those who owned a large flock shared the eggs with others. Many families also raised pigs on their mainland property or even out on the cayes. The raising of pigs and chickens coexisted with small-scale gardening. Gardeners used the manure from their livestock to enrich the poor sand of the peninsula, producing hot and sweet peppers, okra, tomatoes, pumpkin, cucumbers, coco yam, cassava and other vegetables. Not everyone gardened and production was not always abundant, so the traditional Placencia diet is characterized by a notable lack of vegetables. Fruits, however, were plentiful. Besides harvesting wild fruits and nuts such as sea grape, coco plum, craboo, coconut and cashew, people grew salt-tolerant mangoes, lemons and limes, and even bananas and plantains, as well as cultivating other fruit trees such as soursop, tamarind, breadfruit and papaya. Sit-down restaurants did not exist until the 1970s, so home cooking was the order of the day.

During World War II, Belizeans across the country were subject to the British colonial government's price controls on staples, some of which were hard to come by, thanks to rationing in England (belizeinfocenter .org 2012). Almost a thousand Belizeans were recruited to work for the war effort (belizeinfocenter.org 2012; Bilgrami 2004). Black tea, tinned milk, salted beef, flour and rice – staples in Kriol communities closely tied to the colonial system – were difficult to find in Belize during that time. Families sourced them from Guatemala and Honduras; they also ate corn grits and local root crops known as "ground foods" instead of rice (Spang 2013). Some Placencia villagers increased their gardening and farming efforts to compensate for the lack of imported foods. Tea drinkers turned to lemongrass, the bark of the provision tree, and lime-leaf tea. The rationing in England put a real strain on some Placencians, who were used to eating rice and flour as daily staples. One of my research participants recalled that the end of the war was a happy time for people who were trying to provide for their families: "We were picking some coconuts di day we heard my mother say, 'Di war is over, di war is over! Thank God!' She had a big family to feed and it was hard for her."

One informant described to me how in the 1950s and 1960s her father raised pigs on the island from which he would launch his boat to net turtles. During school holidays the entire family would move to the caye, where they would sit under the trees chipping and grating coconuts for oil production. The pigs were fed coconut "trash", the half-dried grated coconut meat left over from making the oil. Coconut oil was shipped to Belize City for sale, traded, and used as the principal cooking oil in the Placencia area. Families rendered lard from their pigs and used coconut milk extensively in cooking and baking. Some people made their own vinegar and sourdough yeast starter. These activities were common across all the families, although some kept more chickens or made more coconut oil than others; any excess was either shared in reciprocal exchange relationships within the village or sold. The villagers I interviewed claimed that no one went hungry in Placencia in the old days. According to them, food was shared freely within and among the families, and seafood was abundant for the catching. That is not to say that the village was an idyllic paradise. There were divisions based on skin colour and clear economic class differences between some households; there were families with "good names" who were more highly regarded than others. However, starvation did not seem to be one of the side effects of racialized socio-economic stratification in this small fishing community.

Before the 1940s there were no real shops; trading took place by boat. A Mr Earl[10] from Sittee River Village was expected to arrive once a week with vegetables and ground foods from his farm. He would fish on his return and sell or trade any surplus in his home community (Spang 2013). Trading ties among the Kriol communities of Monkey River, Mango Creek (across the lagoon from Placencia),[11] Sittee River (north of Placencia Peninsula) and Placencia itself were strong. Trade also occurred across cultural lines: Garifuna people from Seine Bight would barter ground foods and plantains that they grew in small farms across the lagoon for extra seafood from Placencia Village fishermen. When a boat arrived in Placencia Village from one of these communities, word would quickly spread and everyone would come down to see what was available and make their purchases. Fishermen would buy white flour, rice and sugar by the sack "across" in Guatemala, at a shop in Monkey River (a thriving town during the first half of the twentieth century) or up the coast in Dangriga, along with other household necessities such as black tea and sweetened condensed milk.

From the 1940s through the early 1970s, another common way to acquire goods was to place an order with Harley's department store in Belize City (now called Brodies and still one of the country's most famous stores) and have it shipped down on the mail and passenger boats. Placencia locals boarded these boats themselves when official government business or urgent health matters required them to travel to the capital of colonial Belize, then the only metropolis in the country.

By the early 1940s Placencia's first small shops, typically run out of people's homes, began to appear. Hermina James was one of the first merchants, selling soap, rice, flour and powdered milk in five-cent quantities and giving "sugarplums"[12] to children who were running errands for their mothers. These stores filled an immediate demand for goods, especially when a household had run out of something, but were more expensive. Most families continued to acquire things in bulk from outside the village when possible.

THE ARCHBISHOP

It is impossible to talk about the early development of Placencia Village as a community without mentioning the Anglican archbishop Edward Arthur Dunn, an influential figure in the village's history. Bishop Dunn, a son of the Anglican bishop of Quebec, had studied in Pembroke College in England and was appointed bishop of Belize in 1917, a post he held in Belize City until 1936, when he was selected to be archbishop of the West Indies (Kempton 2014). Upon his retirement in 1943 he moved to Placencia, where he lived in a large house until his death on 11 January 1955 (Spang 2013).

Upon his arrival in Placencia, Bishop Dunn had a contractor from Belize City build the village's octagonal wooden Anglican church, which still stands today. The church was the centre of religious and educational activity in the community. Dunn also built a small building called "Coronation Hall", which functioned as a youth centre for the village, and he was responsible for getting the first official nurse appointed to the community. Although he had retired, he played an important role in the spiritual life and education of many Placencia villagers. He was, however, a product of his times; stories about him include his unsuccessful efforts to keep dark- and light-skinned people in the community from marrying (Spang 2013).

Bishop Dunn owned a large piece of property in the middle of the village with five houses on it, four of which he rented to outsiders. He raised pigs and instructed the village men on how to build and use a smokehouse in order to produce his own hams. For a time the only radio and telephone on the entire peninsula were located in his house. One of my research participants recalled listening as a child to the coronation of Queen Elizabeth II, at the Bishop's invitation. Bishop Dunn was also responsible for construction of the first section of Placencia's famous sidewalk, from the tip of the peninsula to his home. Some people credit him with being one of the original supporters of the idea of establishing a fishing cooperative in the village. Around 1945 he started a buying club that sold to its members dry goods, cloth and basic hardware items imported from England. Dunn's shop, one of the first in the village, also advanced credit: five dollars for single individuals and ten dollars for married people.

By the 1930s the last fishing families who still lived on the islands had established main residences on the peninsula. Placencia now boasted a nurse, an Anglican priest, a church, a schoolhouse with a government-appointed teacher, and its very own archbishop of the West Indies (retired). For economic reasons many families maintained another house or a camp on a caye close to the fishing grounds. The founding families were large – ten or more children were common – and by the 1970s so much intermarriage had taken place that almost everyone was related. Placencia Village residents also married people from the nearby Kriol communities of Monkey River, Mango Creek and Sittee River.

THE FISHING COOPERATIVE

The Placencia Producers Cooperative was formed in June 1962, only three years after the first outboard motor reached the peninsula (Carne 2010;

Goetze 2009; Key 2002). It would play a fundamental role in the economic development of Placencia Village. It started with ten members, local fishermen who paid five Belize dollars a share to join. The establishment of the cooperative led to the first radical transformation of this small isolated community (Key 2002). Initially the co-op was run out of the village's old community centre. For the first two years they sold lobster to an American dealer who exported it to the United States. Later the Placencia co-op worked out an agreement with the Northern Cooperative in Belize City. Fishermen crewing small wooden fishing sloops would sail and fish their way north along the reef, sell their product to the co-op, buy ice and then sail south to start the process all over again (Spang 2013). Around 1964 the Placencia Producers Cooperative built a small headquarters with proceeds from their sales to Northern Cooperative.

In the very early 1970s the co-op established a direct relationship with Booth Fisheries of Miami, Florida. This business arrangement kicked things into high gear. Booth Fisheries provided the co-op with large freezers, a four-ton ice machine and a blast freezer to preserve seafood, as well as financing (on credit) the construction of an icehouse and processing plant (PPC 1987; Spang 2013). The cooperative brought in electricity, in the form of generators that helped to run their ice-making machine and the blast freezers, which were used to freeze boxes of seafood for export to the United States. Booth Fisheries' boat, the *Red Diamond*, would dock next to the processing facility and load boxes of frozen lobster, then carry them directly to Miami (Spang 2013).

Residents now had easy access to both electricity and ice, at that time rare luxuries in most of Belize. Placencia was one of the first villages in southern Belize to have electrical power, decades before many other communities (some of whom are still waiting to be connected to the grid). In the late 1970s another company, one that purchased both lobster and conch, replaced Booth Fisheries. This change increased income to the fishermen and the village.

Very few women fished commercially, but the cooperative did not wholly exclude them. The blast-freeze processing facility hired twenty-two people, twenty of whom were women. The best-paid jobs – plant manager and assistant manager – were taken by local men, but the income generated by the twenty cleaning and packing jobs helped quite a few of Placencia's households, especially those that did not include a co-op fisherman. The cooperative's general manager was always a man from Belize City with accounting experience.

The cooperative was a key source of credit in the community. It provided loans and advances to fishermen members to buy boats and engines. Ice was obtained on credit, paid back when the fisherman returned to port with his product. In the early 1980s there was also a cooperative store where family members could purchase groceries and other goods on credit. In 1985–86 the cooperative even had its own gas station that issued gasoline on credit to its members (PPC 1987).

Technical cooperation opportunities arranged by the co-op gave some fishermen a chance to travel to the United States and Canada to learn navigation and "more efficient" methods of fishing, such as longlining, drift-netting and trawling. In 1982 the Placencia Producers Cooperative obtained funds from the government-controlled Development Finance Corporation to purchase three shrimp trawlers, more than any other cooperative in the country owned. By 1985 the cooperative was the second most productive of all the fishing co-ops in Belize. The 1970s until the mid-1980s were a time of peak seafood production in Placencia, but the introduction of new fishing methods sowed the seeds of the industry's own demise. The shrimp trawlers were highly destructive of the abundant reef systems in Placencia waters, scraping up the bottom, capturing every sea creature in their way and breaking up coral beds. Longlines and drift-nets also caused substantial damage to fish populations.

Overfishing, a massive backlog of member debt and outright theft of cooperative funds (blamed on outside managers and accountants from Belize City and elsewhere) led to the downfall of the Placencia Producers Cooperative. The fishing grounds, raked clean by the trawlers, nets and longlines, produced less and less every year from 1986 on (Key 2002; PPC 1987). In 1990 the cooperative was forced to shut down its processing facility, eliminating most of the jobs available for women and ceasing direct export of seafood. Once again the co-op began exporting product through the Northern Fishermen's Cooperative. The Placencia Cooperative had already been forced to close its store and cease providing gasoline on credit; members had failed to pay their tabs and the co-op had taken on more and more debt. The family ties between members, including those on the board, made the board hesitant to take forceful measures to persuade delinquent members to pay their bills.

In the early 1990s the cooperative purchased four more trawlers in a joint venture with a Honduran company, Mariscos de Bahia. This increased pressure on the reef area hastened the collapse of regional fishing grounds. Similar overfishing was taking place across the country. In response to what had become a dire environmental emergency, national fishing regulations were introduced, establishing seasons for lobster and conch and some species of fish (Huitric 2005). Despite regulation, production continued to drop throughout the 1990s and into the twenty-first century.

At the same time, tourism was growing (Key 2002). More and more fishermen became tour guides, working in the tourism sector from November to June and fishing commercially during the slow season (Key 2002; Perez 2003). By 2012 very little was being exported through Northern. Most fillet fish, lobster and conch caught in the area were sold to resorts and restaurants on the peninsula; whole fish went to a Jamaican export company, Rainforest Seafoods, located across the lagoon in Mango Creek (Spang 2013). With the collapse of the fisheries and the corruption and loss of funds within the fishing cooperative, despite the establishment of fishing regulations, the Placencia seafood industry declined rapidly.

TOURISM

Doris Leslie, the matriarch of the Leslie family, was a strong-willed and vocal leader of the community, serving as village chairperson for fifteen years. In 1964 she founded Placencia's first overnight accommodations, the still-operating Sea Spray Hotel (Leslie 2007; Sluder 2010). Located right on the beach, her small guesthouse offered simple rooms with a beautiful view.

The Sea Spray did not stand alone for long. Throughout the 1970s and 1980s a number of small locally and foreign-owned resorts, hotels and restaurants came and went. The Cove and Rum Point Inn were the peninsula's first all-inclusive resorts (Hayes 1975). Foreign-owned, they were relatively small and hired all their staff from Seine Bight and Placencia. They were a key source of jobs, training and income for new (male) tour guides and women who worked in the kitchens and hotels (Carne 2010; Key 2002; Spang 2013). The Belizean-owned Sonny's Resort, Ran's Travel Lodge, King Fisher, E-Lee Hotel and Traveler's Inn, as well as several early restaurants such as the Flamboyant Tree, also provided employment for residents of the peninsula (Key 2002).

Until 1984 the only way to reach the village was by boat or in a tiny plane that landed on a dirt airstrip built by a retired doctor for his own use (Carne 2010; Hayes 1975). There was no real road, only a deep sand track, or *picado*, which ran the length of the peninsula. Between 1985 and 1994 there was no airstrip on the peninsula; visitors flew into Mango Creek, where they cruised by motorized dory to their final destination. Guests were taken fishing and snorkelling by local fishermen (Key 2002).

Visitors to Placencia before independence (in 1981) included British soldiers, government officials on routine visits, sailors making their way down the Caribbean coast of Central America, hippie backpackers from the North American counterculture and other adventurous travellers who came to stay in the several tiny hotels and resorts operating in this remote corner of the world (Key 2002). Some Placencia locals did not like the hippies, claiming that they spent little, stole coconuts, smoked weed and did not bathe or wash their clothes like normal people. Others found their liberal outlook an intriguing alternative to the conservative community in which they lived. For a time, acid and Pink Floyd found a niche among a few Placencia youth (Hayes 1975; Spang 2013).

At the end of the 1970s the commander of the British troops stationed in Belize approached Doris Leslie and asked if she would operate a rest-and-recreation site for the soldiers on her property in the village. The troops were already visiting Placencia but the space they were renting from another villager was not big enough. She agreed, and the Sea Spray Hotel, with its beautiful beach and relaxing atmosphere, became a destination for young British soldiers who needed a break from the deep jungle along the contested border with Guatemala. This was the first regular tourism to take place in Placencia (Leslie 2007). The villagers now had regular contact with outsiders who were in full-on vacation mode. A few Kriol women from the peninsula made money selling them food, and some had children with or married soldiers and left for Great Britain (Spang 2013). A few British soldiers got kicked out of local bars (Connolly 2013, 4; Spang 2013). A few Kriol men made money taking them out fishing on the islands. Friendships were forged and income was generated. Tourism had arrived. Ms Doris received an Order of the British Empire from Queen Elizabeth for her service to the Crown.

INDEPENDENCE, HURRICANE IRIS AND BEYOND: 1981–2018

The past twenty-five years have been a period of rapid change for Placencia Village. Growth of the tourism sector has transformed the peninsula. The changes include the establishment of a series of resorts along the road leading onto the peninsula and more and more restaurants opening in the village and across the peninsula. Tourism has caused a boom in real-estate speculation and the construction industry, especially after Hurricane Iris, which destroyed more than 50 per cent of the buildings on the peninsula in 2001. In the wake of this devastation, some local landowners who did not have insurance on their wooden buildings were forced to sell property in order to rebuild their homes and businesses (Spang 2013). The first real-estate companies, including locally owned businesses such as Yearwood Properties and Ocean Motion Real Estate and, later on, foreign franchises (ReMax and Sotheby's, among others), were quick to respond to this opportunity and open offices in Placencia.

TOURISM POLICY

The initial slow growth of tourism in Placencia was a reflection of colonial policy, which was focused on resource extraction and did not promote tourism as an industry. While home rule was established in 1964, the British still controlled many aspects of the nation. With Belize's independence on 21 September 1981, George Cadle Price, leader of the People's United Party and former premier of Belize under home rule, became the country's first prime minister. A moderate socialist, he was famously against tourism, claiming that it would lead to "a nation of waiters and busboys". He focused the development efforts of his new government on farming, fishing and attaining some degree of self-sufficiency as a newly independent nation (belizeinfocenter.org 2012).

In 1984 the government changed and Manuel Esquivel, leader of the United Democratic Party, replaced Price as prime minister (belizeinfocenter.org 2012). The new government embraced tourism, designated a minister in charge of the sector and began promoting Belize internationally as a destination (belizeinfocenter.org 2012). The United Democratic Party lost the next election but returned to power in 1989. It continued to promote and professionalize tourism, establishing the BTB in 1996 as part of a new Ministry of Tourism and approving legislation that required training and licensing for tour guides and tour operators (belizeinfocenter.org 2012; Sluder 2010). By this time Placencia's fishing cooperative was struggling, and more and more people turned to tourism as a source of income (Key 2002).

At the same time that the United Democratic Party was promoting tourism, Placencia got a (somewhat) all-weather dirt road that connected the peninsula to the Southern Highway (Key 2002). Public "bus"[13] service between the village and Dangriga, the district capital, began in 1985 (Spang 2013). Visitors could come by boat, bus or plane to Mango Creek (and directly to Placencia after 1994), and produce and other goods could more easily and regularly reach the hotels and restaurants that provided services to tourists in the village (Carne 2010). With improved transportation and government support, the local tourism industry began to expand rapidly. The growing tourism-focused economy eventually eclipsed fishing in the late 1990s, especially as the fisheries were declining in the face of trawler damage (Key 2002).

For fishermen who grew up in the 1960s and 1970s, the new tourism industry provided an opportunity to put their considerable sea knowledge to use as tour guides, captaining boatloads of tourists instead of fish (belizeinfocenter.org2012). Sutherland and Huitric both describe this same phenomenon happening in northern coastal Belize (Huitric 2005; Sutherland 1998). Fishing tours combine both activities, and some of Belize's most famous fishing guides began their trade in Placencia in the late 1970s and early 1980s, taking advantage of the world-class fly fishing, drop fishing and trolling available in the area (belizeinfocenter.org 2012). Before 1990, only five or ten men worked as full-time guides at resorts such as Rum Point and Sonny's. Many visitors would go fishing or snorkelling with a local man who fished commercially as his main occupation (Perez 2003). At the Sea Spray, Doris Leslie's sons and grandson engaged in fly fishing and other marine guiding activities along with commercial fishing as a source of income.

Tour guiding grew as a profession in Placencia with the establishment in 1990 of the tour-guide and tour-operator legislation. All new guides were required to go through training, and those who wished to sell tours were required to apply for a tour-operator licence from the BTB (belizeinfocenter .org 2012; Sluder 2010). The first training course at Sonny's Resort in 1990 certified new Placencia guides, while a grandfather clause allowed guides who were already working to continue their careers. After that a number of local Belizeans opened small tourism operations on the sidewalk that runs the length of the village (many have since moved to the main road), selling mainly sea-focused tours.

This alternative livelihood proved increasingly attractive as local fisheries continued to decline (Key 2002). Fishermen turned to tour guiding as a source of income for at least part of the year (Perez 2003). Over time, guiding has become the main source of income for more than a hundred local men, with fishing providing a secondary but important source of funds during the slow season (Perez 2003). Today more than thirty women on the peninsula have tour-guide licences, slowly helping to change what remains a male-dominated segment of the tourism industry. This pattern of fishing in the slow season and guiding in the high season has led to an ironic conundrum: the high tourism season generates the greatest demand for seafood at the resorts and restaurants on the peninsula, but less seafood is available because most fishermen are busy guiding (Huitric 2005).

NATURAL DISASTER

No account of change on Placencia Peninsula would be complete without reference to hurricanes, which are a seasonal threat to the entire Belizean coast. Older residents of the village talk about where they were when Hurricane Hattie devastated Belize City in 1961. While Placencia was not strongly affected, the sea was dangerous that day, and the destruction of the city had national repercussions when the government attempted (for the most part unsuccessfully) to relocate people from coastal communities inland. Silk Grass, Georgetown and Independence, all villages located on the mainland near Placencia Peninsula, were established during this time. Today, Silk Grass maintains ties with Placencia Village and Georgetown houses extended families from Seine Bight.

Most important in recent memory is Hurricane Iris, a category 4 storm that radically transformed the face of the peninsula on 8 October 2001. This storm is so significant in recent peninsula history that local time is divided into "before hurricane" and "after hurricane" (Spang 2013). It was the most powerful storm to make landfall in Belize since Hurricane

Hattie flattened Belize City. Hurricane Iris hit Placencia Peninsula with 145-mile-per-hour winds and produced small, highly destructive tornados that, along with the twelve-foot storm surge, destroyed close to 90 per cent of the buildings in Placencia Village (CDRA 2001; Musa 2001). The few structures left standing could be counted on one's fingers. Some homes were swept into the lagoon and one house floated out to sea (Spang 2013). Most of the peninsula's vegetation was destroyed (CDRA 2001); littoral forest was flattened and huge old mango, cashew and coconut trees, planted at the turn of the century, were scattered like toothpicks across the community. Those trees that remained standing were completely leafless, denuding the peninsula and rendering the nearby islands and the village hot and barren (San Pedro Sun 2001).

More than thirteen thousand people were left homeless in Stann Creek and Toledo Districts (Red Cross 2001); this figure included most Placencia residents. Twenty-four people died, although none from the peninsula (Red Cross 2001; San Pedro Sun 2001). Almost immediately after the hurricane passed, looting took place on the peninsula, with neighbours stealing from neighbours and people from surrounding communities entering the devastated villages and loading pickup trucks with household goods (Spang 2013). The Belize Defence Force was called in to keep looting down but was not particularly effective. Several local restaurants reopened right after the storm and started offering a limited menu, also serving as headquarters for relief workers (Spang 2013; San Pedro Sun 2001). Villagers returning from shelter inland (mostly men in the first several weeks) walked dazed about the peninsula, overwhelmed by loss. The pipe that ran water across the lagoon had been destroyed and no electricity was available. Little shade was to be found (San Pedro Sun 2001). All that was left was a few bare, twisted trees and hot sand littered with the wreckage of the community (San Pedro Sun 2001). About a week after the disaster, the government came in with bulldozers to clear the debris and reconstruction efforts began.

The storm hit only six weeks before the beginning of the tourism high season, the end of November. Placencia Village bore the brunt of the damage and for that reason few locally owned businesses were able to recover in time to participate in that year's season. Up the peninsula, the foreign-owned all-inclusive resort Roberts Grove had suffered minimal damage and opened for business, as did the Nautical Inn near Seine Bight, but they were the exception (San Pedro Sun 2001). More than eleven hotels and resorts, most Belizean-owned, were completely destroyed. Six were never rebuilt, but other businesses recovered and are still operating today.

Because local insurance companies would not cover wooden buildings that did not meet US building code standards, many people did not receive any compensation. Placencia Village found itself economically devastated. It had little surviving infrastructure and the situation became worse when many of those in the tourism sector lost the income from an entire high season. In order to rebuild their homes and businesses, many individuals faced a difficult decision: they were forced to take out a high-interest (16–18 per cent) bank loan with their land as collateral, sell a piece of land, or use their savings (if they had any) together with funds from other sources, such as the Belize government's Development Finance Corporation, which in the wake of the disaster was providing BZ$5,000–$8,000 low-interest loans to qualified citizens (Musa 2001).

LONG-TERM EFFECTS

Because of the devastation and the large number of people trying to sell, real-estate values dropped. Foreign investors were quick to take advantage of the opportunity and land changed hands as Placencia citizens struggled to find the finances to rebuild. At the same time, in the wake of the destruction and the bulldozing of the village, a clean slate emerged for construction. Many foreign property owners on the peninsula began to build homes and vacation rentals; foreign-owned resorts such as Turtle Inn and Roberts Grove took advantage of the situation to upgrade, expand and renovate their facilities (San Pedro Sun 2001). The few locals with insurance did the same, and once the uninsured had secured funds through the sale of land, loans or other means, they also rebuilt as quickly as possible so as not to lose another season (San Pedro Sun 2001). Post-Iris, many businesses, including restaurants such as Wendy's, Omar's and the Galley, began to build concrete structures on the "back road" (which has now become Main Street), leaving the sidewalk, once the centre of commerce, as a quaint and quiet pathway near the seaside (News 5 2002). Some local family members shifted to the "new site", a dredged and filled piece of land on the lagoon side of the road (Spang 2013). The Placencia Peninsula that emerged had more foreign investment and was more oriented towards the tourism and real-estate industries than ever before.

EARTHQUAKE

Although minor compared to Hurricane Iris, in 2009 an earthquake caused damage to important community and private infrastructure in Placencia Village. The Placencia Peninsula lies about thirty miles from a strike-slip boundary where the Caribbean tectonic plate, on which southern Guatemala is located, abuts the North American plate, which Belize sits on (San Pedro Sun 2009). Movement along this fault line holds potential for devastating seismic events in southern Belize. The earthquake that occurred in May 2009 shook the soft sand of the peninsula just enough to split open the ground at the very tip of the peninsula, in Placencia Village. The water tower was damaged and 75 per cent of the village lost water access until it was repaired (San Pedro Sun 2009). Sea water spurted out of the ground through cracks in the tarmac at the end of the road and gushed through cracks in the concrete floor of the fishing co-op's processing facility and icehouse (News 5 2009). The piers at the end of the point were severely damaged, rendering more than half the length of two of them totally unusable. The fishing co-op's pier was almost totally destroyed, leaving only a short section close to the land standing. The Seahorse pier, constructed by a local dive shop of the same name, dropped several feet, flooding the dive shop (News 5 2009). Another pier lost most of its length and a small thatched *palapa*, which subsided underwater.

    The earthquake, like the hurricane, cleaned the slate for accelerated development. An Inter-American Development Bank loan through the central government paid for the construction of a new, multipurpose pier that could accommodate large boats, including yachts (IDB 2007). The pier, finished and inaugurated in September 2013, is now used for fishing, local and foreign boat docking, and evening promenades by villagers and visitors alike. As of June 2017 it also accommodates tenders from a hotly contested mass-cruise tourism port completed in fall 2016 on the island of Harvest Caye, two miles away (News 5 2017).

MIGRATION ON THE PENINSULA

With multiple construction companies building homes and businesses, the demand for labour has been filled by workers busing in from immigrant communities on the mainland, such as Santa Cruz and Bella Vista. These villages are populated mostly by Spanish-speaking Mestizo and Maya immigrants from Guatemala, Honduras and El Salvador who have come to Belize over the past twenty years in search of a better life. Instead of differentiating among their different cultures and nationalities, most Belizeans lump these people together with the descendants of Mexican Caste War refugees who came to northern Belize in the 1850s, calling the entire group "Spanish".

The Spanish presence in Placencia has grown exponentially in the past twenty years, with 363 self-identified Mestizo or Hispanic people living in this historically Kriol village as of the 2010 census (see table 1). According to the census, Mestizo/Hispanic-identified persons now comprise the largest group on the peninsula, with 1,007 individuals living in four communities (SIB 2013). Spanish is heard commonly across the peninsula. Besides the individuals who live in Placencia itself, another 182 live in Seine Bight, while many more commute from the mainland, where the cost of living is significantly cheaper. As of 2013, buses run daily from the mainly Guatemalan immigrant village of Bella Vista to the peninsula and back, carrying male construction workers and mainly female domestic and service-industry workers to their jobs. All these jobs exist as a result of tourism-related growth. Apart from the recent Hispanic immigrants, many Belizeans from different parts of the country have moved to Placencia seeking work. Maya, East Indian, Garifuna, Kriol and Spanish people from Toledo District and Cayo District and across Stann Creek District work on the peninsula. Every day Kriol and Spanish people heading to their jobs crowd the seats of the Hokey Pokey Water Taxi, which takes people across the lagoon from Mango Creek and Independence to Placencia and back.

Immigration from farther afield has also significantly changed the demographics of the peninsula. Thanks to growing international exposure via the tourism industry, Placencia has emerged as a growing retirement/second-home destination for better-off visitors. As early as the 1950s a few adventurous foreigners purchased land and built homes on the peninsula

Table 1. 2010 Census Data for Placencia Peninsula Population by Cultural Group, Placencia Peninsula

	Asian	Caucasian/ White	Creole	East Indian	Garifuna	Maya	Mestizo/ Hispanic	Other	Not Reported	Total
Maya Beach	4	89	3	1	0	25	81	22	0	225
Placencia	15	145	632	38	46	93	363	179	1	1,512
Riversdale	0	8	24	4	16	49	380	73	1	555
Seine Bight	5	22	52	6	822	44	182	31	2	1,166
Total	24	264	711	49	884	211	1,007	305	4	3,459

Source: SIB 2013.

and the Canadian "Maya Beach" real-estate development of the late 1960s also brought in a few outsiders. However, it was not until the 1990s, with the growth of the tourism industry, that investment and immigration from North America became a noticeable phenomenon. After Hurricane Iris, this rapidly expanded and turned into a boom of real-estate speculation, construction and development.

In 1999 the Government of Belize established a retirement programme through the BTB (Peddicord 2014). In the United States companies such as Live and Invest Abroad and International Living promote Belize as an ideal destination for baby boomers who do not want to have to learn Spanish. International Living claims: "As a British Commonwealth country, English is the primary language, making it easy for expats to transition" (International Living 2018). Its proximity to the mainland United States is also an attractive factor for Americans. Qualified individuals, mainly from the United States and Canada, began to purchase land and construct homes on the peninsula. As a result there has been an influx of part- and full-time residents from North America and (to a lesser extent) Europe.

While the economic class of these new arrivals varies, many are middle to middle upper class in their home countries and the great majority are of European descent or "white". First World residents vary from people who visit yearly and stay in their vacation homes for a month or so to retirees and full-time legal immigrants working in Belize. Today roughly five hundred immigrants from North America and Europe call the peninsula their permanent home and several hundred more live there part-time during the winter (SIB 2013). Their growing presence on the peninsula has affected everything from real-estate values to the variety and price of goods at the grocery store. The cost of living has become so expensive that many Belizeans and immigrants from Guatemala and Honduras who work in the tourism industry cannot afford to live on the peninsula itself. These wealthier migrants support the restaurant industry; North American immigrants both own and frequent dining venues across the peninsula, and as customers they keep some restaurants and bars afloat during the slow season.

EMIGRATION

There has been significant emigration of the original Kriol and Garifuna families on the peninsula over the past forty years. Until the 1960s many Belizeans emigrated to England, a natural choice for residents of a British Crown colony. Some served in the British military or obtained scholarships for education in England (Bilgrami 2004). However, after Hurricane Hattie destroyed Belize City in 1961, the United States granted refugee status to dispossessed Belizeans who had lost everything in the storm; a whole generation of adults left their children with the grandparents and headed north to make a better life. Thanks to proximity, American influence has continued to grow since independence, as has emigration to the United States. According to the US Census Bureau, today in the United States there are an estimated 54,925 people with Belizean ancestry (United States 2010). In Los Angeles alone there are tens of thousands of Belizeans and significant populations are also found in New York City, Chicago, New Orleans, Miami and greater Florida. All Placencia families now have members who have made their home somewhere in the United States, Canada or occasionally Europe.

Before the growth of tourism, there were not many paid job opportunities for women in the community. Employment was limited to working as domestic help in one of the wealthier homes, fishing alongside one's husband (when possible), or engaging in a cottage industry such as sewing or coconut oil or Kriol bread production (Key 2002). After 1972 one could clean and pack seafood at the local fishing cooperative or cook and clean at one of the few resorts or hotels that existed on the peninsula at that time. If a woman wanted adventure and a better-paying job, emigration, at least to Belize City, was the only way to get it.

Quite a few people used family or friend connections to move to Belize City or venture farther afield to the United States, where jobs and opportunities could be found. Perhaps as many as a hundred men and women left Placencia Village, a few permanently, others for decades or shorter periods of time (Spang 2013). Some travelled back and forth, living and working in both countries. Those who returned from abroad often brought with them new knowledge, skills and training, and a deeper understanding of the society and cultures of the country they had been living in. This allowed some individuals to effectively enter the nascent tourism industry.

Education was another reason to leave. Until 1989 the closest high school was in Dangriga, Stann Creek District's capital town, which was reachable only by one of the worst roads in the country. Some lucky children from better-off families or those who had scholarships went to Dangriga, San Ignacio or Belize City to get a secondary education (Spang 2013). Many stayed there afterwards to work. A few youth also travelled to the United States, England and Canada for high school, sometimes under the guardianship of early visitors to the peninsula. After 12 September 1989, when a high school opened in the community of Independence, a short boat ride across the lagoon from Placencia, local students were able to commute to high school. This greatly expanded the number of Placencia youth who were able to get a secondary education – an important achievement in a country where high school is neither free nor mandatory.

FOOD SYSTEMS

Tourism and migration have had significant effects on local foodways. The Placencia Village Council decided to ban chickens and pigs from the village in response to complaints that their noise and smell were bad for the growing tourism industry (Key 2002; Spang 2014). While a few clandestine chickens still roam, squawking furtively, around a yard or two at the edges of the community, most have long disappeared into the stew pot. Ironically, some tourists comment on the lack of the chickens that were banned to make their stay more comfortable. Tourists, the village council reasoned, do not care to be wakened by a rooster crowing at three in the morning. Placencians who grew up eating local fowl as a Sunday dinner treat are now dependent on industrially produced chicken and eggs shipped by Mennonite companies such as Dis Da Fi Wi Chicken from Cayo District to grocery stores across the peninsula. These foodstuffs have to be purchased for cash rather than raised on kitchen scraps, cheap corn and coconuts.

Hurricane Iris greatly impacted traditional foodways, as it destroyed most fire hearths in the community. Fire-hearth cooking – traditional Kriol cooking using wood and coconut-husk coals in an outdoor hearth (often made from an abandoned chest freezer or a fifty-five-gallon drum) – was the only way food was prepared on the peninsula until the 1970s, when the first gas stoves entered the community. Until Hurricane Iris many yards still had a fire hearth, which was used for cooking beans, making sweets or baking johnnycakes or Kriol bread for sale. Families could always rely on the fire hearth if the butane bill for their gas stove was too high. The Placencia Village Council Act prohibits the burning of anything, including wood, within the village boundaries, barbecue grills being the only exception. In effect, these regulations prohibit fire-hearth cooking (which nostalgic Belizeans believe produces the best-tasting food). An experienced cook can achieve crisper crusts, better browning and deeper flavour with the great range of heat available on an open fire. The slight smokiness of fire-hearth food is particularly prized. But with the disappearance of many fire hearths, cooking of that kind has become limited to only a couple of yards where members of established Kriol families feel they can use theirs without complaints from neighbours. One such lady is famous throughout the community for her fire-hearth-baked sweets and her tamales, which her sons sell around the village. Her location, downwind of any hotels or inns and with understanding neighbours who enjoy her food, has kept complaints to a minimum.

Any visitor to Placencia Peninsula today cannot help but notice the large number of Chinese-owned grocery stores and restaurants. Placencia Village itself claims six Chinese grocery stores and four restaurants: fast-food (mainly fried chicken) joints catering to Belizeans looking for a late-night meal or a cheap cold beer. They are relatively recent arrivals. The first Chinese to arrive in Belize were brought by the British in the 1880s as agricultural labourers. It was not until the early 1990s that southern Belize began to see a significant influx of Chinese immigrants, mainly from southern mainland China, but also individuals who fled Hong Kong before its transfer in 1997 (Simmons 2001). There is also a large and influential Taiwanese community in Belize, which recognizes Taiwan as the "real China" and as a result has a strong and positive diplomatic relationship with the island nation. The first Chinese-owned grocery on the peninsula, Everyday, opened in 2003. Since then, Chinese-owned grocery stores have opened up and down the peninsula, completely dominating the sector. All other such shops have shut down or, in one case, been sold to the Chinese.

The Chinese have successfully taken over a business sector that few wanted. In close-knit communities like Placencia, grocery store owners are expected to extend credit to their neighbours, who are also their family and friends. Moral obligation does not allow family members to deny one another food, even if there is no money to pay for it. As one grocery store owner in southern Belize said, "I can say no when a man wants credit to buy a pound of nails, but I can't say no when it's a pound of rice."[14] Because of this moral responsibility to give food if requested, Belizean grocery store owners find themselves having to extend credit that is repaid very slowly, making it difficult or impossible to keep the business profitable. Recent Chinese immigrants do not feel the same obligation, oriented as they are towards their own families and the Chinese community, and thus they refuse to extend credit to all but the biggest and most reliable customers. Connections that allow them to access cheap Chinese imports more easily also help maintain a profit margin.

The Chinese-owned grocery stores carry a few vegetables, including onions, potatoes, sweet peppers, broccoli and cauliflower, and sometimes mustard greens and Chinese cabbages in the refrigerator section. They are frequented mainly for their meats, dairy, dry goods and imported processed foods, which line the aisles like a miniature version of a large-scale supermarket. One store, Top Value, boasts wide aisles; when it first opened in 2012, its product line provoked delight among North Americans and Europeans, both recent and long-term residents. They joyfully recounted on Facebook the wide variety of cheeses, familiar brand-name processed food products and other imports carried at this Chinese-owned grocery. These stores carry many imported processed and packaged foods, from sweetened condensed milk (a sweets staple among Belizeans) to frozen bagels, pizza and Kraft mac 'n' cheese. At Top Value, goat cheese, Camembert, Gruyère and real Parmesan impressed North American immigrants looking for the variety of goods they were used to at home.

Wallen's Market/El Garobo Supermarket, established by a Norwegian–Japanese-American couple who moved to Placencia in the early 1970s, took advantage of the newly opened road in the 1980s to begin trucking fish to Cayo District and selling it for vegetables, which Mr Wallen then sold in his store. For a while Wallen's Market was the only reliable source of vegetables on the peninsula. Every Sunday new vegetables would come in and by 6:00 a.m. on Monday, residents would be lined up outside the door, which opened at 7:00 a.m. sharp (Spang 2013). Each customer was given a number, and the first one in got the pick of what was available. The last remaining non-

Chinese-owned grocery in the village, Wallen's, finally succumbed to the competition and closed in October 2015, but the owners continue to operate a hardware business. Their early trading helped to establish links between districts that are important today, as most vegetables available in Placencia come from Cayo District or farther north. Early restaurants and resorts had to either work with a very limited range and unreliable supplies of produce or develop their own trading networks. If they could not find it at Wallen's, they flew in vegetables from Belize City to Big Creek and boated them over.

The paving of the peninsula road, completed in 2010, made transportation of goods easier for fruit and vegetable vendors, who began to come to Placencia by road in the 1980s. The trucks loaded with produce from Cayo District and the Stann Creek Valley initially sold everything out of the back of the vehicle. In Placencia Village in 2016 there were three main truck vendors with permanent outposts – sheds or tents where they sold their products – making weekly trips inland to stock up. These vendors fill orders for restaurants and also retail to individuals. They are the main source of vegetables and fruits in the community, as trading by boat and local gardening have disappeared almost completely. Today anyone with a pickup truck full of pork or plantains is welcome to sell it around Placencia Village for a fee of ten dollars paid to the village council. It is not entirely a one-way situation; several fishermen in Placencia still send seafood to Cayo, where it is sold for double the Placencia price.

At the same time that imported goods have increased in variety and quantity, local commercial food production has plummeted. In addition to the huge drop in the seafood catch and the perennial problem that restaurants and individuals have in acquiring seafood, local production of traditional commodities such as coconut oil has greatly diminished. Only a few people still make coconut oil on the peninsula. No one is drying or corning fish, save occasionally for home consumption. Some of the older women still make guava jelly to sell, but other preserves are rare outside the home. Local cashew wine and nut processing no longer occur on any scale. Craboo are rarely bottled for sale. Baking is still common, but only a couple of people use a fire hearth. Older women bake johnnycakes, meat pies and Kriol bread at home for sale in village grocery stores. A bakery owned by a local Kriol man churns out sliced "pack" bread, Kriol bun and cinnamon rolls every day. Most foodstuffs sold commercially on the peninsula are produced elsewhere. This decrease in local food production and processing has important implications for cuisine development in the context of the Placencia Peninsula tourism industry. Apart from some seafood dishes, the menus of restaurants on the peninsula today reflect little of the area's rich food history.

DRUGS

In recent decades drug trafficking and dealing have become a significant source of income for some people on and near the peninsula. The drug trade is an important underground economy in Placencia. The smuggling of prohibited substances in this area is not new; several of my research participants had ancestors who worked as "rum runners" during American Prohibition. The cultivation and sale of marijuana have long been common in Belize, with many dealers and consumers in Placencia Village and across the peninsula. The drug trade took a whole new direction with the introduction of cocaine in the late 1970s. Cocaine trafficking forms part of much larger transnational networks of organized crime. Since the early 1980s, Placencia Peninsula, like Caye Caulker and Ambergris Caye in the north, has participated in the international cocaine trade that flows from Colombia up the coast to Mexico and the United States.

The repercussions for Placencia Village, the entire peninsula and Belize as a whole have been considerable as money and drugs have flowed into the area (Key 2002; Perez 2003; Sutherland 1998). Over the past several decades, millions of dollars' worth of cocaine has been found at sea or washed up on the peninsula and islands in the area. Locals call finding a bale of cocaine "winning the sea lotto",[15] as each bale is worth more than BZ$100,000 when sold back into the trafficking stream. Some winners have purchased land, built a new home, bought a new boat or invested in their business (Spang 2013). Others burned up their finds in extravagant sprees with friends. Larger traffickers launder money through legitimate businesses, including investments in real estate and construction, often as part of tourism-related development.

However the profits are spent, the cocaine trade circulates significant quantities of cash through the economy of Belize, Placencia Peninsula and

Placencia Village. The side effects of this illicit industry include increasing gang violence in Belize City and an epidemic of drug addiction, which has affected many families and led to increased theft and criminal behaviour countrywide (Key 2002; Perez 2003; Spang 2013).

THE CONTEMPORARY COMMUNITY

Placencia has transformed from a tiny, close-knit Kriol fishing village into a diverse community with international ties, hosting Belizeans from all cultural groups and districts; recent immigrants from Guatemala, El Salvador, Honduras and Mexico (over a thousand on the peninsula); and people from North America and Europe, who number well over five hundred (SIB 2013). First World immigrants often travel regularly back and forth from their home country to Belize, splitting their lives between two countries. Many immigrants from surrounding countries make seasonal trips to their countries of origin and maintain connections with relatives and friends in other ways. These personal networks connect Placencia to communities and countries around the world.

In the past, immigrants were few and they typically assimilated into the social network of the community and made friends with Placencia Kriol people, sometimes marrying into village families. Today migrants are able to build social networks within their own groups. Both the First World and Third World immigrant streams are significant enough that new immigrants may choose to remain insulated within their culture and language and interact with the original Kriol inhabitants of Placencia only for business purposes. This is a new and noticeable change, with profound implications for Placencia's social networks and community cohesion.

All the peninsula's founding families now have branches in the United States, with relatives living in Florida, California, New York, Illinois and many other states. Some emigrants visit home regularly, others return only for major events such as a family wake and funeral, and a few never come back. Young Belizean Americans visit Placencia with their Placencia-born parents for holidays such as Lobsterfest and September Celebrations,[16] bringing with them American tastes and styles and ensuring a continued family connection into the next generation. The village is no longer limited to the peninsula and nearby islands. Today Placencia gossip travels to New York, Las Vegas, New Orleans and Toronto at the touch of a cell phone screen. Social and economic networks stretch beyond national borders and dominate Facebook pages devoted to Placencia news, gossip, community support, food and business.

While Placencia society has changed greatly since the days when villagers would come together to launch a boat or share turtle meat, most active residents maintain that the village still retains some of the strong community spirit for which it was once known. While some new immigrants opt out of village life, others are working hard to integrate themselves into the original Kriol community and become part of local social, economic and mutual support networks.

This community spirit is evident in an event that occurred in June 2013. A young Belizean Kriol man, not originally from Placencia but well liked in the village, was horribly burned in a butane gas tank explosion. His wife, an American immigrant to Belize, accompanied him when he was evacuated to a burn centre in the United States. Through Facebook, led by local Placencians and several immigrant Americans who have assimilated into Placencia Village life and society, fundraisers were organized and international donations made; close to BZ$90,000 was raised. In less than two weeks a transnational Placencia community had rallied around one of their own. The sources of the donations reflect Placencia's internationalized and diverse population. Immigrants from North America, Belizeans from around the country (including Placencia Kriols), Placencia locals who had emigrated to the United States, part-time residents from the First World and even repeat tourists gave generously to help a man whom some of them had never met, all in the name of Placencia.

ENVIRONMENTAL CHANGES AND CONTINUITIES

In the early days of Placencia Village, harpooning manatee and netting sea turtles were common and no fishing laws existed. The British Empire had little interest in regulating resource extraction in a Crown colony founded on the principal of export logging. In 1977, in response to decreasing yields, the Government of Belize established a closed season and a minimum size for conch (Huitric 2005). But it was not until the near collapse of fisheries in the 1990s that the Belizean government created legislation meant to prevent total destruction of the country's unique and splendidly diverse marine ecosystems. Lobster fishing is now regulated in the same way as conch (Huitric 2005). On 8 December 2010 Belize became the third country in the world[17] to completely ban bottom trawling (Oceana 2010; Ramos 2010). Formed in 2008, the Southern Environmental Association (formerly known as Friends of Nature) manages three protected marine areas in Stann Creek and Toledo Districts: Gladden Spit and Silk Cayes Marine Reserve, the Sapodilla Cayes Marine Reserve, and Laughing Bird Caye National Park (AAA 2018; Gille and Riain 2002). The latter two form part of the Belize Barrier Reef Reserve System, which was declared a World Heritage Site by UNESCO in 1996 (UNESCO 2018). These parks are the most popular destination for visitors taking a marine tour from Placencia Peninsula. They showcase the diversity and abundance of marine life that exists when fishing pressure is removed and serve as seeding sites for unprotected areas outside the park's boundaries. Tour guides have a vested interest in the health of the reefs in the area and are increasingly likely to report violators of fishing regulations. The family ties that protect individuals from the law are now being weighed against their livelihoods. Even relatives may risk being reported to the Southern Environmental Association if they blatantly ignore fishing regulations. At least partial adherence to the fishing laws appears to be more common due to concern for the future livelihood of the peninsula's fishers and tour guides and fear of prosecution and possible jail time.

    Despite this, the fisheries in Belize continue to be depleted. The taking of protected species and fishing out of season, as well as illegal fishing by Belizeans and Honduran and Guatemalan nationals (sometimes under the auspices of a Belizean boss), have been common for decades and continue to be a major problem (Key 2002). Some tourists and hospitality providers do not care whether it is lobster season or not, as long as they get one on their plate. Undersized lobster are sold under the table; conch are stockpiled in walled-off caches built by fishers to be killed, cleaned and brought to market the day the season opens; parrotfish and angelfish are filleted at sea and sold as snapper in Honduras and Guatemala and to restaurateurs on the Placencia Peninsula (Spang 2013).

    Environmental effects are not limited to the sea. Thanks to the boom in real-estate development on the peninsula since Hurricane Iris, huge swaths of littoral and mangrove forest are being bulldozed and filled in to make way for hotels, resorts and luxury condominiums.

ENVIRONMENT, IDENTITY AND GENDER

What do these changes mean for Belizeans on the peninsula? Belizean identity, as in many other parts of the world, was historically tied to how people interacted with their surrounding environment. Belizean loggers, the founders of colonial Belize, are so iconic that they are featured on our national flag. In coastal communities, Belizean fishers are equally symbolic.

Like the original fishing communities on Ambergris Caye and Caye Caulker, Placencia remains a very sea-oriented village, with a strong emphasis on a male-centred fisherman's identity (Key 2002). Women are often knowledgeable about sea life, may fish from the shore as needed to supplement the family diet, and also help their spouses fish by boat, especially if the entire family is camping on the cayes (Key 2002). However, captaining a boat and fishing at sea are still considered male occupations, even though a handful of younger Placencia women are now taking their place at the helm. Knowledge of the sea and extraction of marine resources as a livelihood form the basis of this identity. Although commercial fishing is waning as a source of income on the peninsula, the reef, lagoon and river ecosystems continue to be important to local livelihoods and identities, and a macho seafaring/fisherman culture is still strong among many men on the peninsula and in nearby coastal communities. With the increasing disappearance of sea life, this identity is threatened.

A young boy in Placencia would be taken to sea by his male kin and set to work helping with small tasks while being expected to pay close attention and learn everything around him. Over time he would become knowledgeable about his marine environment, amassing a vast body of information that was closely tied to the geography and environment of his region. A skilful seaman in Placencia is expected to know where the best fishing locations are for drop fishing, fly fishing and trolling; the location of productive reefs for conch and lobster and spear-fishing (often down to specific coral heads) and the type of seafood they are most likely to contain; how to hook lobster, pick up conch and spear fish with a Hawaiian sling; how to clean and store seafood; the best snorkelling sites; the names, locations and qualities of local cayes; the spawning seasons for different fish and the best method for catching them; the different types of weather and seas to be expected at any point during the year; how to navigate the treacherous, reef-strewn Placencia waters at night and in bad weather conditions; how to tie basic knots; and – last but not least – how to cook while living in rough fishing camps on the cayes (Spang 2013).

Because much tourism in Placencia is oriented towards the sea and because men were traditionally the seafarers in the community, the tour-guiding profession remains male dominated. While each man is likely to have certain areas in which his knowledge and skill are strongest, all seamen are expected to learn the basics and every Placencia man over thirty-five whom I have met claims to be a good cook because of some level of participation in the seafaring life. Some younger men say the tradition of seafaring is why their fathers ensured that they learned how to cook, even though the big fishing camps of yore are no longer as crowded and young men are choosing increasingly different career paths.

Today job opportunities exist on the peninsula for men who do not find the sea attractive, but those who do choose the seafaring way of life often profess a strong love for it and a sense of naturally belonging in the marine environment. This seaman identity continues to be expressed by those who now work as captains and guides for marine tours. In Placencia today visitors and locals alike still throng to the fish-cleaning tables when someone comes in with a catch. However, as Belize's fisheries continue to decline, the community is increasingly focused on the tourism industry, with both men and women working for hotels, restaurants, bars, resorts and tour operators, and, indirectly, at jobs in grocery stores, banks, real-estate companies and other service-sector businesses. The future of the fishing economy is uncertain, although Placencia-area fishermen and tour guides are passionate advocates for stricter enforcement and regulation to save the fisheries and fishing culture from extinction.

The culinary history of Placencia Peninsula is inextricably tied up in its natural environment: the bountiful sea, the fruitful littoral forest covering the peninsula, the fish-filled lagoon and the pine-ridge hunting grounds. Imported staples such as flour, rice and beans were once paid for with locally caught seafood, and kitchen gardens were common. Today the Placencia food economy is primarily cash-driven and based on ingredients and processed foods imported from the mainland or abroad. Thanks to the demands of the tourism industry and wealthier immigrants, many more ingredients are now available on the peninsula, but at a price that many Belizeans and poorer immigrants can ill afford. Foraging on the peninsula becomes more and more difficult as the coastal forest is bulldozed or fenced off to make way for luxury condos and hotels, and restaurant demand for fish and seafood competes with the local market, limiting availability and driving up prices.

What do these changes mean for the future of local foodways and for cuisine development in Placencia and other tourism zones across Belize? Placencia's coastal location, together with the fishing history of the area and its reputation for delicious fish, lobster and conch, drives a demand for seafood, but few visitors get to taste the dishes that locals most associate with fisherman culture as those are typically prepared and eaten only in private homes. Tourists and immigrants are also unlikely to sample sweets made with the wild fruits of the coastal forest that they drive past. How will Belizeans from Placencia Peninsula present themselves to the world as old Placencia slips into the shadows of history? How is Placencia Kriol cuisine evolving in the face of high levels of immigration, a rapidly growing tourist-service industry and, save for limited commercial fishing kept afloat by restaurant demand, a declining local productive economy? To find out what is happening and its implications for the development of a national Belizean cuisine, we must learn more about the tourism industry.

3
TOURISTS AND THE PLACENCIA FOODSCAPE

TOURISM IS BIG BUSINESS IN BELIZE. ACCORDING TO THE BTB, in 2017 the nation welcomed a record-breaking 1,427,000 people (including cruise ship passengers), almost four times the population of the entire country. Overnight tourism has been the mainstay of the industry, with an established focus on ecotourism and a growing sector of higher-end/boutique resort experiences. Large cruise ships were introduced to Belize City in 2001. In 2013 they became a highly contentious front-page issue for southern Belize when Norwegian Cruise Lines signed a memorandum of understanding with the government to construct a private island cruise port two miles from Placencia Village (Ramos 2013). The port opened in November 2016 and continues to be a source of controversy, as only those contracted by Norwegian Cruise Lines are allowed on the island. Aside from the tourists disembarking from Carnival Cruise Lines ships in Belize City, mass tourism until recently had not been the focus of Belize's young and growing tourism industry, which occupies a high-quality niche among regional offerings. As such it has sold itself as a premium destination for travellers who want to experience what the BTB describes as a perfect combination of nature and culture, of the Caribbean and Central America.

Most tourists coming to Placencia are overnight visitors from North America; they are people of lower-middle to upper-class income who spend at least a week in the country. Placencia is a coastal destination with relatively easy access to the interior, so it receives many tourists (often repeat customers) who spend their entire vacation on the peninsula, with day trips to other locations. How do these visitors influence the ongoing evolution of food systems on Placencia Peninsula? Does their desire to try "Belizean food" and "local food" help drive the development of regional, cultural and even national cuisine? With time and money on their hands and a hunger for entertainment, tourists could have a similar effect on culinary innovation as the bored nobles who are credited with encouraging and supporting the development of French and Chinese high cuisines (Goody 1982; Trubek 2000).

TOURISTS AREN'T ALL THE SAME

Tourists are a heterogeneous bunch and their reasons for travel vary, a fact that has been thoroughly investigated by numerous researchers of the hospitality industry over the past forty years. Differences in visitor identity and their expectations strongly influence how each individual approaches their trip to another country or region, including the food that they consume. Because the tourism industry contributes close to 25 per cent of Belize's gross domestic product, visitors wield outsized and influential purchasing power, just as the aristocracy of France and China once did. Tourist imaginaries and expectations of what Belizean food should be like influence what restaurateurs in Belize offer them. Skinner and Theodossopoulos's (2011) edited volume explores the dialectic dance of host gaze and tourist gaze along the axis of expectations – those of the visitors and of the hosts. Menus and meal and restaurant recommendations from the tourism industry try to fulfil tourist expectations in order to provide a positive vacation experience; this is called good hospitality. The expectations, likes and dislikes of each visitor shape their reactions to food (and everything else) in Belize and guide the actions of people working in the food sector of the tourism industry. The host gaze also plays an important role as Belizeans decide how to respond to visitor expectations (Moufakkir and Reisinger 2013). This feedback loop is not unique to Belize and it is not perfect. A mismatch of expectations between visitor and host can sometimes have strange effects on what is served in restaurants in tourist zones (Skinner and Theodossopoulos 2011). Clare Sammells, in "'Loco-politan' Gastronomy and Bolivian Cuisine", her intriguing contribution to Robert Shepherd's edited volume on cosmopolitanism and tourism, calls these menus "touristic-cosmopolitan cuisines" that reflect (albeit often imperfectly) "how tourists see their relationship to those people (and foods) that they travel to see (and eat), as well as how the toured wish to be seen" (Sammells 2017, 165).

After interviewing twenty-eight different groups of tourists (a total of about eighty visitors), I learned a lot not only about what they thought about food in Belize, but also about the tourists themselves. While most of them hailed from North America, they brought diverse perspectives and personal histories which shaped each person's interpretations and feelings about food in Belize. Prior food and travel experiences influence a tourist's interests, perceptions and expectations. Personal preferences are another factor in whether people have a positive food experience while travelling. Someone who enjoys rice and beans or pasta and seafood would fare much better with the restaurant offerings in Placencia than a person who loves red meat and leafy greens, which tend to be scarce on area menus. All these nuances play into how each visitor interacts with the food environment at their destination.

One Canadian woman told me, "[In] a lot of places I travel specifically for the food or I seek out the food. This is the first place where food had no draw, food had no connection . . . I realize here I travel for the people, for the environment, for the trips and food is not a focus here." This was her second trip to Placencia with her husband and she was not particularly enamoured of the food options; she did not care for rice, beans or pasta, preferring a diet based on meat and vegetables. She also considered much of the food to be like home-cooked, which she could more cheaply get at home. As a result she often cooked in their rental house, something she said she did not do when they visited South Florida and the Florida Keys.

Her statement illustrates the complexity of tourist behaviour around food. A self-identified food lover might select one vacation destination for its food appeal and another because of the people, natural environment or activities available. Guidebooks and key Internet sources for Belize often fail to capture the full depth and breadth of Belizean ingredients, dishes and culinary customs.[1]

Our country is known for its natural environments, Maya archaeology and ecotourism activities. The three S's (sun, sand and sea – strongly associated with the Caribbean and Mexican tourism market) and the less well-known three R's of Belize (reefs, rainforest and ruins) make up the bulk of tourism advertising (Duffy 2002). Until very recently the BTB had done little to market Belize as a food destination. As Wilk (1999) discusses in "Real Belizean Food", most Belizeans, including those who direct the BTB, have only recently begun to conceptualize what Belizean food is and to recognize that our culinary heritage might be of interest to visitors. This realization has slowly begun to change Belize's tourism marketing in the past several years as culinary tourism has exploded globally. While an attempt to start a Belizean food page on the BTB website failed back in 2012, today the BTB embraces food in its advertising line-up. Full-page ads on chocolate making "the Maya way" and on Belizean "fast food" are popping up in American culinary magazines such as *Saveur*. The annual Taste of Belize culinary and mixology competition, organized by the BTB to promote the culinary arts and celebrate chefs and bartenders in the Belizean tourism industry, floundered for several years after 2013, but finally got back on track in 2018. These are positive changes, but food remains at best a supporting player in most advertising and writing about Belize.

It is not surprising, therefore, that the seventeen self-identified "foodies" I interviewed had limited knowledge about Belizean food, despite their pre-vacation research. Out of eighty people interviewed, only one mentioned that she was seeking a particular dish (cowfoot soup), which she had read about in a *Lonely Planet* guidebook.

Twenty of the twenty-eight groups I interviewed were customers of a small tour company that I co-owned at the time of my research. Our company's most popular tours were snorkelling, with a fresh-caught seafood lunch, and a chocolate tour, so interviewees likely self-selected to have at least a slight interest in food. They ranged from a solitary backpacker to a group of nine escaping the rain in a coffee shop. The majority of participants were in their forties, fifties or early sixties and the second-largest group ranged from their mid-twenties to late thirties. Of the twenty-eight groups, only eight included a single traveller and only one was a family with children. The remaining twenty groups all consisted of one or two couples, sometimes travelling together. Two of these groups included a gay couple. All but two participants would be described as "white" by Belizeans. Eleven of the twenty-eight groups were from Canada, while fourteen were from the United States. Participants also hailed from Australia, Scotland, Sweden, Mexico and Israel. My interview sample contained a lot of Canadians but otherwise reflects the general arrivals list recorded by the BTB, in which Americans make up the bulk of Belize's visitors. They are followed by a much smaller but growing Canadian market, behind which trail nominal numbers of guests from Europe, Mexico and Guatemala, Australia and other countries of origin.

GAZING AT TOURISM

In 1990 sociologist John Urry (2002) introduced the concept of the "tourist gaze", which seeks pleasure, novelty and excitement. Since his seminal article on the topic, much has been written about the tourist gaze and the tourists who deploy it in their quest for adventure, leisure and entertainment. Not enough was said about the role of the host (Yuk Wa Chan's 2006 article is a rare exception) until Omar Moufakkir and Yvette Reisinger elaborated on the "host gaze" in a 2011 article and an edited book of the same name in 2013. People who work in the tourism industry are not simply passive objects of the tourist gaze. They use their "host gaze" to determine, create and deliver products tailored to get the best reception, based on their evaluation of the tourist's cultural, national and class background, interests and expectations (Moufakkir and Reisinger 2013). The host gaze can also be used to redirect misguided tourist imaginaries and expectations and to educate visitors without offending their sense of taste, as I will discuss in more detail in chapter 5. During the course of my research I not only observed the use of the host gaze by other industry professionals, I also employed it myself as I evaluated and interacted with my guests on tours. My unique position as both food researcher and tour guide led visitors to ask me questions about food on the peninsula and around Belize and to readily share their observations and experiences. Through participant observation as a guide I was able to observe many different aspects of the vacation experience, including eating while on tour.

Intersecting with and emerging from the crucible of tourist and host gazes are what Noel Salazar, Nelson Graburn and Maria Gravari-Barbas call "tourism imaginaries" (Salazar 2010; Salazar and Graburn 2014). These are "socially transmitted representational assemblages", the products of not only an expectant tourist gaze but also of host gazes, government agencies, corporations and private-sector participants in the tourism industry who create frames of interpretation and fantasy through which to imagine a particular destination and its peoples and environs (Salazar and Graburn 2014). These stem from what Bruner (2004) calls "master narratives", or persistent thematic beliefs about the nature of the "exotic other" that may be encountered during travel (Picard and Di Giovine 2014). Skinner and Theodossopoulos (2011) explore how these imaginaries often lead visitors to have certain expectations about a particular destination or experience, expectations that may or may not be met on the ground.[2]

TOURISM TYPOLOGIES

Starting with Smith, MacCannell and Cohen in the 1970s, sociologists, anthropologists and hospitality specialists have scrutinized and dissected who tourists are and what motivates them to travel. One result of this research has been tourism typologies that distinguish different subgroups of tourists based on attitudes, perceptions, motivation and interests, as well as personality type, age, economic class and education level. These factors influence what particular visitors seek in terms of food-related experiences while on vacation. Mitchell and Hall (2003) have even developed a tourist typology specifically for food. It is important to remember that tourist types really exist on a multidimensional continuum. The discrete categories of a tourism typology are merely arbitrary groupings that simplify the continuum for data analysis.

Tourist typologies do not belong only to academe. Belizeans working in the Placencia tourism industry whom I interviewed also informed me that there are different kinds of tourists. According to my industry informants (and in their own words), some guests want "everything to be like home" while others are "more adventurous". Some have extremely high expectations of their vacation; they want everything to be very luxurious and all their experiences and activities to be perfect, while others are easier-going and understanding ("more relax"). The former guests were considered "pickies" and harder to please. Some tourists are budget travellers (often glossed as backpackers), while others are willing to pay for and expect the amenities of home. The informants said that most visitors to Placencia want to sample local food and culture while still enjoying amenities such as air conditioning during their stay. This emic tourist typology created continuums of least to most adventurous and least to most picky, cross-referenced to a dichotomy of budget travellers and backpackers versus wealthier visitors. While exceptions were noted, most budget travellers were expected to be less picky and more relaxed, while the "pickies" typically emerged from the category of wealthier visitors who spent more money.

This idea that some vacationers are more adventurous than others is a strong theme in tourism research. Erik Cohen (1972), an early pioneer in the sociology of tourism, describes two main dimensions along which tourist identity can develop, based on how much the visitors seek out new experiences and environments versus how much they look for familiar experiences and environments. This is what Placencia industry professionals call "trying something different". Mitchell and Hall (2003) describe this phenomenon as a spectrum of neophilia (love of novelty) to neophobia (fear of novelty). Cohen (1972) divides tourists into four discrete groups: the highly adventurous, novelty-seeking "drifter"; the "explorer", who likes familiar accommodations and transport but is otherwise a novelty lover; the "individual mass tourist", who has a more controlled schedule and itinerary but still ventures out of the tourism bubble to explore; and the generally novelty-hating "organized mass tourist", who rarely sets foot outside the controlled environment of the all-inclusive resort or cruise package.

My research makes it clear that the novelty–familiarity ratio is a continuum with multiple dimensions. Visitors may be very adventurous in some areas and not at all in others, picky in some areas and not others. A large number of my interviewees fell into the more adventurous end of the individual mass tourist category. Quite a few of them described their explorations away from the resort environment as "doing their own thing"; some even said they were "busting out" and "escaping" what they found to be a stifling all-inclusive atmosphere. Most visitors with the latter attitude told me they intended to stay in a locally owned or non-resort hotel in the village the next time they came to Belize. These explorations away from the resort allowed tourists to meet and interact with Belizeans outside the more formalized resort structure, get a taste of local culture at non-resort restaurants, and arrange activities and services on their own, often at a lower price. Some of the visitors with a controlled schedule and itinerary were closer to Cohen's explorer category in that they sought adventure and novelty in most things except accommodations and transportation. They tended to travel as couples or family groups. Many of my guests fell somewhere between Cohen's four points on this spectrum of tourist types.

Cohen (1972) also developed a typology based on the degree to which tourists seek a spiritual connection, a sense of authenticity, through their travel experiences. Within this spectrum he identifies five types ranging from least to greatest need for a sense of authenticity: the recreational, the diversionary, the experiential, the experimental and the existential. The degree to which visitors care about authenticity will shape their activity choices while on vacation, as well as their evaluations of what they encounter during their trip. Whether food is "authentic" or what a "real Belizean" would eat matters to visitors who want a vacation experience that will take them out of the tourism bubble and allow them to "eat like a local". Belizean industry professionals use their host gaze to identify and cater to authenticity-seeking visitors, telling them that they will get the "real local" experience on a particular tour or eat "real local food" at a particular restaurant. The same guide or concierge will typically treat less adventurous guests differently, assuring them that local food is prepared with keen attention to international food safety standards and that it is palatable and delicious to foreign palates. This flexibility in presentation forms part of what I call "culinary code-switching", which is discussed in detail in chapter 5.

MITCHELL AND HALL'S FOOD TOURISM TYPOLOGY

Mitchell and Hall's (2003) typology defines four categories of food tourist behaviour across five phases of the food tourism experience: eating at home prior to travel; eating out prior to travel; food at the destination; vacation experiences – which include exploration, personal indulgence, romance and relaxation, sports, hobbies and learning, and socializing – and eating post-travel. The different categories (gastronomes, indigenous foodies, tourist foodies and familiar foods) span a spectrum from most to least novelty-loving and from most to least interest in the food and foodways of the tourism destination (Yoder 1972). My research sample was focused on people with an interest in cultural tourism, so, not surprisingly, no tourists in the "familiar food" category were interviewed. Seventeen of the eighty research participants identified themselves as being strongly interested in food. Only three of those seventeen could conceivably be categorized as "gastronomes", the other fourteen falling into the "indigenous foodie" category. Six of the seventeen (including the three "gastronomes") claimed that food was often a motivating factor in their travel plans and destination choice. Four participants specifically stated that they were not foodies. The remaining fifty-nine interviewees did not state whether they claimed a food-related identity, but some expressed strong interest in food during their interviews.

Why bother probing the likes and dislikes, desire for prestige, and novelty- and authenticity-seeking behaviours of tourists? Interactions between visitors and locals and in the grey area of retirees, immigrants and part-time residents take place in a power-saturated environment. Without a better understanding of what motivates visitor food purchases and judgements, we cannot understand the often resourceful and creative responses of food industry entrepreneurs to tourist expectations.

CULINARY COSMOPOLITANISM

An individual's degree of attraction to difference or novelty has been identified as a key factor in determining the behaviour and purchasing decisions of tourists. Both Cohen (1979) and Mitchell and Hall (2003) claim that a love of novelty and difference is on a continuum with fear or dislike of novelty and difference. Wilk (1997) argues that taste or distaste for particular foods may be more influenced by habitus, socio-economic and historic background, and a desire to express status and difference (Bourdieu 1979). Simply being new, unusual or local is not always enough if trying a food does not enhance personal prestige. People are more likely to sample foods that build their culinary cosmopolitanism. Robert Shepherd (2017, vii), drawing from Noel Salazar and Ulrich Beck's writings on the topic, defines cosmopolitanism as being "simultaneously rooted in a sense of universal sameness and global diversity" and thus evoking "both the allure of elsewhere and otherness and a solidarity with strangers". A cosmopolitan person is considered to be well-travelled, well-educated, well-read and free to transcend economic, geographic, social and cultural boundaries that bind others in the quest to explore this global diversity. Being cosmopolitan is thus an exclusive identity that is "predicated on privilege and capital, both social and economic" (Sammells 2017, 163).

Culinary cosmopolitanism is the knowledge and appreciation that an individual has for a diverse array of foods from different cultures, regions of the world, culinary styles and even, in some cases, time periods.[3] As part of the tourist experience, it intersects with the concept of being well travelled (Sammells 2017; Shepherd 2017). This knowledge and appreciation selectively draw from (often highly localized) culinary heritage, whether it be across the globe or across town, focusing on that which will build status, particularly with other cosmopolitan people.

With the tourists I interviewed, novelty seeking or avoidance was never on a clear-cut spectrum. Typologies based on this factor alone are not comprehensive, nor do they take into account the many permutations that food interest can take. There are, for example, individuals who do not cook at all or cook rarely and so will not experiment with making dishes from the country they visit, but they have a high level of interest in trying local foods when they are prepared by others. Individuals may be very adventurous about certain categories of foods and not at all about others. New desserts or unusual vegetables or fruits are less threatening to many than unfamiliar meats or seafood. Novelty-seeking behaviour is selective and rarely applies to every aspect of a person's behaviour, while social and status considerations do influence how adventurous people are. The degree of novelty-seeking behaviour that an individual expresses often varies depending on what aspect of life (or vacation) is being evaluated. Each expression may affect an individual's status, position and identity in society.

Highly adventurous "gastronomes" who will swallow a live eel without a qualm may be neophobic about their bathrooms, demanding flush toilets wherever they go. Using unconventional bathrooms does not establish high status in North American society, but eating live eels? In some social circles that is a prestige-enhancing story that places the teller in the same league as daring culinary adventurer Andrew Zimmern of *Bizarre Foods* television fame. In this context, novelty-seeking behaviour around cuisine demonstrates cosmopolitanism, enhancing that individual's status and reputation. Sometimes rejecting fast-food hamburgers and embracing locally grown arugula may be more about expressing class status, education level and cosmopolitanism than loving new flavours. As Sammells (2017, 164) explains, there are great ironies inherent in the fact that relatively well-off travellers, whose adventures depend on sophisticated high-speed transport, high-speed Internet and international banking systems, often "hope to visit places, witness labor forms and sample foods that seem untouched by that same global system" .

This search for "something different" from one's own life and experience, for something "authentic" and "exotic", defines a whole range of touristic behaviour. Leisure time is often treated very differently from the organized, routinized day-to-day working life. In the early days of tourism research in North America,[4] Nelson Graburn (1985, 1989), drawing from MacCannell, Durkheim and Leach, applied the concept of a binary division of sacred and profane to the tourism experience. According to Graburn, the vacation is a ritual, a sacred time and place, a space for renewal and transformation. Victor Turner's (1969) exploration of the liminal, ambiguous, floating, sacred state of being in between one identity/place/status and another describes the (supposedly and ideally) restorative/renewing vacation experience quite well. Thus tourists, exploring life in a liminal state of rest and relaxation, may be more likely to experiment with something new than they would when in their everyday routine state. Following Graburn, Urry (2002, 12) states, "Tourism results from a basic binary division between the ordinary/everyday and the extraordinary." Something the tourist gazes upon must bring pleasure through being different. As Cohen and Mitchell and Hall have argued, it should bring novelty or change from the everyday state. The change must be appealing or pleasurable, or else the experience may be uncomfortable or, at worst, distressing. At the same time, some aspects of the tourism experience, like the amenities in a hotel room, may be familiar or even homelike, since most people are not like Cohen's "drifters" and do not enjoy too much change all at once.

This selective difference that tourists seek is really a projection of their own desires, dreams and expectations through tourist imaginaries (Salazar and Graburn 2014). As Di Giovine and Picard explain in *Tourism and the Power of Otherness*, tourists seek out "otherness" that is a reflection and a projection of their own selves. For this reason, not all differences are equally valued. The projection of self carries with it the social and economic frameworks and cultural background of the tourist. The differences that visitors focus on, seek out and project their home realities onto usually represent an oppositional ideal to the tourist's day-to-day life. It is this difference, these projected imaginaries of otherness, that allows tourists to "liberate and activate their body, consume accumulated economic and emotional surplus, and re-enchant and sometimes also fundamentally change the moral and cosmological order of the world" (Picard and Di Giovine 2014, 2).

When applied to the culinary realm, this projection of self ensures that visitors seek out appealing difference, a domesticated otherness that, while exciting and exotic, does not overtly threaten their personal cultural views of what is edible and palatable. Those few North Americans who hope to shock their home group by tasting something on or beyond the margins of what their culture considers edible typically do so to build prestige and cultivate a cosmopolitan and worldly identity with their peers. Their culinary adventure is thus carried out still firmly within the socio-economic and cultural framework of their home society.

The search for novelty and a search for authenticity are often closely connected. Take as an example Heldke's (2008) exotic/authentic/novelty triumvirate. Novelty, according to her, "marks the presence of the exotic, where exotic is understood to mean 'excitingly unusual'" (181). If the tourist is not familiar with a food, it is therefore exotic, exciting and different, and by default assumed to be an "authentic" representation of the culture being consumed. This may be so even if the visitor dislikes the food in question or does not want to try it, in which case the guest identifies something as authentic but is not interested in pursuing or consuming it. Heldke's triangle ties novelty-seeking behaviour to a search for (and in the case of food, often the consumption of) authenticity. Many of my guests assumed that any food item they encountered with which they were not familiar must by default be an authentic Belizean dish. This belief is key for understanding the ways in which tourism drives cuisine development. If a majority of visitors seek out foods that are different from what they have at home, while also being both palatable to the tourist and prestige-enhancing (*Remember the time I went to Belize and ate the royal rat?*), then that is what the food sector of the Belizean tourism industry will try give them.

But not all travellers are on the search for an "authentic" food experience. According to Urry (2002, 12), the tourist experience is about the inversion of day-to-day work life: "One key feature [of tourism] would seem to be that there is difference between one's normal place of residence/work and the object of the tourist gaze." Any seeking for what are deemed "authentic elements" is important "only because there is in some sense a contrast with everyday experiences" . In other words, Urry believes authenticity is important only if the tourists view their own culture as fake and superficial and thus seek something "deep, real and authentic" as an inversion of their daily experience. This is a quest for an otherness that is a projection of the perceived lack in one's home environment (Cohen 1988; Picard and Di

Giovine 2014). This is a search for the local, the deeply rooted and "real", as an antidote to the "non-places" and supposedly superficial lives which some tourists, hoping to increase their cosmopolitanism, identify and then seek to escape (Sammells 2017).

The tourist gaze is not a homogeneous novelty- and authenticity-seeking radar. Savvy industry professionals use their host gaze to evaluate each guest and determine what they are seeking. In the arena of food, they then use their culinary cosmopolitanism and culinary code-switching to attempt to satisfy the expectations and desires of each guest. Some also try to educate their guests about Belizean cuisine. Cohen's recreational and diversionary tourists may enjoy difference and novelty without questioning whether or not it is "authentic", but authenticity is a critical factor for experiential visitors, who find satisfaction in what they consider to be a "realer" experience. In my research it appeared that experiential, authenticity-seeking visitors often had a higher degree of education and usually worked in white-collar jobs, although I did not collect enough data to run an analysis of this. According to Picard and Di Giovine (2014), these well-educated, well-travelled and well-paid folks are the class of individuals most likely to identify as cosmopolitan. They quote Calhoun, who states that cosmopolitanism

> is the culture of those who attend Harvard and the London School of Economics, who read *The Economist* and *The New Yorker*, who recognize Mozart's music as universal and who can discuss the relative merits of Australian, French and Chilean wines. It is also a culture in which secularism seems natural and religion odd, and in which respect for human rights is assumed, but the notion of fundamental economic redistribution is radical and controversial. This culture has many good qualities as well as blind spots, but nonetheless it is culture and not its absence. (Calhoun 2003, 544)

Some cosmopolitan individuals[5] seem to feel that their lifestyle at home is not as "real" as the lives of some others and that they are not as in touch with the natural world or do not have as much of a sense of community. Di Giovine and Picard argue that these beliefs are a result of the modernist mode of thinking, a projection of power-laden dichotomies upon the world: authentic/fake, self/other, nature/culture, modern/traditional, real/superficial (Picard and Di Giovine 2014; see also Cohen 1988). However, not all cosmopolitans adhere to these views. The postmodern "post-tourist" first discussed by

Feifer in 1985 has supposedly moved past the dichotomy of vacation life and everyday life, which is now seen as a very fuzzy set of interpenetrating and overlapping modes of thinking about, observing and interacting with the world (Skinner and Theodossopoulos 2011).[6] Aware post-tourists understand the "blurred boundaries of the touristy and the non-touristy" and recognize that authenticity and tradition are continually being invented and reinvented (Salazar 2010; Skinner and Theodossopoulos 2011).

Yet the modernist mode of thinking and essentialist authenticity-seeking behaviour has incredible staying power; it continues to pop up even in purportedly postmodern tourist imaginaries. Modernist "structuring structures" still underlie many tourist imaginaries, creating what Kenneth Little (2014, 223) calls "interpretive maps [that] transmit meaning . . . in concert with personal imagining and the global culture industries that act to circulate images of others, natures, cultures, artifacts, histories, adventures and the like". In my research, it appeared that most visitors who worked blue-collar jobs or were small-scale entrepreneurs in industry or the trades appeared less preoccupied with authenticity and they were unlikely to describe their home lives as lacking something that they sought in Belize (except perhaps warm weather in the winter months). Some educated participants in their twenties also seemed less concerned with authenticity, which may indicate a genuine postmodern generational shift in North America relating to how authenticity as a concept is interpreted and applied, although once again my data set was too small to draw any firm conclusions. Further research on the correlations between occupation, education and authenticity-seeking behaviour is needed to make any definite claims about the roles of socio-economic class or age in shaping the projection of modernist thought in a tourism context. However, work on cosmopolitanism indicates that wealthier, more educated segments of society can better afford this perspective.

The exotic/authentic/novelty hypothesis holds true for many tourists in Belize, if by *authenticity* we mean merely that visitors believe a food item that is particularly unusual and exotic to them must be very Belizean. Dishes and foodstuffs that are already familiar as being American or Canadian do not typically garner much attention, nor do they receive strong and immediate labelling as Belizean. Few people feel that a foodstuff or dish can be Belizean if they already consider it to be American or Canadian. That "dual citizenship" is rarely allowed in the world of food categorization is yet another irony of the fundamentally essentialist nature of some "cosmopolitan" thought that claims to transcend such restrictive boundaries, yet systemically seeks out and labels that which is not found at home (Skinner and Theodossopoulos 2011).

One day I was sitting in a Scottish-owned coffee shop in Placencia when two couples from Canada entered, escaping a sudden downpour. I asked them what they thought about the food in Placencia. In the response below, their interest in "ethnic" food and their rejection of a North American menu and ambiance falls in line with the "indigenous foodie" category of Mitchell and Hall's typology. It also supports the idea that many tourists are seeking an experience that is different from what they have at home.

> **First woman:** At Coco Lobo Café,[7] but that was too American.
>
> **Researcher:** What does that mean?
>
> **First woman:** The atmosphere was too American or Canadian – what you call it – too North Americanized. *We don't come here to feel at home* [emphasis added], but we had heard it was a good place to go [and] we went. Like you said, it was like being in Florida.
>
> **Second woman:** Yeah, that's what I felt. Like a lot of places in Florida.
>
> **First woman:** Like Americans that were there – not very ethnic. The food was okay though.
>
> **Second woman:** The food was good. It was kind of fusion – their kind of fusion. When you see it, that's our take on it, 'cause you do get spots of local.
>
> **First woman:** *Fusion* is a good word, because they put their own spin on it. Atmosphere and ambiance affects that too. We walked in and you feel immediately like this could be anywhere in Canada or the USA. Whereas if you go to Marlin or D'Tatch [Belizean-owned restaurants with thatched roofs],[8] now that's somewhere different. 'Cause then I feel like, "Okay, now I'm somewhere different."

An American geography professor also rejected the familiar and evaluated novel foods as naturally being Belizean:

> Garnaches – those are delicious. I absolutely love those . . . I absolutely love them. Those are fantastic. Those I haven't seen in other places, at least under those names. . . . We were completely disillusioned by the hot-dog vendor, the Maya hot-dog vendor. We were like, "Come on! . . . Get rid of it, just get rid of it!"

These educated white-collar individuals' knee-jerk reaction to what was clearly viewed as an unwanted invasion of processed American fast food into their Belizean experience is a clear example of a visitor with expectations of authenticity as something different, novel and exotic that one cannot find in their country of origin. Their disappointment at encountering a familiar food in the form of the hot-dog vendor stems from their belief that a "real" Belizean culinary experience must have no reminders of home. The presence of an imported industrially processed hot dog is a slap in the face for authenticity-seeking tourists who believe that this fast-food snack is an embodied representation of all that is wrong with globalization and American food systems. To this particular visitor, a hot dog was "fake food" that had no business being in a real and authentic space like Belize.

The visitor might be surprised to know that this imported hot dog, this global representative of American fast food, has been transformed and localized in its new Belizean context. In Belize, hot dogs are often sold as a breakfast item and locally made habanero hot sauce is a standard topping. The lowly sausage has been even further Belizeanized in a variation on the gacho,[9] a street food in which the hot dog is rolled up in a flour tortilla spread first with refried beans and cheese. This is "glocalization" in action, undermining the neat binary divisions of modernism and otherness that the cosmopolitan geographer unwittingly unleashed in her response to my query (Picard and Di Giovine 2014; Roudometof 2016).

Urry's tourist gaze is focused on differences more than similarities, especially as some Western commonalities, such as forks, knives and napkins on every restaurant table, are taken for granted. But what are considered similarities differ depending on the origin of the visitor. When I interviewed Mexican backpackers, they highlighted the use of habanero peppers as being something they had in common with Belize, while visitors from the midwestern and southern United States often noted the familiarity of potato salad, coleslaw and barbecued chicken, well-known picnic foods at home.

If a dish or foodstuff that tourists are familiar with from home is also very common in Belize and appears to be an integral part of Belizean cuisine,[10] visitors will seek out differences between the Belizean version and their home version. Thus the dish known as potato salad is Belizean to the degree that it is different from American potato salad. One American couple said how much they liked the potato salad in Belize: "'Cause they put corn and peas [in it]. We don't put that in our potato salad. Potatoes, onions, eggs – we put eggs in ours – but they put everything but the kitchen sink in that thing. But it's got very good flavour. What is the base they use?"

For visitors from the American Southwest who were used to eating lots of refried beans at home, a similar focus on difference occurred in their description of Belizean beans: "The beans are different here. The refried beans we've had here are different than what we have back home, and it's a different bean." Whether the differences are taken as a sign of authenticity – that the dish or foodstuff is uniquely Belizean in a way that other dishes or foodstuffs are not – is not always clear and seems to vary depending on whether the visitor is seeking authenticity or not.

THE POWER OF COMPARISON

Even knowing that the majority of visitors to Belize take novel foods to be exotic, and therefore authentic Belizean dishes, menu designers in Belize's tourism industry still do not have all the answers for pleasing each and every guest. What people consider to be novel varies from tourist to tourist, and restaurants simply cannot cater to each and every individual desire.

To begin with, how does a visitor decide if something is excitingly unusual? The important question is, what are they comparing it to? When a tourist engages with anything local, the cultural background of that tourist becomes the default unmarked yardstick by which all other cultures and foodways are measured (Long 2004). The cultural and class background of each visitor shapes their perception of Belizean foods. And tourists are not limited to comparison with their own cultural background. They use all their personal food experiences, comparing the dishes and foodstuffs they find in Belize with what they have at home, what they have eaten on other trips and in other cultures, and what they have seen in grocery stores or on television and read about in books and online. What they find to be common or to be exotic or unusual and whether they label something as being Belizean will vary depending on their degree of culinary cosmopolitanism.

Culinary cosmopolitanism is similar in some ways to what Naccarato and Lebesco (2012) call "culinary capital", in their book of the same name. They define culinary capital as food and food practices that both challenge and circulate social norms and values while contributing to personal status and a sense of self. They state that "attempts to acquire culinary capital can be read as efforts to participate in projects of citizenship as individuals use their food practices to create and sustain identities that align with their society's norms and expectations" (3). Culinary cosmopolitanism focuses on how food practices, experiences and knowledge are used to distinguish the individual as transcending the strictures of personal upbringing, societal expectation and citizenship through prestige-building culinary exploration, consumption and incorporation of the other. It is the extensiveness of a person's own food-related background, knowledge and experiences. Yet culinary cosmopolitanism is also a product of modernist thought and is still tied, if only through implicit contrast, to social norms and expectations. There is no other without a self, and that self is a product of the social norms of an individual's home society (Picard and Di Giovine 2014). Thus, all subsequent culinary experiences are compared not only to each other but also to the person's earliest food memories from growing up in their home community and culture. The depth and breadth of someone's culinary cosmopolitanism gives them more points of reference for a more sophisticated comparison, shaping their expectations about food as well as how they categorize dishes and foodstuffs that they encounter during their travels. A person who demonstrates a high degree of culinary cosmopolitanism possesses extensive culinary capital that incorporates knowledge about cuisine and foodways from a wide range of different cultures, societies and classes.

As classified by Bourdieu (1979), this knowledge may be acquired through embodied, objectified and institutionalized means. Individuals may gain embodied culinary capital through their experiences growing up in a family that ate adventurously and widely, or by eating local foods while travelling, or by eating with friends from another culture. Reading and using a cookbook or watching television shows or YouTube videos about food from other cultures or places would be an objectified way to expand one's culinary cosmopolitanism. Culinary cosmopolitanism may also be acquired through institutionalized means, such as by taking cooking classes, going to culinary school, becoming a sommelier or getting a doctorate in food studies. People with high levels of culinary cosmopolitanism usually fall into the "gastronome" category of Mitchell and Hall's (2003) food tourism typology, while those from the "tourist foodies" or "familiar foods" groups tend to be less cosmopolitan.

In its embodied form, cultural capital as described by Bourdieu (1979) is part of an individual's habitus, or the norms, dispositions, definitions, beliefs and tendencies that form the basis for that person's thoughts and actions. A person's initial habitus is established during childhood, but it keeps growing to incorporate new elements throughout the person's life and provides, within certain parameters, a flexible, reflexively structured and structuring framework that the individual can creatively apply to life. Culinary cosmopolitanism thus forms part of an individual's cultural capital and is a component of their personal (and ever-evolving) habitus.

Whether they are culinary cosmopolitans or not, all tourists make some kind of comparison when discussing their food experiences away from home. My research participants, both tourists and locals, used their culinary experiences to give them points of comparison when evaluating, describing and categorizing both new and familiar foodstuffs and dishes. The implications for cuisine development are far-reaching. Culinary cosmopolitanism affects how dishes and foodstuffs are experienced, categorized and described to others by tourists, what kinds of culinary experimentation people engage in, and how people think, talk and write about their own food, which is an important part of developing and codifying a cuisine. Culinary cosmopolitanism enables Belizean tourism-industry professionals to engage in effective culinary code-switching, recommending or creating different culinary experiences for different types of guests. Multiple points of comparison allow for a more sophisticated evaluation, where a food or food experience is compared to many other foods and food experiences across a multitude of cultural and class contexts. Food experiences are evaluated based on a number of factors; countries may be compared and ranked according to overall food experience or specific concerns such as food costs, which are important for certain types of budget travellers.

When tourists were asked to describe their experiences with food in Belize, their responses reflected their degree of culinary cosmopolitanism. Most visitors made comparisons based on prior travel experiences (both by country and by region), their experiences growing up and the food from their home context. A visitor from British Columbia whose job took him all over the world made comparisons to other countries and regions but also to his childhood experiences. His culinary adventures around the world had also shaped his tastes, a key part of habitus. But despite his extensive experience and generally neophiliac approach to trying food in different countries, he did not call himself a foodie or use any other food-focused label to identify himself during our conversations. "I am often disappointed in places, and seafood is a big one, because I grew up on the coast. . . . I'm really picky about seafood. It's gotta be fresh and done right and that kind of stuff, and I can't tell you how many times I've gotten rubbery shrimp. And anyway – Placencia, since we got here, I don't think we've had a bad meal."

We do not know what particular negative experiences our visitor was thinking of, nor what countries or restaurants were involved when he ate rubbery shrimp. What we do know is that our visitor had high standards for seafood that were set during his childhood. Given that most guidebooks and Internet sources for travel to Belize say there is good seafood on the coast, most visitors are expecting a great seafood experience when they visit. Fortunately, seafood in Placencia lived up to this guest's high standards:

> **Husband:** This is the first trip [to Belize]. I've been all over the place, but comparing it, say, with Cuba, which is supposed to be famous for its food. . . . Frankly, I think the food here has been a lot better, at least more consistent. . . . I'm always looking for the local – the rice, the veggies, the meat – food, whatever. And I'll eat anything. I've eaten camel and donkey and all kinds of stuff, and I really like it when spices are used to create the flavour of the place. Like the salad [a pineapple, cilantro and cabbage slaw with a lime and olive oil dressing] – if you served that in Canada you would call it "Caribbean salad". It just screamed snorkelling and –
>
> **Wife:** Island and –
>
> **Husband:** Yeah. I mean, this [the salad] is the kind of thing Jimmy Buffet would eat.

Here we see how certain flavours and ingredients are considered evocative not of a particular culture or country but of an entire region of the world. Combining pineapple, cilantro and lime in a coleslaw reflects a tropical influence, and then serving it in the context of an island snorkelling tour only cements the association for our visitors. The husband's reference to Jimmy Buffet, famous for his songs reflecting North American fantasies of a laidback island lifestyle in the Caribbean, reinforces this regional association. The flavours do not evoke a particular nation or the culture of a particular group of people, but rather a certain lifestyle, a geographic context and a generalized daydream of what the Caribbean is supposed to be: islands and snorkelling with a Jimmy Buffet soundtrack (Spang 2011). This common dream of a tropical paradise contrasts with the hectic schedules and enclosed spaces of the suburbs and cities of North America. This is Urry's tourist gaze in action, seeking out and consolidating an attractive landscape that is different from the visitor's everyday life. These are Salazar and Graburn's tourist imaginaries, in this example creating that idealized tropical fantasy world known as "paradise".

Coming from a North American background, our tourist also felt qualified to evaluate his Belizean food experience in terms of what less adventurous visitors from his part of the world might like:

> One of the things is, for a North American palate.... So I've eaten just about – lots of different places, China and places like that – things I normally wouldn't choose to eat.... Here I don't think there is anything that would turn people off. I think it's a safe mix for people. I'm thinking sort of the average American who eats burgers at McDonald's. No reason why they couldn't experience a cuisine that is head and shoulders above what they are used to without going outside their comfort zone.

By situating his Belizean food experience in relation to what he considered to be less agreeable and more unusual food experiences in other parts of the world, like China, he positioned Belizean food as being more appealing to people with his North American background, and even being "safe" and familiar enough for the ultimate neophobe of Mitchell and Hall's "familiar foods" category. He and his wife also compared their Belizean food experiences with dining out in Mexico, Costa Rica and (indirectly) San Antonio, Texas:

> **Wife:** [regarding Belizean food] Awesome. It's exactly what I wanted and expected, a bit more. When I went to Costa Rica, it was all beans and rice and then your protein, and yeah, the seafood is *way* better.
> **Researcher:** Than in Costa Rica?
> **Wife:** Yeah, what we've experienced.
> **Husband:** [asks wife] How does it compare to Costa Rica?
> **Wife:** This is way better, way better. 'Cause everywhere in Costa Rica was rice with black beans and there's a side with sauce and meat, but it's not relying on the sauce, one specific sauce.

Husband: I've been to Mexico a few times and I've never gone to Club Med, anything like that. But I've had local cuisine in Mexico and this is light-years beyond. I'm not saying there isn't a spot in Mexico that is similar, but to me if you get outside the larger areas then it gets very basic. And in the tourist areas it's very Tex-Mex – could be San Antonio, Texas.

While superficial and based on impressions formed during short trips, these travel-based comparisons are an important use of an individual's culinary capital. Cosmopolitanism shapes the tourist gaze. The more knowledge and exposure visitors have to a wide range of foodways and cuisines, the more refined their evaluation of difference when it comes to a food experience. Someone who had not only visited Mexico on a quick trip but also read about the diversity and sophistication of Mexican cuisine would likely make a different evaluation of Mexican food, and thus a different comparison with Belize. In fact, two Mexican visitors had this to say about Belizean food in comparison to their home cuisine: "More chiles, more spices in Mexico than here, but really it has been very good. . . . Well, it's tasty. In Mexico there are regional dishes. Here we haven't noticed much variation except for the introduction of fish in this zone near the coast. My impression is that we haven't seen many differences between the north – like Corozal and the cayes, Caye Caulker and Ambergris – and here in the south."

Both the Canadian and Mexican visitors had limited knowledge of food in Belize, garnered through reading online and in guidebooks and from personal experience during their trip. However, the Mexican evaluation is based on much more extensive, first-hand knowledge of Mexican cuisine, and this affected how it was compared to Belizean food. The Canadian's experiences with food in Mexico and Belize had led him to feel that food in Belize was better and less basic, while the Mexican visitors felt that there was less diversity in Belizean food, with a lack of regional dishes. These evaluations reveal the different habitus and distinctive form of culinary capital that each visitor possesses as a result of their life experiences, cultural and class backgrounds and country of origin.

Why does it matter how visitors evaluate what they eat while in Belize? These comparisons and evaluations have important implications for the development and reputation of a Belizean cuisine that is emerging onto the international market. Tourists play a valuable role in carrying news of food to other parts of the world. Their comparisons help to situate, identify and codify the idea of a national Belizean cuisine in the global arena. Travellers' word of mouth may help to establish Belize as a place with delicious food worthy of being called a cuisine – or to tell the rest of the planet that all we cook is rice and beans.

The presence of tourists also affects the foodscapes within Belize itself, influencing the direction of culinary development. Food options in a tourism zone are often modified to fit what restaurateurs perceive to be the expectations, demands and desires of tourists, drawing from different forms of local foodways to create what Sammells calls "gastro-touristic cuisines" (2017, 166). Some restaurants in Placencia Village are owned and operated by North Americans and other immigrants who project their own culturally framed vision of dining out, further altering the foodscape from what is found in non-tourist areas of the country. Because there are different types of tourists who seek different culinary experiences and because there are different definitions of "local" and different levels of culinary cosmopolitanism among restaurateurs, there are a variety of outcomes for area menus, which I discuss in more detail in later chapters.

EXPECTATIONS

Tourist imaginaries and expectations are the subject of several fascinating books published in the past few years. *Tourist Imaginaries: Anthropological Approaches*, by well-known tourism researchers Salazar and Graburn (2014), and *Great Expectations: Imagination and Anticipation in Tourism*, by Skinner and Theodossopoulos (2011), discuss in great depth the role of imagination in fuelling what people expect to encounter on vacation. They also reveal how the resulting tourist imaginaries and expectations that simultaneously shape and emerge from the tourist and host gazes dynamically interact in the tourism zone.

Imagination is informed by past experience and habitus, and thus culinary cosmopolitanism shapes each tourist's expectations of food in Belize before they arrive. What visitors expect to find when they eat in Belize varies widely, depending on their culinary cosmopolitanism, the amount of research they conducted prior to and during travel, and individual interest and imagination. Expectations are also shaped by the tourist imaginaries –

fantasies of a hidden paradise, of the perfect meal, of a cocktail on a pristine beach – circulated by guidebooks, websites, government institutions, travel shows and tourism advertising (Salazar and Graburn 2014). Someone who has travelled extensively in the Caribbean or Central America, eaten out at restaurants from this part of the world in their home country and read about or cooked food from other countries in the region may expect to find certain ingredients, flavours or even foods when coming to Belize, simply because it is in the same geographic area. Visitors may not even be aware of their expectations until they are surprised by something during their actual vacation experience.

Investigating the gap between the tourist imaginaries promoted by advertisers and translated by personal imagination into specific expectations and a visitor's actual experience is crucial to understanding the success or failure of tourism experiences and destinations, but it is only recently receiving attention in tourism studies (see Hom 2004). A number of the visitors I interviewed claimed that they came with no or few expectations. A young Israeli stated, "I tried to have as few expectations as possible. So my mind would be more open to receive things." A young American man said, "No, not really. I try to go into new places with very little expectations. I try to be very open to what is being offered, what the culture and place can give to me." An older American man explained, "I don't know. I don't know that we expected anything." Regardless of these statements, nearly all the research participants had expectations about food in Belize. Most of the visitors expected wide availability of fresh, minimally processed food, lots of seafood, and fresh fruits and vegetables.

The majority of visitors to Belize engage in some type of research prior to arrival. I found that those who travelled in groups (even couples) typically had a designated trip planner or two. These people would do most of the research and planning for the trip, sometimes looking at food and restaurants. Most guidebooks and some websites have general information on food in Belize. The most commonly used sources of information for visitors planning a trip were the *Lonely Planet* and other guidebooks, Google searches for websites and information on Belize, and TripAdvisor reviews. Visitors who wanted to plan ahead often turned to TripAdvisor to get details about specific restaurants in the areas they were visiting.

Given that Belizean cuisine does not have a strong international presence, most tourists had little information on what they were going to find on their vacation. Most guidebooks give only a short overview on food in Belize, tending to present three options for diners: fast-food burritos, tacos and the like from roadside stands; big platters of Belizean homestyle food at budget-friendly sit-down restaurants; and more upscale restaurants that typically offer non-Belizean fare. The famous staple of rice and beans, as well as the top ten or so dishes found around the country, may be listed with descriptions (depending on the guidebook), but rarely do travel guides engage in a detailed analysis of Belize's cultural cuisines. Unlike in guidebooks on Italy, France or even neighbouring Mexico, Belizean food, while often called "hearty", "delicious" and "filling", is presented as a supporting player to key attractions, not as a notable attraction in itself. Even in touristy areas of Belize, restaurant owners and staff rarely make any reference to their listings in guidebooks. TripAdvisor consumer reviews, on the other hand, are often closely watched. Restaurateurs in Belizean tourism zones know that many visitors look for good reviews and a high ranking on TripAdvisor when deciding where to eat.

A young gay couple from New York who identified themselves as foodies are a good illustration of typical pre-travel research on food:

> **Respondent 1:** Yeah, the food. The food was in *Lonely Planet*. We have *Lonely Planet* and *Fodor's*. Those are the regular guidebooks, right? And they talk about the food being pretty good.
>
> **Respondent 2:** They talk about it being not a staple Belizean, a mixture of different ethnicities. There's nothing that's truly their own. Chinese, Indian, creole . . .
>
> **Respondent 1:** [echoes] Creole.

Individual and organized mass tourists often will plan activities in advance, relying on Internet research, because they have less time for their vacation and want to fit in all the recommended activities and experiences. This may include visits to highly recommended restaurants or a plan to try "local food" at least one night. Self-avowed foodies are more likely to research the restaurant scene online, as one gastronome couple describes here:

> **Wife:** How did we find out about the food? I think, put in the search "Belize restaurants" and you get all different choices. Sometimes you could go to the website and look at menus, like Korea Caribe.[11] I think we're pretty rare that

we pick places based on food. We really enjoy food. That's the highest priority. Really, really. . . .

Researcher: You were looking at TripAdvisor for food before this trip?

Wife: For sure. I'm positive I've been on TripAdvisor, but I googled Belize restaurants and if they had a website, I went on the website and looked at the menu and pictures. So we knew before we came here that we were going to go to Korea Caribe and Coco Lobo Café. Richard's Orchard actually looked good on the Internet.

Husband: Yeah, Richard's Orchard's menu. I think the menu looked good.

But not everyone does research ahead of time. Some visitors chose to be surprised or focused on accommodations, figuring they would work out where to eat when they got there.

Researcher: Any research on Belize before you came down?

Respondent: Not before, no. Totally came in blind.

Another respondent: By the time we had decided where to stay, I guess, I didn't really look at the food thing. We just pretty much figure that out when we get there.

Word of mouth also seemed to influence visitor expectations among the sample of tourists that I interviewed. This typically took three forms: (1) the expert at home: a friend or family member back home who had travelled to or was from Belize and recommended visiting; (2) other travellers whom visitors encountered once they arrived in Belize; and (3) local knowledge: suggestions and recommendations from Belizeans and foreigners who lived in Belize. Individuals from all classes of tourists ask for recommendations; what varies is whom they ask. For example, many research participants asked me for restaurant recommendations. My respondents sought out venues, particular dishes and foods like fish through recommendations from their hotel concierge, the lady at the gift shop, their tour guide, someone they sat next to on the local bus, other tourists staying at their hotel or with whom they went on tour, and friends of theirs who had visited Placencia before.

Visitors often described food in Belize as being "healthier" or "fresher" than what they found back home (see table 2). Nineteen of the twenty-eight groups interviewed used the adjective *fresh* or *fresher* at least once, and two

Table 2. Terms Commonly Employed by Tourists in Food Interviews

Term	Total Number of Times Mentioned	Number of Groups Who Mentioned the Term
Fresh/fresher	61	19 (of 28)
Fish/seafood/individual names like lobster, conch, shrimp.	299	22
Fruit	71	16
Rice and beans	59	21
Stew chicken	11	7

male fitness-focused travellers used the term thirteen times during our conversation. This food was explicitly contrasted with North American fast food; visitors to Belize often express their happiness at finding no familiar fast-food chains. American-style dishes such as hamburgers, hot dogs and french fries received notable attention from guests. Many visitors who were looking for something different from what they found at home in North America explicitly stated that they are not in Belize to eat burgers. Burgers and fries symbolized what they were trying to get away from: a fast-paced, overprocessed, unhealthy way of life. Less adventurous travellers and visitors who spent an extended time (three weeks or more) in Belize were more likely to have eaten a hamburger while in country, but most of my interviewees on ten- to fourteen-day vacations claimed to be trying to avoid North American fast food. It is likely that the veracity of these claims may be skewed by attempts of some of my research participants to present themselves to the food anthropologist interviewing them as adventurous and cosmopolitan.

An image of the neophobic "ugly American" tourist who refuses to experience anything new and lives on a diet of hamburgers and pizza seemed to hover, ghost-like, in the background of these conversations. Out of the eighty tourists with whom I spoke, quite a few made a point of distancing themselves from the "burger and fries" set, likely in recognition of the status to be gained from being a more adventurous eater in today's world of Anthony Bourdain and Andrew Zimmern. Here are the responses of a mixed group of Canadians and Australians:

Man: I don't wanna, didn't think I'd find a Big Whopper. Out there.

Researcher: Were you hoping you wouldn't find one or? [laughs]

Man: I wouldn't have one here if it was here.

Researcher: Okay. Yeah, there are no McDonald's, no Burger King.

Man: No Starbucks.

Researcher: No Subway, no –

Second man: You don't look for that when you come here.

Woman: I only expected different, and it's been different.

Researcher: Different from what?

Woman: Exactly, exactly. Yeah, so it's been really great not to see any fast food, any McDonald's or Subways or anything like that. That's fantastic not to see here. You just don't want burgers. You don't want fries or all of that.

Researcher: Are you surprised they aren't here?

Woman: Uh, no, I'm not actually. I'm not surprised. I don't know why, but I'm not. I'm pleased they are not.

A middle-aged couple explained: "We try not to eat foods we would have in the States. . . . Like, I've been chowing down on the plantains. . . . No burgers and fries on this trip!" They then went on to say, regarding their resort restaurant, "Oh, they have a great menu. You can get a cheeseburger. We would *never* get one, but it's there! No Italian, no pizza, no Chinese. We wanted local. And what were those chips I had yesterday? Cassava chips. I liked those. That was the closest to American I got . . . fries." A Canadian visitor quoted earlier also made sure to distance himself from the hamburger-eating neophobic traveller: "Everywhere I go I sample local cuisine. And yeah, I'm not claiming to be any kind of connoisseur or anything like that, but I don't eat burgers and fries. I'm always looking for the local – the rice, the veggies, the meat – food, whatever."

So if burgers and fries were the stereotypical food to avoid, what were tourists expecting to enjoy on their trip? What did they actually experience when they arrived that they felt was worth mentioning? What did they know about food in Belize? Within the broad category of fresh food, several foodstuffs were mentioned repeatedly. Twenty-two of the twenty-eight groups mentioned some type of seafood at least once, and one couple used the words *fish, lobster, conch, shrimp* and *seafood* a total of thirty-eight times in their interview. The words *seafood* and *fish* and the names for individual species such as lobster, conch and shrimp came up a total of 299 times in all the tourist interviews, far more than any other word. The adjective *fresh* was often associated with seafood in these conversations.

Some visitors expected to find seafood only on the coast, while others thought it would be available across the country. Some visitors were surprised by what they considered to be a lack of seafood. They were expecting to see many fishermen with lots of fresh fish and seafood for sale down by the docks and were surprised to find that getting hold of fresh seafood to cook in their vacation rental was not as easy as expected. As a middle-aged American man staying in a vacation rental with his wife explained,

> **Man:** I expected a lot of fish, I guess. I was surprised to not see it, but I can understand why, because there's so much demand for it, it's essentially sold before it gets off the boat.
>
> **Researcher:** When you say "seeing it", you mean buying it?
>
> **Man:** Yeah, buying it myself. Or even in the restaurants it's pretty unusual to see it. I guess the higher-end restaurants buy it all up before it comes off the boat and we just didn't – we haven't seen very much. . . . We went to the co-op [but] they said, "Well, come back in a few hours when the boats are here, but you better be here when he gets here."

This man had not yet eaten out at many places in Placencia and may have had a skewed view of seafood availability in restaurants, but he was not the only visitor to comment on the difficulty in obtaining fish to cook. This demand for seafood is a major challenge for restaurant owners/operators and chefs, who are always on the lookout for the freshest fish. Even locals keep a sharp eye out for opportunities to purchase fish when personal connections and fishing for themselves are not options. But despite the difficulty of purchasing fresh fish for cooking, almost all the restaurants in Placencia serve seafood as a daily special or on their permanent menu, so visitors have no trouble indulging in fish, shrimp, lobster and conch when in season.[12]

After seafood, rice and beans was the second most mentioned food and the only dish (as opposed to a foodstuff or ingredient) to get significant attention – not surprising, given its ubiquitous presence on Belizean restaurant menus and its constant mention in guidebooks. Thanks to online research, guidebooks and word of mouth, most people had heard of these staple foods before arrival, although they were not always aware of the different ways of preparing them. Guidebooks such as the *Lonely Planet* series make an effort to educate potential visitors on the difference between the one-pot dish of rice and beans and stewed beans and rice, but not all visitors learn this before arriving (Brown and Vorhees 2013). If they did not do any research they soon found out the importance of both rice and beans and beans and rice in Belizean-owned restaurants in Placencia and across the country. Rice and beans is normally served with stewed chicken or some other stewed meat, forming a de facto national dish with potato salad and fried plantain. This meal – what Mintz (1996) calls a signature or significant food – was once the Kriol Sunday dinner. Wilk (2012) details how it became Belize's national dish after being disseminated far and wide by the earliest Kriol-owned restaurants. This is one meal that most visitors are aware of through pre-travel research, as it is mentioned in all the guidebooks and most websites about Belize.

Another common expectation is tropical fruits, which are also often described with the adjective *fresh*. Sixteen of the twenty-eight groups mentioned fruit at least once when discussing their expectations and experiences.

> **Researcher:** Did you have any expectations about what you would find in Belize, food-wise?
>
> **Woman:** No, not really. Just we figured there would be lots of seafood.
>
> **Researcher:** Why is that?
>
> **Man:** 'Cause you have a big coast. [laughs]
>
> **Woman:** *Lonely Planet* and *Moon* and those have a little section on food: places to eat and –
>
> **Man:** – and tropical fruits that actually have flavour, unlike in Canada, where you get tropical fruits that taste like –
>
> **Woman:** – cardboard.

DASHED HOPES

Despite some visitors seeking out new and different foods, there is always demand for familiar foods as well, especially for those on an extended stay in Belize. The search for foods common back in North America or Europe was the most reliable source of disappointment. The most common surprises and complaints were a lack of vegetables in local foods, especially at Belizean-owned restaurants; lack of American-style beef and steak culture; lack of good coffee (visitors often assumed that because our neighbour Guatemala is famous for its coffee that we would be as well); and the fact that some tropical produce such as avocados and mangoes, which North Americans are used to finding year-round in their grocery stores, are seasonal in Belize. For the same reason, some visitors were equally surprised that dishes like guacamole were not commonly available in restaurants. Some research participants also mentioned the cost of wine and cheese and the relative scarcity of crusty European-style breads. A few visitors were surprised that fruits were not more often incorporated into entrées and several also wondered why coconut water was not more widely available.

Generally, tourists were more excited about the taste, quality and availability of fruits in Belize than they were about vegetables, which some found to be scarce, both on some restaurant plates and in the Chinese-owned supermarkets.

> **T (husband):** Well, a perceived problem by some members of the party.
>
> **J (wife):** Those who like vegetables.
>
> **Second man:** Well, J likes lots of vegetables all the time everywhere, and yes, there's not very many vegetables available in most of the restaurants in Placencia.
>
> **J:** So there isn't even the option of ordering just a salad or sides of vegetables, which sometimes they'll provide if you ask, and often sometimes there aren't even vegetables included on the plate. You know, you get chicken and rice or rice and beans, whatever. So that's important to me, but T's quite happy.
>
> **T:** It's a bonus. [laughs]

Some expectations flowed directly from the personal experiences of the tourist in question. Most of Belize's visitors are from the United States and Canada and are used to huge grocery stores stocked with thousands of items, regardless of season. Regional culinary stereotypes also shaped expectations of food. Some visitors expected to find jerk meats or Mexican-style foods, depending on whether they thought of Belize as being more Caribbean (like Jamaica) or more like Mexico. Although a Belizean Garifuna restaurant was featured on Guy Fieri's popular Food Network show *Diners, Drive-Ins and Dives*, and Andrew Zimmern visited Belize for his show *Bizarre Foods*, Belizean foodways do not have the strong international profile of Jamaican or Mexican cuisine.

WHAT IS BELIZEAN FOOD?

In my interviews with visitors I asked them how they would describe Belizean food to a friend who had never visited the country. Participant responses confirmed that most visitors are exposed to a very limited selection of Belizean dishes, ingredients and preparation techniques. Fresh seafood and tropical fruits and the dish of rice and beans (or beans and rice) and stewed chicken were by far the most frequently mentioned examples of what visitors considered to be Belizean. Dishes such as pibil, chimole, serre, cowfoot soup, boil-up, poch and curry cohune cabbage,[13] which are found around the country or associated with specific cultural groups, were rarely discussed.

The couple J and T, repeat visitors who own a time-share in Placencia, explain what they tell friends about Belizean food:

> **T (husband):** Well, the common [dishes] seem to be fish and chicken. A lot of fish and chicken.
>
> **J (wife):** Rice, beans.
>
> **T:** Where did we have that really good salad? Was that the lunch that...
>
> **J:** That was at Dominico's,[14] on your plate, but I ordered one. I ordered it extra. I ordered a pasta dish, they provided a side salad. The other thing that I always tell people, we have great local fruit, so papaya, bananas, pineapple and sometimes others when it's in season. Papaya, bananas and pineapple have always been available whenever we've been here. And oranges of course. The oranges are great for juice but they don't look very appealing.
>
> **T:** They're great for the juice, though! That's about getting over the North American expectation of how they look, but they're great, great oranges.
>
> **J:** When we have company, we kinda describe [that] you can go out and have traditional Belizean, which is either chicken or fish, either grill [or] jerk, whatever, beans or rice or coconut rice and, if you're lucky, vegetables. Or you can go to some of the other restaurants with usually expat chefs, who do more interesting things with –
>
> **T:** More international things.

J: Well, often with local ingredients, hon. But there's great food.

T: Lots of good food. Well, there's good variety.

When talking about food to be found on the peninsula, the time-share couple make an important distinction between Belizean and non-Belizean-owned restaurants in the Placencia area. Later in this chapter I address the implications of this distinction.

Regardless of the type of tourist, pretty much everyone mentioned rice and beans when attempting a description of Belizean food. These couples from Louisiana and Arizona also discuss fry jacks, puffy fried dough pieces which are a common breakfast item on the menus of Belizean-owned restaurants in Placencia:

> **Researcher:** How would you describe Belizean food?
>
> **Louisiana man:** Hmm . . .
>
> **Louisiana woman:** Probably the beans and the rice. . . .
>
> **Arizona woman:** That's on my list too. I've got lots. [laughs] Just kind of skipping breakfast, though I do want to try one of those stuffed fry jacks. We had regular fry jacks but I want to try one. We had the plain ones. It's kind of like fry bread or empanada or something like that. It's poofy and just *awesome*. . . . They were good. We got that at Wendy's – not like the redhead Wendy's. [They all laugh.] That place was good too. What did you have there? Stew meat, chicken?
>
> **Researcher:** For lunch?
>
> **Arizona woman:** Breakfast. And fry jacks.
>
> **Louisiana man:** Especially in Monkey River. If that wasn't an authentic Belizean meal [rice and beans, stewed chicken and fried plantain] I don't know what was. Made by this woman in this tiny kitchen.

A more sophisticated analysis of Belizean food was made by the American geographer who rejected the Maya hot-dog stand. This individual has visited Belize multiple times, as well as other countries in the region, and was preparing to teach a "geography of food" class at her university that year.

> **Geographer:** Coconut rice and seafood, but also a lot of chicken. Certainly chicken. Um, beans, but the beans are done more in the Central American style than the Caribbean style – the refried beans. More refried beans than black beans, which you actually see a lot in the Spanish Caribbean. I think in

the anglophone Caribbean you see the red beans. Um, tortillas, of course. I think what happens is the Belizean food gets conflated with the Mexican food and to a lesser extent Guatemalan food, because people are exposed less to it in the States. But I think it gets conflated in there, and that's why I think it's a tough question, because you've almost got Belize – It's an interesting identity because it's in Central America but it has a Caribbean identity, which is slowly changing. And in the border areas I can certainly see more Guatemalan and Mexican food and Salvadoran, from Salvadorans who live there. They live there, which is a long-winded way of saying it's all over the place.

Geographer's boyfriend: Seafood for one. Lobster and stuff that's good, fish. And coconut rice. And ceviche, yeah.

It is clear that visitors to Placencia, even if they have travelled through other parts of Belize, rarely move very far beyond the rice, beans, chicken and seafood paradigm. It is true that Belizeans eat more chicken than any other kind of meat and that beans and rice are daily staples for many people, but such a superficial analysis of Belizean food would be similar to a visitor to the United States saying that all Americans eat is potatoes, usually as french fries, and beef in hamburger form. Without proper marketing and educational outreach, tourist food experiences will remain limited, as will perceptions of Belizean food. This is problematic for the national tourism industry, as one of the fastest-growing areas in the international tourism market today is food-focused travel (UNWTO 2012).

TOURISM IMPACT

How do tourists in Placencia affect the food scene? The presence of tourists influences not only what restaurants sell but also how many food venues exist in the village, who owns them and the prices of their dishes (see table 3). In Placencia Village itself, there are approximately twenty-three sit-down restaurants and bars, along with at least eight cool spots, a number of cart vendors, and people who sell food on the street out of Tupperware containers and buckets – what anthropologist Douglas Reeser (2012) calls "bucket food". Since January 2014 the numbers have changed in this crowded and dynamic sector; a foreign-owned real-estate office replaced a foreign-owned restaurant, for example, and cool spots opened and closed.

Table 3. Food Venues in Placencia Village and on Placencia Peninsula, June 2014

Venue Type	Owner Type	Location	Total # of This Type & Location
Sit-down restaurant (no bar)	Born-Belizean[1] owned	Placencia Village	4
Sit-down restaurant (no bar)	Immigrant owned	Placencia Village	2
Cool spot	Born-Belizean owned	Placencia Village	7
Cool spot	Immigrant owned	Placencia Village	2
Sit-down bar and restaurant	Born-Belizean owned	Placencia Village	5
Sit-down bar and restaurant	Immigrant owned	Placencia Village	8
Food cart	Born-Belizean owned	Placencia Village	2
Food cart	Immigrant owned	Placencia Village	1
Sit-down bar and restaurant	Immigrant owned	Maya Beach and rest of peninsula	8
Sit-down bar and restaurant	Immigrant owned	Seine Bight	1
Sit-down restaurant (no bar)	Born-Belizean owned	Seine Bight	3

[1]The term *born Belizean* is an emic label used by born Belizeans and long-term immigrants to refer to Belizean citizens who were born in Belize, thus rendering them "born Belizean". The implication remains that born Belizeans are more Belizean than those who were born elsewhere, no matter how young they may have been when they arrived in Belize.

On the rest of the peninsula are another twelve sit-down restaurants, seven of which are at resorts, and various vendors and cool spots. The foreign-owned Maya Beach Bistro, located in the mainly North American immigrant community of Maya Beach, eight and a half miles north of Placencia Village, has been selected as the number-one restaurant in Belize by the BTB for three years in a row. Placencia Village has 1,512 residents. Being an international tourism destination is a key factor in explaining why the village hosts ten times the number of restaurants than other similarly sized communities. Seine Bight, a neighbouring village of 1,166 people only five miles up the peninsula road from Placencia, is surrounded by resorts and housing developments to the north and south, but there are only four sit-down restaurants in the village proper. Tourism affects price as well. More than a dozen restaurants offer dishes on their evening menu that cost more than BZ$25, which is high compared to the normal price range for restaurants that cater to Belizeans.

Eighteen restaurants on the peninsula are owned by North American immigrants. Their prices, atmosphere and dishes tend to reflect North American trends. According to my interviews with business owners, part of the reason for this is that the North American immigrant and retiree community, along with some better-off Belizeans, represents a financially essential year-round customer base that they must satisfy along with the seasonal tourist boom. Fresh seafood and fruit prepared in ways that fit the structure of North American dishes, along with an array of pastas, salads and the requisite chicken, pork chop or steak for non–seafood eaters, are served in an atmosphere considered appealing by North American standards.

This seems to be a successful equation for North American–owned restaurants, whose focus is the evening meal. Belizean-owned sit-down establishments tend to serve a Belizean lunch special at midday for BZ$10–$12, catering chiefly to Belizeans and other residents, and then offer a pricier evening menu that is similar to those of the North American–owned venues. For North Americans living in Belize, eating at a place with a "North American" atmosphere, reflecting current food and style trends from outside the country, represents a different experience from the norm and is often a welcome reminder of home. For this same reason, some tourists are disappointed when they encounter a North Americanized menu or atmosphere. What customers consider "different" and "exotic" depends on what their everyday baseline experiences are. Tourists' and North American immigrants' desires may not always line up, even if they are originally from the same part of the world.

T and J, the couple that vacations yearly at their time-share in Placencia, suggested that restaurants with "expat" (North American or European) chefs are more creative, with more interesting food that reflects an international palate. As repeat visitors to Placencia they have a different perspective from one-time or first-time tourists. Whether a person is visiting for the first time or the tenth, as well as the length of their stay, also influences what they are looking for and how they evaluate food in Belize. A couple in their thirties, on their first trip to Belize, stated that they felt restaurants in the tourism zone were Americanized.

> **Visitor:** It's hard for us to really tell [what is Belizean] too, because in Placencia the restaurants are very Americanized. [There are] a lot of American-style dishes that we've seen. Crossroads had that, Coco Lobo Café. There seem to be a lot of people who have originated in the US.
>
> **Researcher:** What do you mean, "American-style"?
>
> **Visitor:** Burgers, french fries, mashed potatoes, steamed vegetables. Coconut rice – we don't have a lot of that in the US.

These items do not fit into the category of "something different" that some neophiliac visitors are seeking. However, the dishes satisfy a range of customers: they appeal to Belizeans looking for something different from a plate of rice and beans, cater to North American immigrants who crave home food, are preferred by less adventurous visitors, and are often consumed even by those who seek "different" food experiences. Few visitors to Placencia want every meal to be completely unfamiliar, as the same couple demonstrates:

> **Man:** Seems to be a lot more seafood on the coast, but that would be natural.
>
> **Woman:** A lot more touristy food on the coast.
>
> **Man:** Yep.
>
> **Woman:** Well, you can get hamburgers and a grilled cheese sandwich and –
>
> **Tour guide:** – pork chop.
>
> **Second woman:** Catering to North Americans. Cheeseburgers and all that stuff. Pizza.
>
> **Tour guide:** Smoothies
>
> **Man:** Gelato, but it's good!
>
> **Woman:** We love the Belizean gelato and the Belizean Italian restaurant. [laughs]
>
> **Man:** Yeah, yeah. I would never come to Belize and look for a steak! I love the

seafood. In fact, if we go to a restaurant that's what I'm having. It's a rare thing if I order a hamburger.

At the point the woman chimed in. They both said they had had hamburgers twice in the whole month, so that's not much. The man said the Sandy Bar had a good cheeseburger.

The qualifying *but* with the mention of gelato illustrates that even for an adventurous eater something familiar can still be an acceptable and enjoyable part of a vacation experience, as long as it is memorably delicious. Especially when visitors are spending an extended time abroad, the desire for a familiar meal is likely to arise during their trip, regardless of their overall neophiliac tendencies. Sometimes you just want a burger, an American-style salad or some nachos with that Belizean Belikin beer.

IMPLICATIONS FOR CUISINE

Does the scrutiny of the tourist gaze push Belize towards a simpler, more homogenized cuisine, or does it promote diversity and the proliferation of culinary categories? Most visitors hail from North America, but what they seek can vary widely; for that reason, tourism pushes food marketing in multiple directions. Depending on the tourist, their gaze may be more or less novelty-seeking, and even the most extreme neophile may occasionally want a familiar meal. Those who seek unfamiliar foods are usually more interested in novel items that are prestige-enhancing and thought to be "authentic" Belizean food. Many visitors are most interested in foods that are different yet still appeal to the taste sensibilities they developed in their own culture. They want a safe yet authentic Belizean culinary experience that does not push their boundaries regarding what is considered palatable. Their degree of culinary cosmopolitanism often helps to determine the breadth of those boundaries. A gravid female iguana cooked with its eggs may be too unusual even for tourists who claim to love trying new foods. A small minority are actively seeking boundary-pushing culinary experiences, often for the story-creating potential and prestige they may garner from being so daring, but most visitors are not so adventurous.

Cultural marketing may better fulfil the demand for novelty and authenticity by providing multiple culturally distinct food categories instead of offering only "international" and "Belizean" food. Neophiliac visitors may be more excited about trying Garifuna, Maya, Mestizo, East Indian, Kriol and perhaps even Mennonite food on their trip to Belize. People who fall into Mitchell and Hall's "tourist foodies" and "familiar foods" categories want to simply enjoy tasty comfort food from home or Jimmy Buffet–inspired generic "tropical" vacation food: margaritas, nachos, burgers with a slice of pineapple or jalapeño on top (Spang 2011). They may seek out a "local" restaurant for one or two meals during their stay, but beyond that they are not interested in experiencing Belizean foods and do not care whether or not their meals are "authentic", as long as they are tasty and familiar.

In response to these diverse demands and to the bottom line, the most successful restaurants cater to a broad range of customers – North American–owned restaurants with the formula described above and Belizean-owned restaurants – by providing culturally marketed dishes alongside more internationalized "tourist food" such as burritos, burgers and pork chops. Trends in both directions often appear on the same menu; for example, Omar's features dishes such as "creole conch" as well as jumbo burritos. Tropicalized American fast foods, such as burgers with cilantro and jalapeños on top, are common at local bars alongside local favourites like breadfruit chips and conch ceviche.

Tourism marketing typically uses simplistic definitions of culture that can be easily commoditized. The nachos and dishes flavoured with jerk seasoning found on menus around Placencia Peninsula are responses to visitor expectations that they will find certain dishes or flavours which they associate with the region. At the same time, demand for authentic Belizean food creates space for cultural marketing such as that carried out by Omar's Creole Grub,[15] which sells itself by using a Kriol ethnic framework and intentionally playing off American knowledge of Louisiana creole cooking, which some visitors confuse with Belizean Kriol.

Sammells (2017) argues that there are four types of "local":

- local/native: the foodstuff is originally from the area and has long been used in local cooking, such as habanero peppers and corn in Belize.
- local/domestic: the foodstuff is not native but is domestically produced and has long been adopted into local cooking, such as rice and mangoes in Belize.
- local/expertise: locally rooted types of preparation and serving tech-

niques used to transform the foodstuff into a dish, such as cooking meat or fish in waha leaf or rice with coconut milk in Belize.
- local/evocative: how diners understand particular dishes as grounded in place and experience, such as a dessert that combines imported sweetened condensed milk and local craboo fruit to stimulate memories of childhood treats for Belizean diners.

According to Sammells, different restaurants represent different (often multiple) forms of localness. She calls those that play with separating and integrating distinctive types of local for tourist consumption "local-politan" or "haute-traditional". Such restaurants take different forms of localness and creatively recombine them in their menus, typically referencing an imported French-derived culinary grammar or framework in order to be considered cosmopolitan by visitors (Douglas 1972; Sammells 2017).

To be considered Belizean by most Belizeans, a dish should not only be local/domestic and local/expertise but also local/evocative, something hard to achieve for foreign chefs with little understanding of Belizean foodways. The burgers with tropical toppings (pineapple, tamarind) found in Placencia bars may use a few iconic local/domestic or local/native ingredients, but the final product is not local/evocative. Rather, it is a cheeseburger in paradise: a very specific yet totally generic Jimmy Buffett–derived "tropical paradise" tourist imaginary (Spang 2011).

A third direction for culinary development has arisen, in part to cater to tourists at high-end resorts but also in response to the more cosmopolitan tastes of well-travelled Belizeans and returned Belizeans from abroad. It is what Belizean chef Sean Kuylen calls "inspired Belizean cuisine", which falls squarely into Sammells's (2014, 2017) "haute-traditional" local-politan category. This path takes the flavour combinations, dishes and ingredients common to the different cultures and regions of Belize (local/native, local/domestic and some local/evocative), melds them with outside flavours and dishes, and innovates and elevates them by using international (French-influenced) cooking techniques and high-end restaurant presentation. This formula – local ingredients and flavour combinations + foreign technique and presentation = elevated cuisine – has begun to pop up in more expensive and experimental restaurants across Latin America. It is seen by chefs like Kuylen as a way to create an integrated and dynamic national cuisine where none existed before (see Kuylen's afterword to this book). While this approach allows plenty of room for experimentation, it is predicated upon a European-style culinary grammar. The menu design, plating and meal structure, as well as many of the cooking techniques, are imported from the French-derived professional culinary framework found in the high-end restaurants of Europe and North America. But why are European-derived culinary technique and training granted the power to elevate? Should a national cuisine not draw from an indigenous culinary framework? It is not coincidental, as Sammells (2017) notes in the case of Bolivia, that often the majority of the customers at such restaurants are foreigners of European ancestry. At this time there is no one restaurant on Placencia Peninsula that has fully embraced the idea of inspired Belizean cuisine, although it is likely that one may emerge soon.

Tourism and tourism-related immigration, along with the continued emigration of Belizeans to other parts of the country, have led to shifting demographics and a diversifying international environment on Placencia Peninsula. In order to understand the effects of these different groups' expectations and culinary imaginaries on the local food scene and the implications for cultural and national cuisine development, we have to unpack their heterogeneity. Visitors' or immigrants' culinary capital affects their expectations and the way they evaluate their food experiences in Belize. People with a high level of culinary cosmopolitanism will have a wide range of food-related experiences to draw upon as they compare and evaluate the food that they encounter in Belize, while someone who is not a culinary cosmopolitan will assess food experiences differently. This is particularly noticeable in how visitors determine whether a food is truly Belizean or not. Someone with a wide range of food experiences tends to associate fewer food items exclusively with Belize, while people with little culinary cosmopolitanism find many foods to be new to them and tend to assume that means they must be uniquely Belizean. Cuisines do not grow in a vacuum but, like all human creations, evolve through dialectic processes of imagination, awareness and experimentation. Thus the habitus of each person affects how visitors and immigrants to Belize evaluate, label and categorize food, which in turn influences the shape of cuisines as they develop in our young and diverse country. This process is accelerated in restaurant-dense tourism zones where a multiplicity of expectations and imaginaries are deployed by a diverse and constantly changing population.

Visitors' neophiliac or neophobic behaviours, their quest for food-related status, their degree of culinary cosmopolitanism, their imaginaries and expectations – plus how they are feeling on a given day – will determine on a meal-by-meal basis whether they seek out new and different food experiences, want something familiar and comfortable, or fall somewhere in between. Because their time in Belize is limited and part of the liminal holiday experience, they may be more willing to experiment with novelty than they would during their normal day-to-day lives. In the next chapter I examine how this approach differs from that of immigrants, who must learn how to *live* in a new country with different food-supply chains and foodways.

4

"FOREIGNERS" AND "ALIENS"
IMMIGRATION AND THE PLACENCIA FOODSCAPE

TODAY'S PLACENCIA VILLAGE HAS EXPANDED UNDER THE INFLUENCE of migration and tourism far beyond the loose boundaries of its original Kriol identity. First World[1] tourists, retirees, part-time and full-time residents and labourers from surrounding nations stream to Placencia for work or leisure purposes, altering the foodscape of the village as they do so.

Labels abound. The term *local* is highly contested. Does or does it not include those "foreigners" – usually "white" North Americans from the United States or Canada – who have decided to spend some or all of their time dwelling on the peninsula?[2] What about the "aliens" – the Spanish-speaking recent immigrants from surrounding countries who flock to Placencia Peninsula to work at construction and service jobs? And let us not forget the Chinese immigrants who own most of the grocery stores across Belize and on Placencia Peninsula. And Belizeans in the village are no longer limited to Placencia Kriol as people from nearby districts flock to the area to work.

Motivations for coming to Placencia vary widely. North Americans who immigrate via Belize's retirement programme are not allowed to work or generate income of any kind while in country, although some do illegally. Most Spanish-speaking immigrants from surrounding nations are seeking jobs, as are Belizeans from other districts. Non-retiree migrants from North America and Europe seek work permits in Belmopan and open small businesses or join in on the peninsula's real-estate boom as formal or informal developers or real-estate agents. Immigrant business involvement in the food sector is an important part of the multinational culinary landscape on Placencia Peninsula and other tourism destinations across the country.

This broad range of new arrivals has had a noticeable impact on local food culture and foodscapes, driving up prices and changing menus and grocery store offerings. How has tourism-driven migration changed food and identity on Placencia Peninsula, and what are the implications for the development of cultural and national cuisines? The culinary traditions that immigrants bring with them, the foods they seek in area stores and restaurants, and the food-based businesses they establish all contribute to creating a diverse culinary milieu on Placencia Peninsula. This atmosphere facilitates the demarcation and development of cuisines by providing ample opportunity for cross-cultural and cross-national comparison, contrast and experimentation. Comparison increases awareness of the differences and similarities among foods associated with specific countries and cultures. Even Belizeans who have never left their country have the opportunity to experience food from other cultures and places, especially from tourists' and immigrants' home countries, and to observe visitor reactions to and evaluations of the foods they grew up eating. Individuals identify similarities and differences and use them to categorize and label the food they encounter around them, an essential step in cuisine creation. To understand this comparative process we need to examine the culinary imaginaries, expectations and experiences of these various immigrant groups and how their desires and needs shape food availability, marketing and business across the peninsula.

WHO AND WHY

In Belize the term *foreigner* is typically used to describe visitors, immigrants and part-time residents from North America and Europe, Australia, New Zealand and other "developed" or "First World" countries with a European-derived dominant culture. Belizeans make a distinction between countries dominated by people of European descent and the rest of the world, and perception of "foreigners" is strongly racialized. Belizeans expect people from this category, whether visitors or immigrants, to be "white", and for the most part they identify as such, although there are several exceptions among the North American immigrants to the peninsula, and tourists are increasingly diverse.

Every year more and more "foreigners" – the majority from North America – make the decision to move to Belize. According to 2010 Belize census data, the foreigner category included 2,834 American-born and 685 Canadian-born people, plus the "other" group, comprising 3,886 people born outside of Central America, China or India, a number which would include any Europeans, Australians and other immigrants born in developed countries. If half the "other" group were from the First World, the total number of foreigner residents would be around 5,462, a number which seems low, given that there are over 2,000 immigrants on expat group pages on Facebook alone. The figure would not include part-time residents who were not in the country at the time of the census, which was conducted in July, a month when most foreigners or snowbirds with second homes in Belize have returned to their countries of origin (Hall 2014).

With the economic downturn and the baby-boomer generation beginning to retire, more and more Americans are looking abroad to stretch their social security dollars and live at a different pace. There is a long history of this type of migration, starting in the late 1940s in Mexico, but the large wave of adventurous baby boomers has caused a recent upturn in overseas real estate and retirement. Panama and Costa Rica, as well as the Dominican Republic, are popular destinations for retirees and other First World immigrants. Belize – English-speaking, relatively peaceful, with an incentivized retirement programme and only a two-hour flight from the continental United States – is an attractive destination for First Worlders looking for a new or second home. The impact of these immigrants on real-estate values and housing access is beyond the focus of this book but worth mentioning here. As C. Michael Hall notes (2014, 123), "In some locations . . . second homes only further highlight the increasing disparities in wealth in many societies which is reflected in competition between the mobile and the immobile for access to housing stock."

There is extensive promotion of Belize as both a retirement and a "live abroad" destination: on television, on websites like expatbelize.com and internationalliving.com, in books such as Lan Sluder's (2016) hyperbolic *Easy Belize: How to Live, Retire, Work and Buy Property in Belize, the English-Speaking Frost-Free Paradise on the Caribbean Coast*,[3] and by companies such as International Living and Escape Artist. These companies offer services, conferences, a website, newsletters and advice (for a fee) to North Americans on how to move and live overseas, including to Belize. The International Living report for Belize, sent free to subscribers, is titled "Belize: The Top English

Speaking Retirement Haven in the Caribbean". Or for US$399 you can buy their virtual tour, "Blueprint for a New Life in Belize", which promises to take you on a full "lifestyle and investment tour" of Belize, including all the "secret places" that experts will reveal (International Living 2018). For those looking for free information, there are many online resources. There are at least fourteen blogs[4] written by North American immigrants, including the popular *San Pedro Scoop*, and two closed Facebook groups catering to First World immigrants (one with 4,282 members, the other with 11,250 members), as well as the Belize Expat Exchange forum and the expatbelize.com website. Several recent North American arrivals have established websites and consulting services that claim to guide you step by step through the process of migrating to and settling in Belize. Migration is big business.

Emigration to Belize from these First World destinations is inextricably tied up with the growth of the country's tourism industry. While contested as simplistic, the pattern referred to as a "tourism-area life cycle", initially described by Butler (1980) in his early sociological research on tourism development, reflects some of the changes that happen over the lifespan of a tourism area. According to Butler's model, tourism development follows a five-stage life cycle: (1) exploration; (2) involvement, development, consolidation; (3) stagnation; (4) social and environmental deterioration; and (5) the final part of the cycle, which is either stagnation or rejuvenation, depending on the direction taken by investors and the tourism industry. This artificially stable model does not take into account the role of unpredictable yet powerful factors in development such as social and political movements, natural disasters and the state of international financial markets, but despite these limitations it can help us understand the changes that Placencia Peninsula is experiencing. The peninsula's tourism development has so far followed the stages laid out by Butler, and his model gives us some idea of what to expect in the future if no changes in direction occur.

From the beginning, visitors to Placencia Peninsula fell in love with its peaceful atmosphere, beautiful seaside and slow-paced communities and wanted to live there. According to local sources,[5] some of the earliest leisure travellers to the area purchased property in the late 1940s and early 1950s. However, the peninsula could only be reached by boat and had no electricity, so only a few adventurous travellers came through the area and even fewer decided to stay. This was the exploration stage. Those who did visit let others know and over time the trickle of visitors and immigrants grew until the 1970s and 1980s, when the first small resorts opened. In the late 1980s the United Democratic Party government targeted the area, along with Caye Caulker and Ambergris Caye, for tourism development and marketing.

As a particular destination becomes popular with tourists, it gains a public profile. Marketing and word of mouth from satisfied tourists spread the word about the beauty and allure of a particular place. In response to tourist demands, the destination also gains amenities such as wireless Internet access, coffee shops, sports bars, yoga classes, paved roads, air conditioning, boutique shopping, more diverse and upscale dining options and so on. With the growth of restaurants to service the tourist trade, local grocery stores slowly begin to stock a wider array of goods, and services like vehicle rentals and tour companies facilitate visitor experiences. This is what has happened in Placencia during its ongoing development and consolidation stage; it has significantly more "First World" amenities than similarly sized villages that have not been promoted as tourist destinations.

This is the case for dining establishments as well, as Placencia Village has many more places to eat than a village that is not a tourism destination. I define a restaurant as a venue that has seats and tables for diners located inside a building (which in Belize may or may not have walls), has a menu and serves food on a consistent basis. This includes most bars on Placencia Peninsula, all of which have reasonably extensive menus and daily meal specials. It excludes cool spots, which usually have their seating outside, and vendors who do not have seating. By my definition there are some twenty-six restaurants (some of which are bars) and roughly six cool spots in Placencia Village itself, with twelve more sit-down restaurants (seven located at resorts) on the rest of the peninsula, as well as several additional vendors and cool spots in Seine Bight Village. Eighteen of those sit-down restaurants are owned by immigrants to Belize.[6]

Tourists often enjoy Belize so much that they return again and again – with the encouragement of the BTB and Belize Tourism Industry Association. Some visitors have been vacationing in Placencia every year since the 1970s. But not all visitors want to stay in a hotel. Early on in the tourism-area life cycle – during the exploration phase – property values had not yet risen substantially and land is cheap. On Placencia Peninsula, early entrepreneurs and foreigners looking to invest for the long term were able to buy land quite cheaply both for investment purposes and to provide themselves with a vacation home. In 1999 the BTB launched its retirement programme and began promoting it across North America (BTB 2018). Placencia, as a growing tourism destination with a beautiful beach, affordable property and some First World amenities, was one of the spots that attracted retiree attention and investment. Local real-estate values rose in response. After Hurricane Iris in 2001, a whole new wave of tourism infrastructure development took place (Spang 2013). People who had purchased land prior to the hurricane decided to build on it. Property values rose again, as did foreign demand for beachfront real estate. Today real-estate "for sale" signs line the road to the village. Several hundred North American and European immigrants and part-time residents live on the peninsula: in Placencia, Seine Bight, Maya Beach (locally known as a mostly North American immigrant community), Riversdale and all points in between.

According to the 2010 national census, 473 "white/Caucasian"-identified persons lived on the peninsula (SIB 2013). Since few born Belizeans identify as white – typically labelling themselves as light-skinned Kriols, Hispanics, Mennonites or of Lebanese descent – these 473 people likely formed the bulk of "foreigner" immigrants to the peninsula, although there are several "black" and "Asian" First World immigrants as well. The total number has certainly increased since the 2010 census, especially if we include part-time residents. Some form part of the new wave of retirees, some work remotely and some own businesses locally or work for foreign-owned resorts. Some are part-time residents who go back and forth between Belize and their home countries, spending part of the year in each, or own a vacation home or time-share on the peninsula that they occupy for only a few weeks out of the year. Meanwhile, others have made a complete move from their home country and go back only to visit family and friends (Hall 2014).

ALIENS

Who are "aliens"? This term, used by the press and many Belizeans to refer to recent immigrants from surrounding Spanish-speaking countries, was particularly popular during the 1990s, when a wave of immigration swept the nation. The majority hailed from El Salvador and Guatemala, both of which had recently experienced horrific civil wars, and more recently from

Honduras. According to the 2010 census, 7,087 immigrants hailed from El Salvador, 2,240 from Mexico, 19,432 from Guatemala and 6,995 from Honduras (SIB 2013). These numbers seem low; they do not reflect the large number of illegal immigrants in a country with porous and difficult-to-patrol borders. Most of these people are seeking work, better wages and a more peaceful life with more opportunities for their children.

Some recent Spanish-speaking immigrants live in Placencia – according to the 2010 census, 1,006 "Hispanic/Mestizo"-identified people lived on the peninsula, 363 in Placencia Village itself (SIB 2013) – but because the cost of living is so high,[7] many more live in nearby communities on the mainland. Mango Creek/Independence, Bella Vista and Santa Cruz are all within commuting distance of the peninsula and they are also near shrimp farms and banana and citrus plantations that hire cheap immigrant labour. On Placencia Peninsula recent Spanish-speaking immigrants (usually glossed as "Spanish" by local Kriol and Garifuna people) often work jobs that are low-paying, labour-intensive or both. With the growth of tourism and the opening of more resorts and hotels, as well as the immigration of First World foreigners who want gardeners, housecleaners and caretakers for their property when they are away, those jobs have proliferated.

Placencia Kriols and First World foreigners alike claim that the Spanish are better, more reliable caretakers than the original Kriol and Garifuna population of the peninsula. Jobs such as yard and housework – historically performed by poorer Kriol people, children and Garifuna men and women from Seine Bight – are today dominated by Spanish immigrants. (A small group of Kriol and Garifuna men still do yard work on a "catch and kill" basis.) Men rake beaches and do yard work, landscaping, construction and mechanic work. Women clean, cook, keep house and do sewing and laundry. Some work in the homes of wealthy Belizeans or First World immigrants, others in kitchens or as wait staff in restaurants and resorts. Young men and women may be found stocking the shelves of Chinese-owned grocery stores or assisting at the two fruit and vegetable stands in Placencia Village owned by Spanish immigrants.

Some Spanish immigrant women work alongside Belizean Maya women in Chinese-owned restaurants or bars on the peninsula where it is reputed that their sexual services may be available. Bella Vista, about an hour's drive from Placencia Village, is considered a hot spot for prostitution (along with

Mango Creek, also known for its brothels). Some Placencia Kriol men joke about visiting its "butterfly farms", low-end whorehouses run by the Chinese and others. Belizean-born women also work in the sex industry, but young, sometimes illegal immigrants from "across"[8] who may not have extended family networks in Belize are easier targets for this type of work.

Entrepreneurship is the ultimate goal for some recent immigrants. For several years one of the most popular mechanic shops on the peninsula was owned by a man originally from Nicaragua. Four Spanish women operate a popular and successful food stand on the main road that is frequented by many other Spanish-speaking immigrants as well as Placencia locals, tourists and foreigners. The grandmother of one of these women runs a small sewing business while also working as the cleaner for several properties owned by a member of one of Belize's wealthiest and most powerful families. On Sundays she sets up a table and sells *baleadas* (flour tortillas filled with refried beans, fresh cheese and sour cream), a specialty found only in Honduras, her home country, and unknown in Placencia. While these women live in tight quarters with their families in Placencia Village, at least a hundred more Spanish people commute daily to Placencia from Bella Vista and Santa Cruz.[9] In 2013 someone started a daily bus service from Bella Vista, through Santa Cruz, to the peninsula and back. Every evening scores of men and smaller groups of women, some from the resorts, some dirty from cleaning yards and working on construction sites, cluster along the road running the length of the peninsula, waiting patiently to catch the bus home.[10]

In this dynamic environment, identity is often contested, multiple identities are common and a person may be labelled or categorized as belonging to different cultures depending on the beliefs and attitudes of the individual doing the labelling. In a notable example of contested cultural affiliation, Kriol, Garifuna and even Maya and Mestizo people themselves regularly gloss together Mestizo and Maya identity, often erasing Maya languages and identities in the process (Medina, 2003; Wilk and Chapin 1988). New Kekchi-speaking Maya immigrants from the highlands of Guatemala join Spanish-speaking Guatemalan Mestizos in Bella Vista Village, a source of much manual labour on Placencia Peninsula. Individuals may identify as Kekchi Maya in one context and Mestizo in another, or there may be a change in self-identification between one generation and another. A person of acknowledged Maya ancestry may switch cultures, speak only Spanish and English, and identify as Mestizo/Spanish in order to gain status in a society that still puts down the Maya as ignorant "Indians"; this practice has been well documented among the Yucatec Maya of northern Belize and southern Mexico (Loewe 2010; Medina 2003; Wilk and Chapin 1988). Because of this fluidity and movement of people between the two groups, because both Maya (mostly Kekchi, although there are some representatives of other Maya groups from the Guatemalan highlands) and Mestizo immigrants from Guatemala know how to speak Spanish, and also because of perceived similarities in their culture and food, Kriol Belizeans in Placencia tend to lump them all together regardless of their personal self-identification. As a result, some born-Belizean Kekchi Maya I spoke to were quick to make it clear that, although they lived in Bella Vista and knew Spanish, they were *Belizean* Maya and not recent immigrants.

TOURISTS, MIGRANTS AND THE PLACENCIA FOOD SCENE

Anne Sutherland (1998, 77) describes Belize as "a postmodern ethnoscape replete with recent migrations, immigrations, emigrations and the resultant demographic changes in the country". Twenty years later this still holds true for Placencia Peninsula. Placencia Village was a Kriol community for over a hundred years, but today it has diversified culturally, as has the entire region. These changes are a direct result of regional socio-economics and the growing tourism and real-estate industries.

In chapter 6 I will discuss in more detail the meanings of the different foodstuffs mentioned here. Suffice it to say that culinary heritage is a highly fluid field that is constructed, contested and changed in both public and private spaces through communal, institutional and individual decisions and choices regarding the transmission, transformation and implementation of culinary practices (see, among others, Di Giovine 2010; Picard and Di Giovine 2014). Culinary heritage can be highly politicized as part of a gastronational or cosmopolitan project, deployed as a form of resistance or loyalty to dominant social and economic powers, cherished as an intimate expression of valued kinship ties (Grandma's recipes) or rejected as a symbol of poverty (DeSoucey, 2010; Picard and Di Giovine 2014; Wilk 1999, 2006; Williams-Forson 2006; and others). The foodways of immigrants have received special attention from social scientists as they are carried from one country to another. Foodways function as symbols of difference and unity within migrant groups and as a connection to the homeland, and as such they may be embraced, rejected or altered to accommodate new forms of identity and ways of living in the receiving country (Davidson 1983; Halloran 2016; Koc and Welsh 2001; Ray 2016; and others).

"ALIENS" OR "SPANISH" IMMIGRANTS

One of the biggest visible effects of recent Spanish immigration on the foodscape of Placencia has been the proliferation of taco stands, which to my informants was a clear representation of the arrival of Spanish or Mestizo culture to a Kriol (and therefore white-flour-eating) village. Before 2010 there were no places that consistently sold tacos, but in the past nine years multiple locations vending a variety of corn-based foods have opened and closed; six remained in business in 2019. One of the first people to start a cart selling what are commonly called "corn foods" alongside flour tacos and burritos was a Belizean Kekchi Maya woman, originally from a Maya village in Stann Creek District, who now lives in Mango Creek. She started her business in Placencia in March 2010, after ten years of vending in Mango Creek. Her stand offered corn and flour tacos, burritos, hot dogs and tamales. Her customers were diverse: local Placencia Kriol and Spanish migrant labourers and Belizean Maya. Her regular customers drove taxis, worked in construction or in the service industry at low-paying jobs, or sold crafts to tourists. Few tourists stopped by her cart, save the occasional budget backpacker. She spoke Spanish with the Spanish immigrants, Kriol to the Kriol, and Kekchi to the Kekchi Maya and served everyone cheap and fast food. She closed down her stand after several years when competition increased, but she has now returned to Placencia to establish the peninsula's very first tortilla factory. There corn is put through the nixtamalization process of being boiled with calcium carbonate, then ground into masa and mechanically formed into corn tortillas. They are sold by the pound to all the new taco stands, restaurants and individuals who want to eat corn tortillas at home.

The woman's competition appeared not long after her initial foray into business in Placencia in 2010. Another stand a few hundred yards north, owned by a Belizean Kekchi Maya couple, began serving the same basic items, minus the homemade tamales. A scant fifty yards south on the village's main road, a pair of Spanish sisters operated another cart. One of them had run the same business in Dangriga but decided to move to Placencia, where there was less competition, and her older sister, who had worked at several local restaurants, joined her. Kriol locals typically refer to all the owners of taco carts as "Spanish", although several identify themselves as Kekchi Maya. A Honduran immigrant woman, known as "the panades lady"[11] by many, complements these carts, which typically close in the mid-afternoon, with her early evening rounds of the village. She sells fish panades every evening and freshly fried doughnuts dipped in cinnamon and sugar every morning.

In competition with the carts and the panades lady, a burrito/garnache/salbute/taco stand with countertop seating opened in 2012 on the roadside near the basketball court. The little wooden cool spot[12] houses two separate businesses with two shifts of young Honduran immigrant women. One business takes over the space from 6:00 a.m. until noon, and then the other pair of women come in from 12:30 p.m. until after dark. This particular stand has been very successful because of the quality and variety of its food. Because it has more space and a two-burner stove, the women can prepare fried tacos and salbutes, which the carts do not offer. They offer beef and chicken burritos instead of just chicken and dress them up with homemade salsas and hot sauce. Fresh juices are in the fridge. The cart vendors have limited space and no electricity and have to move everything when they close, so they cannot offer a broad menu. The (albeit limited) seating at this taco stand qualifies it as a cool spot – a casual, usually outdoor food venue where one can sit and eat.

At least four other Kriol-owned cool spots currently operate in Placencia Village, but this is the only Spanish-owned one and the only one that serves tacos, salbutes and other corn foods on a daily basis. Many members of the Spanish immigrant community in the area make daily stops to buy food, alongside Belizeans of all cultural backgrounds, tourists and First World immigrants. Almost every morning a number of Belizean and Spanish-speaking immigrant men – mechanics, personal trainers, construction workers, truck drivers and labourers – stop for breakfast or a *cafecito* with the ladies who work at the stand before making their way to their jobs. Mothers drop by with their children for some tacos to go on the way to school. Tour guides grab a quick bite before heading out with their guests.

"Corn foods" dominate the menu at the carts and the Honduran cool spot, although flour tortillas and fry jacks also make an appearance at some venues. While corn has always had some presence on Placencia Peninsula, it was not until the late 1990s that corn tacos became regularly available. Corn tortillas were not part of the daily Kriol diet and were not consistently available on the peninsula until after 2001, when the first ones were sent by boat from Spanish immigrant-owned and operated *tortillerías* in Mango Creek (Spang 2013). In Placencia, imported white wheat flour has historically been the basis of Kriol bread, johnnycakes, fry jacks and other breads. These wheat flour–based foods were a product of colonial-era frontier staples, barrels of flour and salted meats that the British imported from English farms for creole labourers to eat (Wilk 2006). Now freshly made corn tortillas can be purchased every morning in several of the Chinese-owned grocery stores on the peninsula and at the new tortilla factory.

Another important arena for the role of Spanish immigrants is the provision of fruits and vegetables to Placencia Peninsula. Three main vendors sell fruits and vegetables on a daily basis in Placencia Village. Two of these businesses are run by Spanish-speaking couples originally from Guatemala. One is run by a Kriol man who used to work for a business out of Belize City that provided produce directly to restaurants. That business closed and he started his own, and then began selling to the public as well. One of the Spanish couples has been coming to the peninsula to sell produce for seventeen years, braving the rough road that was unpaved until 2010. They provided fruits and vegetables and meat from Cayo District to both restaurants and the public. In the 1990s they kept the kitchens of both foreign- and Belizean-owned restaurants and bars stocked at a time when Placencia had only one grocery store, with a weekly vegetable delivery from Cayo. The other couple started coming to the peninsula around 2006. Both couples started with just a truck and sold their goods out of the back, but they now have permanent stands situated a safe distance from each other along the Placencia road. They shuttle back and forth between Cayo District and Placencia on a weekly basis.

ADAPTING TO BELIZE

Most "foreign" immigrants, whether part- or full-time residents of Belize, come from the same countries as tourists: the United States and Canada; a few from England, France, Italy, the Netherlands, Germany, Spain and Russia; and the occasional far-flung Australian. While the national, cultural and class backgrounds may be similar, the experience of being a part- or full-time resident is significantly different from being a tourist. Immigrants bring with them their culinary heritage when they commit to living in a new and different foodscape (Koc and Welsh 2001; Halloran 2016; Ray 2016). One "expat in Belize" website did interviews with ten North Americans and Europeans who have moved to the country. They asked the migrants what, if anything, they missed the most. Six listed a specific food or beverage item (cheese, meat, good ice cream, sushi, chocolate) or stated that they missed "Good Food AND Good Wine!"; "the variety of food places, oh yeah and beer"; "the pubs"; "good cheese and meat, ok, really good restaurants for that matter"; and even, occasionally, fast-food places from their home country.

Many "old-timer" immigrants warn those who may have visited as tourists and now want to move to Belize that vacationing here and living here are two different things. While someone on a trip for ten days or a couple of weeks may be using a tourist gaze, seeking out difference, novelty and excitement, most migrants to Belize find that they cannot live in a permanent vacation state, even if they are retirees. Once people have moved to Belize, they establish routines, even if for some it is spending the day hanging out at the beach bar with a rum drink. Those who have a hobby, job or business have work to do, and those who own property have errands to run and chores to deal with, or at least people to hire to do it for them.

While some adventurous tourists try to avoid familiar foods for their entire vacation, knowing that their favourite low-fat vanilla latte is waiting for them at home, foreigners living in Belize have to make permanent adjustments to what is available. Eventually even the most adventurous eaters start craving "home food" that may be difficult or expensive to find or make in Belize. Tourists who miss tender steaks and good coffee, goat cheese and French bread, or wine and McDonald's hamburgers can always wait a few days and get it when they go home. Foreigner immigrants, unless they spend a lot of time in their home country, do not have that option. Few visitors cook, and those who do still tend to eat out quite a bit during their stay. Those who live here for at least a good part of the year are faced with the task of learning how to shop, cook and eat in a new country. While every year a greater variety of foodstuffs are available in Belize and on Placencia Peninsula, most immigrants still have to adjust their diet. Old favourites may be exorbitantly expensive or simply not available. And one-stop shopping is rarely an option.

I found that foreigner expectations often depended on how long they had been in the country and on the peninsula. "Old-timers" who arrived in the 1990s and before remembered the days when produce stalls did not exist, truck vendors had to brave a rough, unpaved road that would wash out in the rainy season, and customers had to pick a number and stand in line to get vegetables at the village's only grocery store. Newer, post–Hurricane Iris immigrants may complain about the quality of the lettuce or wish they could get avocados year-round, but old-timers and Belizeans from the peninsula laugh at those comments and recall when even carrots could be hard to find.

Immigrants from neighbouring countries encounter less culture shock as they adjust to Belizean food systems. Much grocery shopping in Guatemala, Honduras and El Salvador is also done at small stores, produce stands and markets. Street vendors, hawkers and many staples (rice, beans, corn and flour tortillas) are common in all Central American countries.

I met a pair of upper-middle-class white Canadian women who had purchased house lots on Placencia Peninsula with their husbands. They were visiting to investigate how it would be to live on the peninsula when their homes were eventually built. They had not yet decided if they were going to live in the houses or simply vacation there, and food was one of the factors that they were analysing as they looked at their options. Because they were trying to determine how it would be to live in Belize, they were not eating out as much as they would if they were on vacation.

> **Woman 1:** We wanted to know if we could feed ourselves here without eating out. We've been eating in a lot. We are still going to try and make some of those [restaurants] before we go. We did all the, I guess you want to say high-end ones, and they were okay, but we are trying not to do the same ones all the time. But yeah, we are still testing the waters to see how it goes.

The women discussed what foods they had tried that were acceptable and noted what adjustments they might have to make if they decided to live in Belize. They come from a part of the world where beef is a major component of the diet. Like some of the tourist participants, they noted that beef in Belize did not live up their expectations.

> **Woman 1:** The chicken, and the steak of course, because it's Brahmin [sic]. That isn't our beef cow where we come from. Ours are all grain-fed and yours aren't, so we have found it to be tough, though we had some yesterday that wasn't bad.
>
> **Woman 2:** Some pieces were tough and some weren't.
>
> **Woman 1:** Fish . . . Well, N and M have been catching a lot of fish and it's been interesting. Some of it is pretty fishy. We had grouper the other day and it was really fishy. N is but the rest of us aren't real fish eaters, so it's been an adjustment for us. We had conch – we liked that. We've had mackerel and barracuda which they caught, so those were okay. I don't know the breakfast sausage that we've had is good. And that Italian sausage we had the other night, it was good. The bacon is fine down here. Ham not so much; N wasn't impressed with that. What else did we have? We noticed lots is done with coconut oil, coconut juice or coconut, which I am not particularly a fan of.
>
> **Woman 2:** That coconut oil is a good cooking oil. A lot healthier.
>
> **Woman 1:** I think you just have to get used to it.

For beef eaters, moving to Placencia does require some change in diet. One recent immigrant from Canada commented that he and his wife had switched from eating a lot of red meat to eating a lot of fish. This is echoed by a number of North American immigrants to Belize. He described his first visit to Canada after moving to Placencia:

> My first trip back to Calgary was red meat. There's lots of red meat in Calgary. I grew up with T-bone steak, rib eyes. And [with] all my friends it was steak on the barbie, steak on the barbie. But then I missed fish when I was there!

He went on to say that he had eaten more fish since moving to Placencia than in his whole life, because the fish is really fresh and tastes better. "So that was sort of like what we changed. We eat more chicken and fish now that we are here."

I conducted an informal survey of a "foreigner immigrants" group on Facebook, asking members, "Did moving to Belize result in any changes in your diet? What and why?" One response from an American woman who has lived in Placencia since 1998 was pretty typical:

> Few, if any, processed foods. No beef, very little pork, some chicken. More rice, less pasta. Meals are made from scratch. More rum, less wine, unfortunately. (Wine is better health-wise, than rum, but too expensive.) More fish. Fewer traditional vegetable choices, but introduced to lots of good new ones, including my now favorite green of all time, callaloo. Finally learned to make my own pizza crust and can now bake my own bread and crackers.

In a second comment she added: "No beef, except a hamburger about once a year. (Also have a coke about once a year, whether I need it or not.)"

North American immigrants often said that Belize food is healthier, fresher and less processed than back home. Some claimed to have lost weight simply by moving here. At the same time some immigrants, like some tourists, claimed that most village restaurants do not provide a lot of vegetables. One man who does not cook at home remarked about his daily meals at restaurants in the village: "I don't eat enough vegetables. I've never eaten so much chicken in all my life. Yeah, I don't eat vegetables, man. [Before moving here] even when I went out dining it always came with vegetables; everywhere I went came with vegetables. Here, vegetables are coleslaw."

Diet is affected by what is available – and for immigrants on Placencia Peninsula that means shopping.

> **Husband:** We like to cook a lot, so we've been trying local ingredients. New things all the time. Well, there is a lot available, that's the thing. What did we eat back home? A lot of rice; it's easy to get. But back home [we] ate pasta and rice. You can get almost everything [here]. There are some things that are hard to find, like fresh mushrooms.
>
> **Wife:** When you first get here, you are like I *can't this and I can't that and I can't find this* and *I can't find that*. And then you adjust and you work with the ingredients here, so maybe we have to rethink it instead of going, "You can't." 'Cause we hear a lot of that in the market: "Oh, they don't have this." We miss broccoli. They get it, but it's from Mexico.

According to Hasia Diner (2001), many European immigrants came to the United States in the nineteenth century because of poverty and hunger, seeking a place of opportunity with access to abundant and cheap food. Why then would their descendants leave that Eden, that home of drive-through restaurants and supersized markets offering every foodstuff imaginable from all corners of the globe, to live in little Belize? According to my informants, the reasons rarely have to do with sustenance for the body. Instead, some First World immigrants to Belize appear to be seeking food for the spirit: a more relaxed or slow-paced life with more opportunities to be part of a small community or to commune with nature.

Food, instead of being an attraction, is often a challenge for new immigrants from wealthier lands. Foreigner immigrants have to adjust to a new shopping scenario. North American immigrants, who make up the bulk of the "foreigner" arrivals, are used to being able to do one-stop shopping at huge grocery stores stocking more than twenty-five thousand items year-round. Even the biggest grocery stores in Belize City do not come close to that. It is an adjustment for these immigrants to shop at mom-and-pop fruit and vegetable stands for produce, then go to a small Chinese-owned grocery store for dry goods, frozen meat and dairy products.

AVOCADO SUPPRESSION UNIT

Part of the art of food shopping in Belize involves insider knowledge and accessing informal markets. Recent work on informal markets and tourism focuses on the role of Internet-based platforms in providing informal accommodation (such as Couchsurfing, Airbnb and the like) and their effects on area housing markets, as well as on how tourism is used by government institutions as an excuse to gentrify spaces and physically displace informal businesses (see, among others, Bromley and Mackie 2009; Chen 2017; Guttentag 2015; Picard and Buchberger 2013). There is also a large body of work on how tourism drives informal and often illegal markets in sex work.[13]

Tourist desires for "authentic" housing that will provide a more personal cross-cultural experience than a hotel, and for sexual and/or romantic intimacy with locals, are seen by most researchers as part of the search for and consumption of the "exotic" (and therefore "authentic") other as discussed by Heldke (2008) and Picard and Di Giovine (2014). In some cases these attempts to incorporate the other may also be an expression of a tourist's efforts to recognize universal commonalities, while also incorporating or consuming the appealing differences embodied in the other, as part of a cosmopolitan project (Beck 2006; Calhoun 2003; Shepherd 2017).

Food also provides a daily opportunity for cross-cultural experiences and intimate interactions with locals. Small food businesses and informal food-procurement practices are an important part of the Belizean economy. Most research on the intersections between tourism, food and informal markets focuses on street vendors in Southeast Asia, but informal markets intersect with tourism across the globe (see, among others, Henderson et al. 2012; Hsieh and Chang 2006; Tinker 2003; Truong 2018). Belize street vendors, casual restaurants and, as discussed here, produce-stand owners often engage in informal procurement strategies to obtain foodstuffs that are rare, imported, out of season or highly seasonal.

In Belize, signs, marketing and advertising are scarce in comparison to North America, even in a visitor destination like Placencia where levels of signage are much higher than in non-tourism communities. Some of the best and freshest food is sold through informal channels. No licences, sales tax or business registration is involved in these exchanges along often-short supply chains between the actual producer (farmer, baker, butcher) and the consumer. You might have to ask around to track down a particular food item, or hawkers will bring it right to your door in a pigtail bucket or wheelbarrow – but only if you know enough to call them over as they pass down the street. The best whole-grain coconut bread is baked to order out of someone's home and sold, via text message, only to those in the know. Finding fresh seafood in Placencia on a given day often involves the application of kinship networks, cell phone contacts, the exchange of "favours" and patient waiting for the right boat to come in. Belizeans know to buy fresh butchered pork out of coolers in a pickup that comes around town now and then. First World immigrants, especially recent arrivals, who complain about the frozen meat in the Chinese grocery stores may not realize that something tasty is also for sale – or they may be squeamish about purchasing meat out of the back of a battered four-by-four. Obtaining out-of-season or imported produce often requires asking around or special orders. In Belize, the consumer is expected to take the initiative.

While most produce vendors on the peninsula do source a few imported items such as apples, celery and pears, the majority of the produce found in Belize is grown in Belize and is thus limited by its climate, what local farmers are growing and the seasons. One produce vendor in Placencia is famous for acquiring items of particular interest to foreigners who live on the peninsula. He buys vegetables and fruits such as butternut squash, Mexican avocados (when Belize's avocado trees are not producing) and even Brussels sprouts, asparagus, fresh rosemary, blueberries, Ocean Spray cranberries and Driscoll's strawberries from smugglers who bring in these items from Mexico and sell them illegally on the black market. Avocados may not legally be imported because they are produced in Belize (albeit not year-round) and thus subject to laws meant to protect the agricultural sector. Other protections, licensing requirements and import laws make it difficult for small purveyors to legally import fruits and vegetables from out of country, so smuggling is common. This is the case not only in Placencia but also in other tourism areas like San Pedro, Ambergris Caye, where there is high demand for fruits and vegetables that are not available year-round. The outcome of this demand includes hilarious Internet threads about where to find illegal Mexican avocados, like this one on the AmbergrisCaye.com forum:

> Hey ———, how's it going.... Look ... I need 10 kilos of stuff.... Right away, I don't care what the price is, I have customers lined up asking for it. I know the border has been tight as of late and they're lots of checkpoints, but call your guy and make it happen ok?
>
> Perhaps those bringing avocados into Belize should pack/disguise them as drugs, thus allowing freer movement about the country???
>
> That said, we might (?) have some here.... Come to the back door and knock three times ...
>
> And if anyone is looking for some mangos, decent carrots, or some pretty killer romaine, I might know a guy who knows a guy.

While light-hearted in nature, this thread foreshadowed a more recent incident in Belize. Avocados became headline news in March 2018, when an avocado dealer (later found to have legally procured his out-of-season produce) was physically assaulted in Belize City by police officers who believed that the avocados were smuggled from Mexico (Shoman 2018). There was huge public outcry against the police in the wake of this incident, especially as yet another drug plane full of cocaine had escaped police capture that same day. A meme called "Avocado Suppression Unit" showed a police officer holding an avocado vendor at gunpoint and saying "Drop those avocados or you're guacamole"; it was circulated widely on social media and jokes about the dangers of vegetable shopping lingered for months.

Despite this unsettling incident, the produce stands of Placencia continue to source fruits and vegetables that are sought after by North Americans living on the peninsula. I learned about butternut squash and cranberries through Facebook one day, when a North American immigrant enthusiastically posted on the "Placencia Food and Restaurants" page[14] about the latest delicacies for sale. Immediately other North American immigrants flocked to buy up all that the vendor had to offer and then responded to the original post expressing their excitement and satisfaction and discussing what they intended to make with their coveted acquisitions. These ingredients are not well known in Belize except in canned form and they play little role in Belizean dishes, but they are iconic foods for Americans. This is especially true in the fall months, when winter squashes and cranberries are associated with Thanksgiving, an unequivocally American food-centred holiday which nonetheless has begun to appear on the menus of a large number of Placencia restaurants in November. These Thanksgiving dinners cater to the culinary heritage of homesick American immigrants and also offer something different yet familiar to Belizean diners, who have watched many a Thanksgiving feast on American cable television networks. The idea of the Thanksgiving feast has been transformed into a Belizeanized "turkey dinner" found across the country: an American-Belizean mashup that includes rice and beans, stuffing (usually out of a box) and turkey, often served with a side of canned cranberry jelly and Marie Sharp's hot sauce.

Both locals and immigrants make requests for specific produce from their vendor of choice. Immigrants whom I spoke with reported that you had to ask for smuggled Mexican avocados because they were "hiding in the back", or that if you asked so-and-so, they would bring you all the basil you wanted or track down dates for the holidays. "But you don't know about it unless you ask" was a common refrain. This was insider knowledge, the kind of information that long-term immigrants share with recent arrivals, sometimes on Facebook-hosted closed groups established for that very purpose.

EXPAT EFFECTS

The presence of immigrants from North America and Europe and the growth of foreign-owned restaurants have influenced what is available at produce stands and in local grocery stores. In an informal Facebook poll of a closed group where First World (mainly North American and a few European) immigrants share information, I asked members if they had asked any grocery stores to bring in food items, and what items they had requested. Twenty-one responses indicated that members or their spouses or families had requested things from grocery stores or produce vendors. Requests included packaged processed foods: whole-wheat pita bread, whole-wheat pastas, ready-made hummus, couscous, almond milk and ranch dressing. Imported cheeses such as Brie were also mentioned, along with gluten-free products, nuts and frozen foods – peas and corn, blueberries and sweet peas.

The largest Chinese-owned grocery store in Placencia Village, which opened in May 2012, was lauded for being especially responsive to requests for special items. One woman, an immigrant from the United States who has been living in Placencia since 2008, explained:

> Items I asked for the owners of [store name] to bring before they opened their store was . . . Pita whole wheat, whole wheat pastas, large variety of pasta, Cheer Free N Clear Detergent, Oxy Clean Stick, Garbanzo Beans, Tahini, Ready Made Hummus, Brie and a large variety of imported cheeses, variety of nuts, frozen blueberries. All of the items I would get at Brodies or Sav U in Belize. The other store owners said they wouldn't bring them in because no one would buy them. HA! Now everyone shops at [store name] and the items fly off the shelves.

When the store in question first opened, a North American immigrant posted on Facebook about how many different cheeses the new grocery carried. Other immigrants joined in and a lively conversation ensued as the "foreigner" community shared what latest hard-to-find imported item had appeared at the new store. Earlier stores had also responded to customer requests. A respondent to my Facebook survey stated, "Couscous is good example of food which wasn't available down here which Wallen's brought in due to requests from customers, but it always sold out very quickly, now with all the big Chinese supermarkets they all have most of the time."

RESTAURANTS AND DINING OUT

Another area where foreign immigrants have affected the food scene in Placencia is the restaurant industry. There are approximately forty-one food venues on the peninsula where you can sit down to eat; this includes resort restaurants, bars that serve food and cool spots. Of these venues, eighteen are owned or owned and operated by immigrants from North America or Europe, four by Chinese and two by Hondurans. As mentioned in the previous chapter, in non-tourist areas on the mainland with similar population densities, the number of sit-down food venues is much smaller. The four Chinese restaurants are mainly fast-food places frequented by Belizeans and immigrants wanting a quick fried chicken or late-night burger, but they also offer simple Chinese-style dishes (typically stir-fries, chow mein and chop suey) to customers looking for something different. The Chinese restaurants as a whole do not tend to cater to tourists, although one venue (defunct as of 2017) did advertise to visitors. The two restaurants owned by Honduran immigrants have a mixed customer base of tourists, immigrants and Belizeans. Most restaurants on the peninsula cannot survive without resident support, since during the slow season, particularly in September and October, very few tourists come to the area.

The restaurants owned by "foreigner" First World immigrants tend to be higher-end places that are more dependent on tourist and First World immigrant customers. Unlike the immigrants interviewed by Krishendu Ray in *Ethnic Restaurateur* (2016), these restaurant owners, while they have brought their own food culture with them to Belize, do not usually highlight that culinary heritage or the cultural background of their dishes in their menus or marketing.[15] This is likely because their target customers are mainly of the same general cultural background (North Americans of pan-European descent). Despite a growing body of experienced professional cooks in Belize, many resorts still bring in chefs from other countries. At least two such chefs, brought in from North America, opened their own restaurants on the peninsula after leaving jobs at foreign-owned resorts. There are also many foreigners who have immigrated to Belize with the specific goal of opening a restaurant. Three foreign-owned restaurants in Placencia are in their second generation of foreign (American) ownership, sold to other immigrants at prices few Belizeans could afford.[16] One very popular American-owned restaurant was started by a couple with Culinary Institute of America degrees; they signed a lease agreement while on their honeymoon in Belize and three weeks later shipped down a container load of supplies to set up their new venue.

Apart from the stand-alone venues, a number of restaurants are associated with three all-inclusive resorts north of Placencia Village. All three are under North American ownership. The same goes for specialty food stores: the only two coffee shops are owned by First World immigrants, as is the peninsula's only ice-cream shop. Misleadingly listed as the "number-one restaurant" on TripAdvisor is Tutti Frutti, Placencia's only gelato shop, which is owned and operated by an Italian couple who combine secret ingredients from Italy with Belizean cream and fruit, making it an extremely popular dessert spot for everyone. Tourists, Belizeans and immigrants of all types love their gelato. Residents of the village pine for their creamy treats when the shop closes for two months every slow season, while the owners make their annual visit back to Italy. Cognizant of the large foreign influence on food in our tourism zone, one visitor joked to me that they loved the "Belizean gelato" and "Belizean pizza" available on the peninsula. How "glocalized" these foodstuffs are is debatable. The gelato and pizza are made with many domestically produced ingredients and thus are indeed local/domestic, but pistachio gelato and pepperoni pizza cannot be local/evocative. (The one exception may be Tutti Frutti's seasonal soursop gelato, a flavour combination that for many Belizeans evokes childhood memories of eating cold soursop pulp with a drizzle of sweetened condensed milk.)

During the slow season, particularly in September and October, many restaurants close for at least a few weeks, and some for a month or two, because there is simply not enough business. Tourists alone are not enough to keep a restaurant in business on a peninsula overloaded with dining choices. During the slow season even resort restaurants offer "local" prices (for people residing in Belize) to attract business and make ends meet.

Apart from owning and operating almost half the restaurants on the peninsula, "foreigner" First World immigrants are also avid customers. With at least four hundred foreigners dwelling on the peninsula and more staying over the winter months, a reasonably sized customer base frequents the foreign-owned (and Belizean) bars and restaurants, helping to keep them afloat during the slow season. First World immigrants, despite coming from the same countries as Belize's tourists, make their day-to-day lives in Belize and have a different perspective on food experiences. Novelty-seeking is not as likely to be enhanced by the ludic lens of the tourist gaze; instead, immigrants have to learn new and different patterns of shopping, cooking and eating along with experiencing dishes and staples that are different from those of their home countries. The same restaurants and bars that some more neophiliac tourists call Americanized, and reject as not reflecting the "different" feel of Placencia, attract homesick First World immigrants who are seeking a dining experience that reminds them of their home countries.

Demands for foods from home have changed the offerings of local grocery stores as the number of First World immigrants on the peninsula continues to rise. Financially secure immigrants are willing to spend more money on expensive imported groceries and dishes at restaurants than most Belizeans. Along with tourism, First World immigrant presence has driven up food prices and increased grocery diversity. Couscous, frozen English muffins and goat cheese have nothing to do with the fishing history and diet of Placencia Peninsula, but now they can be found in area stores. Immigrants from the neighbouring countries of El Salvador, Mexico, Guatemala and Honduras may learn how to cook Belizean-style rice and beans, but they also bring with them a wide array of corn foods that have expanded the variety of inexpensive street food available in Placencia. Thanks to them, corn tortillas are now widely available at Placencia grocery stores and produce stands. Chinese immigrants have also diversified grocery store offerings: Chinese-owned grocery stores are well stocked with items such as rice flour, spring roll wrappers, canned bamboo shoots, dried mushrooms and oyster sauce, while plastic bags stuffed with bok choy and mustard greens lurk under the rows of soft drinks and beer in the refrigerator section.

Immigrants play an important role in cuisine development in Belize by creating a diverse foodscape that encourages cross-cultural and cross-national comparison, driving culinary categorization, experimentation, development and marketing. With the arrival of immigrants and tourists from across the world, identity and citizenship have become increasingly important and controversial issues. Dialogue and debate have arisen over the parameters of Belizean identity, including its expression via food. As immigrants involve themselves in the food sector of the tourism industry and influence the local food scene, what people eat increasingly becomes a question of identity rather than simply a matter of making do with what is available (Halloran 2016). As we will see in the next chapter, how that identity is expressed is an important part of the work that tourism personnel do to effectively engage with and sell to their guests.

5
COSMOPOLITANISM, CULTURAL CAPITAL AND CODE-SWITCHING

AS THE PREVIOUS CHAPTERS HAVE EXPLAINED, FOOD FORMS part of a complex, constantly changing and diverse environment in international tourism zones. On the Placencia Peninsula there are more than forty restaurants and cool spots, multiple cart and "bucket food" vendors, and the presence of a varied array of culinary traditions, thanks to immigration and tourism. How do individuals living there navigate these murky waters to their advantage? In such a diverse environment, more cosmopolitan individuals with higher levels of cultural capital have a better chance of competing successfully. People with the necessary knowledge and awareness use identity work, including code-switching and strategic deployment of cultural capital, to advantageously position themselves in a globalized and competitive world. Given the high level of immigration that is a secondary effect of a growing tourism industry, even individuals who do not directly work in the tourism sector find themselves in a new socio-economic environment as prices rise on everything from groceries to real estate. As the world comes to their doorstep, they are pushed to be cosmopolitan "global citizens", to develop and deploy what Bunten (2008) calls commodified personas, to draw upon their stores of cultural capital and to code-switch between cultures in order to be economically successful, all in the face of often dramatically unequal access to financial and educational resources. Those who do work in tourism have to navigate identity on a daily basis, not only on the local level but also as national and international "representatives", or, as the BTB puts it, "ambassadors of the nation".

COMMODIFICATION, CODE-SWITCHING AND IDENTITY

I learned about entrepreneurship on the peninsula from daily observation and field notes, informal interviews, twenty-five food life-history interviews and ten semiformal business interviews, as well as participation in the tourism economy as a small-business owner. I culled information regarding code-switching, self-commodification, cosmopolitanism and cultural capital from my pile sorts, interviews, field notes and extensive participant observation of tourism zone interactions.

Code-switching is a term typically used to describe changing from one language, dialect or form (register) of speech to another, but I expand the idea to describe identity work where an individual switches from one culturally mediated expression of self to another. Code-switching falls squarely under what Dell Hymes famously labelled "communicative competence", which is the sum of an individual's linguistic (grammar, syntax, vocabulary) and sociolinguistic (understanding social context when using language) knowledge (Hymes 1972). Sociolinguistic communicative competence is essential to seamless code-switching in the multicultural environment of Placencia's tourism zone, where different languages, accents and linguistic registers are markers for the expression of distinct identities.

Face work – what Erving Goffman (1967) labelled the activities involved in representing oneself to others in a way that brings about social approval – is an important aspect of these forms of identity work. Identity work is particularly active in tourism areas because people of many different cultural and national backgrounds are constantly meeting and interacting. But because Belize is such a diverse country, many Belizeans were familiar with code-switching before the arrival of the tourism industry. In the Placencia tourism zone these are daily practices that came up again and again in all my research activities. This is especially true for what the tourism industry calls frontline personnel, those people who directly interact with tourists in the course of their jobs.

DEFINING TERMS

Before discussing identity work in Placencia, I would like to define the terms I use throughout this chapter. What is a *commodified persona*? When individuals engage cross-culturally in a tourism setting, they often practise self-commodification, which Bunten (2008, 381) describes as "a set of beliefs and practices in which an individual chooses to construct a marketable identity product while striving to avoid alienating him- or herself". In essence, a commodified persona is the result of self-branding: a selective, strategic presentation of personal identity meant to appeal to tourists. This is not a new concept in the world of tourism. From entrepreneurs to hustlers, tourism-savvy individuals knew about and utilized the self-branding concept long before Tom Peter's 1997 article "The Brand Called You" excited American office workers and ushered in a new era of Internet-based self-commodification.

Individuals engaged in self-commodification practise a delicate balancing act as they try to appeal to visitor interests and expectations without "selling out" their own sense of self. In the tourism encounter, there is space for individuals to use their host gaze to evaluate and respond to dominant socio-economic forces and visitor stereotypes and even to confront these structuring forces (Bunten 2008; Moufakkir and Reisinger 2013). It is up to individuals how they construct a commodified persona, but if they do not keep in mind the demands and requirements of the job, the market value of the persona may not measure up. They might not make as much money in tips or be popular as a tour guide or waiter. Clients' expectations must be fulfilled if frontline personnel want visitors to return, and repeat customers are an important part of overnight tourism in Placencia. Performance is an intrinsic part of the commodified persona: trying to keep a balance between fulfilling client expectations and not buying into their stereotypes of the "other" that the individual may represent.

As discussed in chapter 3, *cosmopolitanism* – exposure to a wide range of experiences outside of your own class, culture, religion and country – is an important component of identity work in a tourism zone. Having a broad range of experiences builds cultural capital. Cosmopolitanism enables individuals to effectively build appealing commodified personas and to communicate and form personal and business connections across cultural, class and national lines.

Code-switching from one identity to another is a way of expressing cosmopolitanism as a form of cultural capital. When individuals strategically deploy a commodified persona meant to appeal to a tourist consumer, they engage in face work, consciously shaping and presenting their personal, cultural and national identities. When cross-cultural communication takes place between a visitor and a Belizean in a tourism zone like Placencia, cosmopolitan Belizeans with knowledge of the visitor's culture and country will alter their speech and self-presentation. They shift to English when speaking to the visitor, shake hands instead of offering a "buck" (fist bump) and change their topic focus from everyday village affairs to a visitor's welcome and information session. This code-switching can be very persuasive and useful in the international tourism industry. Depending on context and speaker objectives, individuals may exercise their communicative competence, engage with tourism imaginaries, and accentuate one or combine a number of cultural, national, racial, cosmopolitan, class and gender identities in order to more effectively forge a personal connection.

Frontline personnel regularly give advice and information about the local restaurant scene and Belizean food to foreign visitors. Frontline personnel include (but are not limited to) wait staff, concierges, tour guides and taxi drivers. Visitors often expect these individuals to act as cultural brokers, to understand and be able to translate between different cultures and societies. Frontline personnel use their host gaze to learn what guests expect and want in order to provide good service and advice. They have to know enough about each visitor's cultural and culinary background to be able to give comparisons and explanations of local dishes. *Culinary code-switching* is the term I used to describe this food-focused identity work. Being able to switch from whole fish to boneless fillet, from rice and beans to mashed potatoes and steak or sashimi and salad is a crucial skill in this highly competitive industry, where tips for excellent service can be an important part of income.

Culinary code-switching allows an individual to demonstrate how cosmopolitan their culinary capital is. As mentioned in chapter 3, depending on their degree of cosmopolitanism, visitors are able to make more or less sophisticated comparisons and evaluations of foods encountered while travelling in Belize. The same applies to Belizeans and other residents in the Placencia tourism zone. Being able to culinary code-switch requires an individual to experience and appreciate different foodways and cuisines and understand at least superficially the underlying organizing principles and how they differ from one culture or nation to another. The more cross-cultural and cross-class culinary experiences people have had, the better their sociolinguistic communicative competence and the more sophisticated their culinary code-switching can be. Cosmopolitan Belizeans not only know that North American tourists do not usually like bones in their fish, but they also offer their hypothesis of why that is and can tell a visitor exactly why Belizeans would rather eat their animals bone-in.

CODE-SWITCHING

In my research I constantly ran across examples of this type of identity work. Culinary code-switching is not a simple culinary diglossia with individuals choosing between a high-status acrolect (foreign food) and a low-status basilect (local food). In colonial Belize, Wilk (2008, 102) claims, "while the cultural superiority of European food was not challenged, a variety of cuisines developed that were intermediate in status between European and local rural (often 'ethnic') cuisines". These mesolects also make an appearance in culinary code-switching. Serving fry jacks with jam and butter on the side reflects a culinary code-switch from the locally preferred plate of fry jacks with refried beans, eggs and cheese to a mesolect that incorporates North American preferences for sweets at breakfast. When a restaurant owner instructs her staff to give a North American visitor a plate of stew meat with no bones in it, reserving the bones for Belizean customers, she is engaging in culinary code-switching between the acrolect of American food desires (no bones) and the basilect of local preference for bony cuts. The same thing occurs when a guide on a snorkel tour serves visitors lobster tail and takes the chopped-up head home for his mother to stew. Or when a concierge, asked to tell visitors about local food, indicates the places with the best grilled fish fillets, then for her own lunch eats some garnaches or a plate of rice and beans and stewed oxtail from her favourite cool spot. When a restaurant owner offers coconut rice and fried plantain or mashed potatoes and green salad as side options, that is culinary code-switching between Belizean and American tastes. Following Wilk's hypothesis, replacing the mashed potatoes with a coco yam–coconut milk purée would result in a mesolect option that blends American fondness for pulverized starchy root vegetables with local ingredients. But in today's dynamic tourism zone, one person's mesolect might be another's acrolect or basilect. Whether a particular ingredient or dish is a higher-status acrolect or a lower-status basilect depends on the perspective of the individual evaluating the menu. It is in this complex foodscape that frontline personnel must (if they wish to be successful) acquire and strategically deploy their knowledge of the culinary imaginaries and expectations of their guests.

When a Belizean describes the cultural and socio-economic background of beef in his country and how it has shaped his preference for a well-done steak today, and then compares that with North American steak culture, he is displaying his culinary cosmopolitanism. His argument that hygiene was the reason for not ageing beef in pre-refrigeration days in Belize is acceptable and persuasive for visitors from countries that have strict sanitation codes and social concerns about food and cleanliness. In these examples the Belizeans doing the culinary code-switching are using their cosmopolitan cross-cultural knowledge about the foodways of the tourist to make decisions about what they think the visitor is looking for, would enjoy or would want to avoid. They can express themselves in a range of culinary registers and may experiment at home, mixing together ingredients and dishes associated with different points on the culinary "foreign to local" continuum. Belizeans who engage with the tourism market use their host gaze (informed by their level of cosmopolitanism) to determine and deliver tailored products that they think will get the best reception, based on their evaluation of the tourist's cultural, national and class background, interests and expectations. They may also create culinary imaginaries that reflect and redirect tourist expectations.

Expressing a commodified persona and engaging in code-switching are possible only with the exposure and awareness discussed by Wilk (1999) in his paper on real Belizean food. Self-awareness is particularly high in communities that participate in the tourism industry. While television, the Internet and other media forms bring the world to people's doorsteps in many communities in Belize, tourism zones take cross-cultural exposure to a different level. In tourism zones, thousands of visitors embody their culture and social norms in restaurants, on the street, at bars and clubs, on the beach, at the hotel and during tours. During high season in Placencia visitors are everywhere, and respite may be found only in the relatively private sphere of one's yard and home (although even then a lost motorist might end up turning their car around in your yard or a pedestrian might wander near your house on the way to the beach). Everyone cannot help but have some level of exposure to people from different cultural, class and national backgrounds. This exposure increases awareness of the differences and similarities in attitudes, perceptions, behaviours and beliefs between and among different groups and individuals. Some awareness of the different identities available in the world must be present before individuals gain enough communicative competence to effectively code-switch or commoditize their own identity (or identities).

TOUR GUIDES

Tour guides are frontline personnel in the tourism industry who spend entire days, sometimes even weeks, in sustained contact with visitors. Bunten (2008) describes Tlingit tour guides as participating in both Euro-American and Tlingit cultures as they guide. Many Belizeans also participate in multiple cultures, particularly those from less dominant cultural groups who must know about and participate in the dominant Kriol culture. In a small and diverse country like Belize, some level of participation in more than one culture is the rule rather than the exception. Close to a quarter of Belizeans in the 2010 census identified as belonging to more than one cultural group. Tourism further increases the need for awareness and participation in other cultures. A Kriol tour guide in Placencia must know at least the basics of North American society, particularly "white" Euro–North American middle-class culture, in order to interact effectively with his or her guests. In recent years the number of Canadian tourists has grown significantly. Tour guides who were used to dealing chiefly with Americans now have to learn about Canada as well. An understanding of the cultural norms of Euro–North American societies helps tour guides understand the basis for visitor expectations and to more effectively customize their product.

Despite the focus of tour descriptions on destinations and activities, the guide is an essential part of the tour product, and self-commodification is part and parcel of tour guiding. Many guides have little stories or lines that they use over and over again which they feel represent themselves and their identity in a way that tourists will like. A Placencia tour guide and captain with more than twenty-five years in the industry, Mark Leslie regularly informed guests that he was the product of "four generations in Placencia: pirate, fisherman, tour guide".[1] This phrase paints an exciting picture of the history and culture of Placencia, linking the guide's identity to the sea and the pirate history of the Belizean coast. Mark's story engaged with a common tourism imaginary by describing and authenticating the tour guide's credentials as a real local with deep roots in the area. These narratives help to build a picture, a commodified persona that the tour guide uses with his or her guests. As a tour guide specialized in culinary and cultural tours, when I tell my guests about getting my first machete as a birthday present at age four, that helps to establish my credentials as a cacao farmer from the jungle.

These anecdotes tie into master narratives and tourism imaginaries of local peoples' connection to their natural environments, building a persona that is appealing to visitors. Storytelling of this type walks a delicate line between what the visitors expects and wants to see and what the tour guide believes to be his or her identity. This balancing act is most successful when tourist expectations overlap with the guides' personal vision of themselves. A tour guide in his early thirties told me a story of how cooking is in his blood, passed down from his father and his ancestors:

> **Tour guide:** Well, it tells me that, hey, they praise my dad and I got his blood, so they praise me too. [laughs]
>
> **Researcher:** Maybe it has less to do with blood and more to do with efforts, no? [laughs]
>
> **Tour guide:** Well, a lot of it has to do with blood, trust me. Cooking runs in our family, in our blood.

These kinds of essentialist assertions are appealing to visitors who are seeking authenticity, because it helps them to feel that the tour guide they are interacting with is truly from and part of the place they have come to visit.

Sociologist Dean MacCannell problematizes the quest for authenticity, discussing staged space and performance in his famous article "Staged Authenticity: Arrangements of Social Space in Tourist Settings" (1973). Using Goffman's idea of front and back stages, MacCannell argues that there is a (sometimes infinite) continuum of "false backs" in the tourism industry which tourists enter believing they are experiencing "authentic" local culture. The private back area that a tourist sees is not really the "authentic" back area, as it would be were it not prepared for tourist viewing. It is a *staged* back area, a private space that claims to be authentic but has been intentionally altered for public viewing. MacCannell argues that it is almost impossible for tourists to actually get to an unstaged (and thus authentic) backstage, but does seem to accept that one may exist somewhere (Goffman 1956; MacCannell 1973). According to MacCannell (1973), the mere fact that a tourist is seeking out an authentic place, material object or personal interaction means that the experience will be in some way transformed – staged – for that tourist, rendering its authenticity problematic. Following this argument, authenticity is predicated on a lack of performance, so according to MacCannell's argument, Bunten's commodified persona, as well as the act of code-switching in self-presentation, confirms that tourists see an inauthentic "staged" product made for tourist consumption.

As discussed in earlier chapters, the presence of tourists leads those in the tourism industry to adjust the content of their front and back stages. But can we accept MacCannell's argument that this staging somehow destroys the authenticity of the experience? What makes something real? Is authenticity really negated by performance (see Taylor 2001; Zhu 2012)? Cohen (1988) argues that authenticity is a product of modernist thought that rejects modern society as inauthentic. Those who accept this premise search abroad for the "authentic other" as a means to anchor personal identities cut adrift by the advent of the industrial era in First World countries (Picard and Di Giovine 2014). As a social construct, Cohen asserts, the meaning of authenticity is negotiable and thus open to interpretation, which ideally should allow for staging without destroying the "realness" of the final product.

Bunten (2008) rejects the idea that natives in the cultural tourism business create and present an inauthentic product. She says the whole cultural presentation involved in a cross-cultural encounter is much more complex and that native tour guides in her research put together commodified personas that drew from multiple cultural frameworks. They are, she says, "sophisticated culture brokers" (382). Guides have the power to choose how they respond to the tourist gaze (Moufakkir and Reisinger 2013; Salazar 2010; Urry 2002). A person who is self-commodifying can resist being stereotyped, despite pressure to perform for clients.

Power and agency are most important here. MacCannell was focused on the wrong thing. The question is not whether the identity represented is staged but, rather, who is evaluating and judging the authenticity of someone's identity (see introduction, Salazar and Graburn 2014). Psyche Williams-Forson (2006) addresses these power struggles in her work on black American self-representation through food. She argues that the process of self-definition, in order to be successful, must be supported by a deep understanding of the power structures at work behind external definition and stereotyping. In the case of tourism between "developed" and "developing" countries, these include economic and educational inequalities that support essentialized stereotypes of the exotic – often seen as primitive, naive and un(der)educated – "other" that circulate as part of tourism imaginaries and expectations. Frontline personnel have an opportunity to use their host gaze to evaluate the expectations of visitors and resist, correct or support stereotypical tourism imaginaries (Salazar 2010; Salazar and Graburn 2014; Skinner and Theodossopoulos 2011). Bunten (2008) describes tour guides highlighting parts of their personalities which conform with tourist expectations while at the same time "correcting" visitors' exoticizing tourist gaze, by showing them other parts of their identity that the guides feel are important and authentic aspects of who they are as modern Tlingit people. The result is a commodified persona that conforms in part with visitor expectations but also corrects, redirects and educates the tourist gaze. To achieve this goal, tour guides selectively utilize circulating tourism imaginaries, tapping into master narratives about the histories, cultures, environments and destinations at hand (Bruner 2004). Guides rework these narratives according to their own beliefs and knowledge before (re)presenting them as "seductive tourism tales" to a tourist audience, responding to and "glocalizing" popular tourism discourse (Salazar 2010).

Bunten's term "sophisticated cultural broker" is an apt description of the identity work performed by frontline workers in Placencia. Processes of self-commodification are flexible, form through human interaction and reflect the structured agency that Bourdieu (1977) discusses in his analysis of cultural capital and habitus. This agency in self-presentation allows frontline personnel to adapt to a wide range of guests with different interests and expectations, as long as they know what the visitor is looking for. Astute tour guides ask questions and quickly read visitors, using this feedback to inform what they say and how they present themselves to their guests (Salazar 2010). Many people do something similar, if less consciously, on a regular basis in job interviews and other contexts where our personalities and identities are under scrutiny. Does identity work somehow inauthenticate the interaction?

In Placencia and in my informal encounters in other parts of the country, most tour guides strongly believe their self-representations are accurate depictions of their identity; they would reject or might even be insulted by the idea that their story is somehow not authentic. Identity work reflects the struggles over agency and power that underlie a constant negotiating process between the tourist gaze and the host gaze about who determines what Belizean culture is. How could an outsider determine authenticity? Even if someone's identity goes beyond the appealing "pirate, fisherman, tour guide" imaginary, that does not mean they consider that partial self-representation to be inaccurate or inauthentic. This self-commodification is simply emphasizing a certain part of their total identity, a part that is particularly appealing to tourist consumers.

What visitors deem authentic reflects Heldke's (2008) novelty/exotic/authentic triumvirate. Something that is novel to a person's experience is often considered exotic and, because of its novelty and exotic nature, authentic to the culture being explored. As I discussed in chapter 3, the authenticity of something very similar to what tourists experience at home is more likely to be questioned, especially if it does not fall in line with their preconceptions. Because they ate it at home in America, several tourists who participated in my research questioned the authenticity of potato salad as a Belizean dish. Mark Leslie, the Placencia tour guide mentioned earlier, knew that emphasizing his "exotic" pirate and fisherman ancestry would be a more effective use of his personal identity than emphasizing his childhood in a relatively well-off home. Both parts of his life experience are real and shaped his adult identity, but his ancestry was a better opening line in conversation with potential clients. As a tour progressed, he would exhibit the parts of his identity that he believed conformed with his visitors' expectations, but he also educated them about himself and local culture. Some of those topics and facets of his identity were things most tourists in Belize might be unaware of and may even clash with their general preconceptions of the area and its people. A guide, through one-on-one interaction and the strategic deployment of commodified personas, can direct, expand and correct visitor expectations and preconceptions of Belize and its people. The tourist gaze is turned back upon itself, questioned and redirected through the agency of Belizeans who, acting in the same way as the Tlingit guides that Bunten described, refuse to restrict their commodified identities to visitor expectations.

Visitors also prefer a tour guide with enough cross-cultural knowledge and interpersonal skills to understand and cater to their interests and allay their concerns or fears. The more understanding guides have of the social background and cultural heritage of their guests, and of the tourism imaginaries that drive their expectations, the better they will be able to "perceive the everyday world around them through the eyes of tourists" (Salazar 2010, 51). Visitors appreciate a guide who is cosmopolitan enough to be able to chat with them about a wide range of topics beyond interpretation of the country and explanations of tour activities. Cosmopolitanism is an important component of commodified personas in a tourism zone and one that challenges common visitor stereotypes of untravelled, uneducated natives who live a "simple" life exclusively tied to their culture, history and surrounding environment (for examples, see Adams 1997; Ardren 2004; Volkman 1990). It asserts categorical equality, even if the Belizean engaged in the interaction is economically poorer or has less formal education than the tourist. Mark established his authenticity and identity as a "real Belizean" by using his "pirate, fisherman, tour guide" story, but he also made sure to let his American guests know that he had travelled to thirty-six states across the United States. If the visitor was from a place he had visited, he let them know where he had been and his experiences in their home state. This often surprised guests, but it also helped them feel more comfortable and opened up room for conversation and personal connection, leading to good tips, repeat tours and good reviews online.

IDENTITY WORK AND ENTREPRENEURSHIP

In a crowded public sphere, self-commodification or branding allows individuals to stand out as unique products that visitors want to support, interact with and "consume" (Peters 1997). Code-switching allows individuals to market themselves and their products to a wide range of potential customers from different cultural and national backgrounds.

CREOLE ECONOMICS

Self-commodification and code-switching are important components of what Browne (2002, 2004) calls "Creole economics" – informal, flexible, opportunistic economic activities that demonstrate the cleverness of the entrepreneur. Browne's research in Martinique shows how the Caribbean models of reputation and respectability shape attitudes and practices of entrepreneurship.[2] She argues that reputation in the economic realm in Martinique is achieved through businesses which demonstrate cleverness and cunning and are often extra-legal or off the books. These entrepreneurs demonstrate independence, worldliness, intelligence, personality and capability. These same qualities are necessary to be a successful frontline person in the tourism industry (although cunning and illegal activities may be penalized). Browne (2002) claims that the cultural emphasis on these qualities derives from the unique history of creole peoples in the Caribbean, a place with the world's longest (and, some say, most brutal)[3] colonial history.

The creole economics that Browne has identified and described in Martinique constitutes a specific cultural model of economic behaviour that may be found, in varying forms, across the Caribbean. In Belize, one form of creole economics is called "catch and kill", a term describing opportunistic money-making behaviour that typically involves one-off jobs or entrepreneurial opportunities that have a limited time duration and a cash pay-out and are usually part of the informal economy. Individuals who are not working at a steady job will often describe themselves as living by catch and kill. People exploit money-making opportunities when they arise and may also actively seek them out ("hustling"). Food is an important part of catch and kill in the Placencia Peninsula tourism zone.[4] Sales of homemade food from a roadside table to a holiday crowd, of bottles of cold water on a particularly hot day or of a box full of ripe fruit from one's tree during mango season are all examples of catch and kill. Creole economics is also practised to a greater or lesser extent in some "legitimate" food businesses in Placencia, including Kriol-owned cool spots and even some restaurants, such as when ingredients are obtained "free" in return for a favour.

REPUTATION AND RESPECTABILITY

Creole economics is based on a foundation of reputation-enhancing entrepreneurial activities. Successful business owners enhance their status through clever entrepreneurship. I have found that men often engage in reputation-building activities more overtly than women, but I question the gender-exclusive way in which Wilson originally defined respectability and reputation. I agree with Besson (1993) that many reputation-building activities can be found among women and in a wider range of places and spaces than Wilson (1969) initially considered. Independent food businesses can be an important avenue for women to build reputations, as savvy business owners, as purveyors of excellent food and as people who have access to useful contacts and connections (also see Freeman 2007, on Barbados).

In Placencia cooking is an arena in which men and women compete for reputation. The paid and thus to some degree professionalized cooking activities of tour guides, adapted from the necessary cooking by fishermen at sea, continue a tradition of male cooking that is explicitly contrasted with women's cooking at home. Men cook at sea as part of their job as tour guides and at home only when they feel like it, while women are expected to produce three meals a day, seven days a week, no matter how they feel. A good housewife is expected to "cook, wash and mash"[5] on a consistent basis. Placencia attitudes towards who cooks what, when and where are very similar to the European and North American dichotomy that describes male cooking as paid professional work, usually performed in the public sphere, with male home cooking done only for special occasions or employing special techniques and equipment, such as barbecuing (Swenson 2013). Female cooking, on the other hand, is regarded as an unpaid labour of love, performed to nurture the family in the private sphere of the home as an everyday "domestic duty".

In Belize there is a long history of food businesses operated by women outside the home that challenges this dichotomy of professional cooking versus unpaid housework by putting women into the public sphere, where they build reputations that are not based exclusively on kin networks.[6] There are ample opportunities for women to engage in creole economics via the food sector and connect the home with the public sphere, even if they do not have a cool spot on the road. Some women who operate food businesses out of their home have a village-wide reputation for their delicious food that transcends the public–private distinction.

Ms Brenda, the proprietor of the cool spot located next to the village piers, engaged in self-commodification as she flirted with tourists, made jokes and called to them from across the street, loudly inviting them to come try her barbecue or rum punch.[7] She used culinary code-switching in her menu and marketing, selling serre, or fish stew, and calling it gumbo and regularly preparing and selling her version of jerk chicken, which is considered a Jamaican dish by Belizeans but which tourists often expect to find. She also made cuttobrute, a local sweet of raw brown sugar and half-ripe coconut cooked together, and sold it as "coconut macaroons" to visitors. They became famous, and the proprietor's over-the-top personality garnered her a listing on TripAdvisor, an important global online review site and app for hotels, restaurants and activities. The main draw was her personality, as mentioned repeatedly in her TripAdvisor reviews: "But the best part of going to Brenda's is her personality. Such a fantastic person. I miss you my friend and will see you again next year." Another person mentioned both the famous "macaroons" and the owner: "Ms Brenda is the sweetest (and possibly funniest!) person we met in Belize! Her jerk chicken was by far the best meal we ate in Placencia. And the macaroons were to die for!" Another stated: "Brenda lured us in with a plate of fresh fruit. She was quite charming." Another reviewer noted: "As the other reviews state, Brenda is quite a character and you may hear her before you see her as she likes to sing." Even a bad review gave points for personality: "I gave it a 2 because Brenda is jovial and the food taste[d] good generally."

Another example of creole economics and self-branding in action is the Coconut Man. Originally from Belize City, the Coconut Man reinvented himself in Placencia. He was reluctant to give out his real name, but his nickname "Coconut Man" was known throughout the village and to visiting tourists. He wove mats and made hats and baskets out of free coconut leaves, doing his work outside in public spaces where visitors could watch his craft. He walked the beach, the sidewalk and the street shirtless and wearing one of his signature hats, selling his coconut crafts to visitors and local businesses. One American-owned bar even hired him to teach a "Coconut College". Tourists and foreigners paid ten dollars each to receive an education on all aspects of the coconut tree and its fruit; the event culminated with his peeling a coconut with his teeth, a trick often featured in competitions at Belizean fairs and festivals.[8]

Here the act of self-commodification creates a personal brand that allows very small businesses to carve out a niche in a competitive market. This focus on the individual and flexibility in self-presentation is a key component of creole economics. The use of cross-cultural knowledge to engage in effective marketing through code-switching is also found in larger establishments. Omar's Creole Grub uses *creole* in the restaurant name and menu descriptions knowing that some American visitors associate that word with Louisiana and good food. The owner described how it works: "Creole wah ring a bell because da south da states da creole. Some tourists tink its Cajun creole of Louisiana. We say no, it's our own creole, di real creole, no French creole ... Dis no patois business here! Dey say, 'Okay, we try it,' and dey say, 'Oh, it's good!'"[9] This understanding of the potential for a different interpretation of the word reflects the owners' culinary cosmopolitanism. Their savvy use of *creole* as an adjective in their restaurant name and menu helps to sell their dishes.

NOT A LEVEL PLAYING FIELD

Cosmopolitanism, code-switching and self-commodification can help small-business owners and individual employees stand out and compete more effectively, but identity work cannot fully compensate for major structural inequalities in education and access to investment capital. And not everybody has the same level of cosmopolitanism. Without communicative competence, code-switching will not be effective. Knowing what to talk about and when is an art which requires cross-cultural knowledge that goes beyond the superficial.

Some people living or working in Placencia Village have not travelled and work in jobs or have businesses that do not cater directly to tourists. They have less exposure to and awareness of the cultures and identities of the different groups that visit Belize. As a result, there are different levels of skill in code-switching and effective self-commodification. It's easy to learn that Americans like hamburgers and pizza, but a whole other level of culinary cosmopolitanism is required for a non-American to understand and communicate the difference between Texas and South Carolina barbecue. A Belizean who wants to successfully advertise food to an international, culturally diverse clientele has to learn about the food and dining expectations of those clients. In Belize today, many homes have access to American cable television and the Food Network is often a source of more detailed information about American culinary imaginaries, foodways and food preferences. Those who do not possess this knowledge tend to sell to other Belizeans. These entrepreneurs sometimes say that it is "too much work" trying to attract both Belizean and visitor clientele and instead they focus on developing a loyal local following.

A good example of different degrees of culinary cosmopolitanism is the making and selling of guava jelly in Placencia. An older Kriol woman who bakes Kriol bread and makes jelly out of her home sells the jelly bottled in reused Nestlé coffee and other jars. She tapes a handwritten label to each that says "Mirna's Guava Jelly".[10] Several grocery stores in the village buy the jelly from her and retail it on their shelves alongside Marie Sharp's and imported jams and jellies.[11] Recently a local Kriol restaurant owner also began making and bottling guava jelly to sell out of her family restaurant, Omar's Creole Grub. Using the name "Creole Gial Guava Jelly", her family created a brand name and logo (a painting of a guava fruit) and made laminated full-colour posters which they hung up in their establishment and several other places around town. They purchased small one-cup jars to hold the jelly and put full-colour labels with the brand name and logo on each jar. The family then sold each jar for double the price of Mirna's jelly. Both women had learned to make guava jelly from older relatives who knew the technique and the quality of the product is the same. The restaurant owners' product, thanks to savvy marketing, has more visibility and appeal to visitors, which enables them to sell their jelly at a much higher price. This is culinary cosmopolitanism at work. With their years of experience interacting with and marketing to visitors in their restaurant, the owners knew what would appeal to tourists. They captured visitor interest with an eye-catching culturally framed logo and brand name and used smaller jars that could be easily carried home as gifts and souvenirs.

In Belize it is common to name a business or product after the person who runs or made it. Many restaurants and other businesses across Belize are named after their owners, allowing the personal reputation of the individual to speak for itself. But tourists whom I interviewed seemed to enjoy venues and products with funky eye-catching names that they felt reflected the culture and environment of Belize. A venue named "Mary's" does not necessarily capture the tropical vacation experience that these visitors are seeking, for it means nothing to a visitor who does not actually know Mary and her extraordinary cooking skills. For this reason several bars and restaurants on the peninsula (mostly foreign-owned) are named after local plants and animals. In the case of the Omar's Creole Grub guava jelly, calling it "Creole Gial" reflects the culture and language of the village in an appealing way. Instead of promoting the individual who made the jelly by selling it under her name, it generalizes her identity by branding the product in accordance with her gender and her cultural identity. Guava jelly is no longer just something to spread on your morning toast but also a visible expression of (commodified) Belizean Kriol culinary heritage (Picard and Di Giovine 2014). Using Kriol orthography for the name further differentiates and exoticizes the product by tying it to Belizean Kriol culture.

The other guava jelly maker does not regularly interact with tourists and is not thinking about how to market her product to them, nor is she aware of how much she might be able to charge for her jelly with effective promotion. Unlike the restaurant owner, she does not have access to someone in her family with computer and visual arts skills who could do the design work for free if she did decide to brand her product. Finally, she does not have the level of financial security and capital to invest in making labels and buying jars, nor does she have her own venue where she could sell the jelly without an intermediary taking part of the profit. Villagers know that she makes excellent guava jelly and seek her out to buy it directly from her, but tourists are likely to overlook her product on local grocery store shelves.

IDENTITY WORK AMONG BELIZEANS

As long as the Kriol woman can sell her guava jelly and make enough to live on, there is not necessarily a problem. Code-switching and self-commodification are not always for tourist consumption. Not all businesses in Placencia want to cater to tourists or First World immigrants; some rely on Belizean and Spanish immigrant clientele. Most of the taco and hot-dog stands in

Placencia sell to Belizeans and Spanish-speaking immigrants, with some North American immigrants and the occasional backpacker thrown in. The individuals who run these stands still engage in code-switching but do not think a lot about North American society and culture. These entrepreneurs make and sell cheap food that residents eat for breakfast on the way to work or as a snack between meals. They may speak Spanish to one customer, Kekchi Maya to another and Kriol to a third, making culturally appropriate conversation and serving them all the same portable meals of tacos, hot dogs, burritos or tamales.

In all areas of entrepreneurship and business in Belize, cross-cultural knowledge is an asset. Many Belizeans have some degree of communicative competence in code-switching between different Belizean cultures. Being able to speak even two words of another cultural group's language helps a Belizean navigate a diverse society by smoothing the path for cross-cultural interaction. It demonstrates that the individual has enough interest in others to bother learning something of their idiom and is a sign of respect. The same applies to food. Knowing about and enjoying the dishes and ingredients that are significant or specific to another cultural group, especially a minority group, shows respect, demonstrates cosmopolitanism, facilitates personal connections and enhances one's reputation.

Identity work is an important component of daily life in such a small and diverse society as Belize. In an international tourism zone like Placencia, where an even greater number of cultures and even nations are represented through tourism and migration, identity work is essential, particularly for frontline personnel in the tourism industry. Code-switching and self-commodification allow individuals working in a tourism zone to flexibly exert agency, compete in business, educate the tourist gaze, move between cultures and classes, and display cosmopolitanism as cultural capital. Culinary code-switching allows Belizeans to demonstrate culinary cosmopolitanism, express cultural and national identity, connect with visitors through a symbolically important daily medium, and effectively market food products to a wide variety of visitors and residents.

But what exactly is Belizean national identity? Who is Belizean? What does Belize's cultural diversity imply for the development of a national identity and, by extension, a national cuisine? Similar questions can be asked in any culturally diverse country. The answers help us better understand the role of food in the development of cultural, regional, national and cosmopolitan identities around the world. In the next chapter I examine the role of race and cultural politics in shaping national identity in this diverse nation.

6

WHO IS A "REAL" BELIZEAN?
THE CULTURAL POLITICS OF GASTRONATIONALISM

HOW DOES FOOD RELATE TO THE CONSTRUCTION AND evolution of national and cultural identity? This question is most salient in a rapidly changing and heterogeneous place where the power relations and relative positions of different groups of people are in flux. In that context, material expressions of identity become particularly meaningful and visible ways of claiming political, economic and social space. In post-colonial Belize a culturally diverse population attempts to understand and express itself on cultural, local, national and international levels while dealing with the effects of a growing tourism industry and major demographic changes resulting from emigration and immigration. At each of these levels food is part of the processes of identity construction, differentiation and expression. In this pressure-cooker environment, cuisines are being forged.

People who live in a tourism zone or work in the international tourism industry are exposed to a wide range of cultures and nationalities and develop heightened awareness of and differentiation around their culinary traditions. Food-based distinctions are simultaneously politicized and commoditized. People celebrate them as expressions of multicultural harmony or international cosmopolitanism, deploy them in identity discourse to express culinary pride or personal preferences and use them as marketing tools to attract tourists. They create, vigorously defend or completely ignore boundaries, depending on context. Some foods are more controversial than others. The edibility of armadillo, a once common bush meat, is now questioned by some Belizeans who have read about its role as a carrier of leprosy, while gibnut continues to be a popular meal. Experimentation and adaptation are encouraged while traditional foodways are lauded.

In Belize food categories such as "Kriol", "Belizean" and "local" are defined and applied differently depending on the context, the actors involved and the model of nationalism employed. Food categories and the process of food categorization reflect the relationships between different models of nationalism, the status of the different cultural groups that make up Belize's diverse society, and how all of these interact with the rest of the world. At local, national and international levels people engage in culinary code-switching, creating and strategically employing culinary categories, experiences and "signature foods"[1] to legitimize identity claims and express cultural capital in highly competitive environments. The complex socio-political negotiations that undergird competing discourses of nationalism in modern Belize have resulted in a hierarchy of overlapping cultural and national food categories cross-cut by class considerations. As discussed in chapter 4, new immigrant groups occupy an uncertain position in relation to national culinary identity even as their presence is substantially altering the foodscapes of Belize.

GASTRONATIONALISM, TOURISM AND THE POST-COLONIAL NATION

Gastronationalism describes the way food is harnessed to express national pride and identity in response to the homogenizing pressures of neo-globalization (DeSoucey 2010). This chapter takes a hard look at the cultural politics underlying processes of national culinary expression in Belize.

In the context of a booming interest in food and international travel, culinary tourism has expanded beyond its traditional territories such as France and Italy and is emerging in post-colonial nations where the development of a "national cuisine" may still be in process (Cusack 2004; Wilk 2006). Around the world individuals, tourism agencies, governments, businesses and ethnic groups have sifted through their cultures, selected aspects considered to have visitor appeal and commoditized them for the international tourist industry. It is a messy and often controversial process that may involve informal feedback from guests, personal beliefs about what will sell and market research funded by government or non-governmental organizations. As a daily necessity and a means through which to explore other cultures, food has taken an increasingly important place in the tourism market. Not only individual cultures but the foodways of entire nations may be promoted as part of the tourist experience (Cusack 2004; Hall et al. 2003).

Wilk's (1995) concept of "common difference" refers to the way in which differences are standardized at the international level, allowing them to be compared across cultures and nations in a global arena. This difference gives value to tourism destinations, products and experiences, including food, by allowing them to be compared with one another at an international level (Urry 2002). I argue that common difference is a prerequisite for cosmopolitanism, as this standardization allows individuals to evaluate and incorporate the appealing differences that they encounter during their international explorations. The ability to compare and the valuation of difference lead to a proliferation of discourses about foods pertaining to a particular country, culture, region, town or even neighbourhood. These can be used to promote a patriotic feeling of national or even global (cosmopolitan) unity or to divide people into groups along cultural, class, gender, religious or geographic lines.

Expressions of gastronationalism typically appropriate and utilize cultural, regional and local foodways as symbols of national identity. Concerns about cultural belonging and citizenship are expressed through food categorization and marketing. What part does food play in the discourses of nationalism, belonging and cultural identity in Belize? How do these interconnected conversations affect food marketing in an increasingly cosmopolitan, professionalized and competitive international tourism industry?

WHO IS A "REAL" BELIZEAN?

How do we define Belizean food, and what does that say about who we consider to be Belizean? The symbolic importance of material culture in creating a sense of national identity cannot be overlooked (Hobsbawm and Ranger 1983). Food, the most necessary and ubiquitous of material objects, is strongly imbued with culture, symbolism and, often, national pride. Having a national cuisine is also useful for marketing to tourists.

The way my research participants defined Belizean food reflects a specific model of national identity. Belizean anthropologist Laura K. Medina (1997) published an insightful piece on race, ethnicity and competing forms of nationalism in Belize. Drawing on Caribbean anthropologist Nigel O. Bolland's

(1987) typology, Medina states that three main models of national identity coexist in Belize. The Belizean government officially promotes pluralistic nationalism, which defines Belize and Belizeans as a harmoniously diverse multicultural society, with each culture group possessing its own attractive cluster of traits – language, food, music and "traditions" – in the context of an overarching national identity, what Wilk (1995) calls "domesticated" or "safe" nationalism. In this model, well-groomed and socially acceptable diversity is an asset. This model of nationalism is used by the BTB in its publications and international advertising that urges visitors to experience "the many cultures of Belize". Synthetic nationalism, promoted early in independence, attempts to create an overarching "national" Belizean culture which is different from and more powerful than each cultural group's identity and that blends traits of different cultural groups. This national Belizean identity supersedes the ethnic identities of individuals and mutes cultural difference.

Hegemonic nationalism is not promoted by the Belizean government but is, according to Medina, an "unofficial" model which has been embraced particularly by Kriol and Garifuna Belizeans in the face of large-scale Spanish immigration from surrounding countries. This discourse racializes Belizean identity, claiming that Spanish-speaking Belizeans (a term often broadened to include all Maya groups as well) are not real Belizeans, and that only those with some degree of African heritage truly represent the nation. Most of my research participants reflected the influence of hegemonic nationalism in their definition of Belizean food, marginalizing Belizean Maya, Mestizo, East Indian and sometimes even Garifuna cultures while exalting Belizean Kriol culture and foodways at a national level.

RACE, ETHNICITY AND HEGEMONIC NATIONALISM

Why isn't the "Belizean food" category more inclusive? And why, at the same time that Kriol food is nationalized via the Belizean food category, are more restaurant owners in Placencia advertising the same dishes, on a cultural basis, as "creole"? Given the powerful influence of Kriol cooking on national cuisine and the early conflation of the two at the time of Belizean food's emergence, it is interesting that some people have begun to market certain foods as "creole" in a way that seems to reflect a more ethnic orientation. The use of this adjective to distinguish some Kriol dishes from a nationalized Belizean food and from the food of cultural groups such as the Garifuna (well known in Belize for their foodways) reflects a public debate that has emerged in the past twenty years: whether the Kriol should be regarded as an ethnic group, as "real Belizeans" who are the living product and representation of the country, or as black-identified members of a transnational pan-African movement. This debate has taken place mainly among the Kriol elite of the country, but its publicizing via newspapers and other media has made most of Belize's population witness to the discussion.

National identity in Belize is ethnicized and racialized (Medina 1997). While the official government narrative is one of multicultural harmony, the popular hegemonic nationalist discourse is tied to certain essentialized and racialized conceptualizations of ethnicity (Medina 1997). In Belize, the most powerful group continues to be the Kriols. Under the British, the Kriol were the socio-economic and politically dominant group during the colonial regime. Problematically but commonly described as a mixture of African and European immigrants, and thus a product of colonialism, they have long been associated with the birth of the nation as a British colony in the heart of Spanish territory (Judd 1989b; Shoman 2010). For most of the history of the colony[2] they comprised the largest population, and prior to and after independence in 1981 they were associated strongly with the nation and Belizean identity (Judd 1989b). Ties to the rest of the British-controlled Caribbean are reflected in the fact that some of the ancestors of some Kriol people were brought to Belize from Jamaica as part of the empire's slave trade.

As a result of a growing influx of refugees and economic immigrants from surrounding Spanish-speaking countries, combined with steady emigration of Kriol Belizeans to the United States and elsewhere, the Kriol are no longer numerically dominant. Since the 1991 census they have continued to dwindle in number as compared to the heterogeneous "Spanish" or "Hispanic" group.[3] According to the 2010 census, the Kriol now represent only 21 per cent and the Spanish (Hispanic) a full 50 per cent of the total population. So far the Kriol remain politically, economically and culturally dominant, although they are well aware of their shrinking demographic position. The arrival of growing numbers of Spanish-speaking and "white" (chiefly North American) immigrants on Belizean soil has resulted in a complex process of differentiation, demarcation and defence that Kriol individuals enact along often ethnicized and racialized national boundaries and/or often nationalized ethnic boundaries. Food is a powerful and ever-present medium for these processes, as illustrated by Kriol assertions that Spanish, Chinese and white immigrants' food is not as thoroughly and properly seasoned as Kriol cooking.

The role of race and African ancestry in Kriol identity is important in shaping the hegemonic nationalist model of Belizeanness. Because the British officially founded the contemporary nation of Belize, narratives of belonging often converge on ties to British colonial rule. In the creolization narrative, both African and European ancestry – but only if tied to Belize's colonial past – are acceptable claims to Belizean identity, but a mixture of the two is ideal (Judd 1989a, 1989b). The hegemonic model of national belonging equates Belizeanness with having some degree of African, or "black", ancestry. According to both narratives, all Maya, Spanish and non-Kriol individuals of European ancestry ("white") are denied real Belizean identity (Medina 1997).[4] Assimilation into the Kriol cultural group is sometimes possible for newer "white"- and "black"-appearing immigrants; a range of European and African phenotypes are acceptable as Kriol if individuals learn and use the language and adopt Kriol cultural norms. However, because of the role that physical appearance plays in determining Kriol identity, it would be significantly more difficult for a Maya person to be considered Kriol. Publicly most Belizeans adhere to the official pluralistic model of multicultural harmony promoted by the government and educational institutions, but the creolization and hegemonic narratives are clearly expressed in the way that research participants categorized Belizean food.

Cross-cutting these racialized nationalist narratives, groups have organized themselves along ethnic lines, most prominently the Yucatec, Mopan and Kekchi Maya, via the National Maya Council, and the Garifuna, through the National Garifuna Council, both established in the 1980s. Palacio (1988), among other Belizean scholars of ethnicity, argues that socio-political and economic marginalization form the basis for the ethnic consciousness that led to creation of these councils. In 1995, after the 1991 national census showed that the Kriol had become an (albeit substantial) minority in the country, prominent Kriol leaders formed the National Kriol Council and the Kriol Language Project and began to publicly describe the Belizean Kriol as an ethnic group, seemingly in opposition to pre-existing nationalist narratives of Kriol identity.

Meanwhile, others such as Evan X Hyde, founder (in 1969) of the United Black Association for Development and promoter of pan-Africanism in Belize, have argued strenuously for decades that Kriol people should call themselves black and ally themselves with their brethren in Africa and across the African diaspora. His push for pan-Africanism and black nationalism in Belize and the new ethnic orientation expressed by the National Kriol Council reflect two different frameworks for approaching Belizean Kriol identity. Both are predicated on an acknowledged shared ancestry: in Hyde's case an African heritage shared with a broader transnational diaspora of black people, including the Garifuna, and in the case of the Kriol Council, an ethnic identity with acknowledged African and European ancestry, but strongly rooted in the specific social, cultural, historical and geopolitical context of the development of Belize as a wood-cutting settlement, British colony and, finally, independent country. The approach taken by the Kriol Council ties Kriol identity and ethnic group formation to the emergence of the Belizean nation-state, while Hyde rejects nationalism in favour of an international black identity.

This difference is strongly reflected in the different approach of each camp to the historic mythology of Kriol identity as arising out of the very events (such as the Battle of St George's Caye) that formed the nation as a British creation in Central America (Judd 1989b; Shoman 2010). In these narratives – rejected by Hyde and embraced by the Kriol Council – Kriol identity is conflated with the nation: Kriol people are not only representative of the country: they *are* the country (Judd 1989b). As the prototype of Belizeanness, they are glossed as representative of the nation, despite a pluralistic governmental narrative which celebrates Belize as a "multicultural paradise" (Judd 1989b; Medina 1997). Their African and European heritage is important as part of the Kriol creation myth, as a mixed people arising proudly out of the British Caribbean colonial context; Kriol identity is not focused on Africa or Europe but rather on Belize.

According to the Kriol Council, Kriol identity is Belizean identity; they are a people born out of the same historical context that gave birth to the country. The Kriol "ethnicity" promoted by the Kriol Council is thoroughly nationalized. This attitude is not limited to Belize. Creole groups in some other nations of the Caribbean basin also adhere to this creole nationalism approach (Bolland 1998; Khan 2001). However, in Caribbean island countries few indigenous groups remain to claim first rights to the nation. Belize is a special case among Caribbean nations because it has a Maya indigenous population. It is also different from other Central American countries because more than 30 per cent of the population claim genetic or cultural ties with Africa.

The attitudes and tensions around these different models of identity and belonging are reflected in the way food is described, categorized and marketed in Placencia. Research participants who used a hegemonic nationalist model prioritized the food of the dominant Kriol (and sometimes, to a lesser extent, their Garifuna "cousins") over other ethnic groups, while the few who had a pluralistic nationalist perspective were more likely to include the food of the Maya and other cultural groups in the category of most Belizean food.

Despite a shared African heritage, the Kriol as a group express ambivalence about the Garifuna people, who have both African and Carib (the original Caribbean islanders) ancestry. While intermarriage has increased, especially in areas such as Belize City, and while some Kriol may ally with them under the guise of pan-Africanism or label their food Belizean because of hegemonic nationalism, many Kriol people in Belize still distance themselves from the Garifuna (Palacio 2018). In part this is an outcome of a history of separation established and enforced by British colonial policy. In Placencia a few Kriol ignore or downplay their African heritage in the community, claiming to be a mixture of exclusively European ancestors (Spang 2013). These same individuals tend to focus exclusively on the African ancestry of the Garifuna people in Seine Bight while ignoring their Carib heritage. Despite this, some point out that certain dishes are the same in both Kriol and Garifuna cooking, just with different names. One such dish is what the Garifuna call *hudut,* a dish made of boiled and pounded plantain that is called *fufu* (a West African name) in Kriol culture.

How does cultural politics affect gastronational expression in Belize, and how could we measure those effects? When conducting my field research, I used pile sorts that revealed participants' models of nationalism. I made a set of cards covering a range of foods found in Belize, with a photo on one side and the name on the other. I conducted both "free list" and "Belize continuum" pile sorts with these cards. For the free-list exercise, research participants sorted the cards into whatever groups made the most sense to them. They were then asked to describe each group to me. The purpose of this was to determine how important national or cultural labels were in food grouping. I conducted this pile sort with fifty-five people. The Belize-continuum pile sort asked participants to sort the cards to show how Belizean they considered a particular food to be. A food card could be placed in the "most", "least" or "in-between" group on a scale from most to least Belizean. We then went through the groups one card at a time and participants were asked to explain why a specific food had been placed in a specific category – what made this food most, least or in-between Belizean? Forty-two people did this exercise.

Regardless of the model of nationalism or the cultural affiliation of the participants, Kriol food was always placed in the "most Belizean" category. Kriol (and even some non-Kriol) research participants regularly conflated *Kriol* and *Belizean* when sorting foods. It was clear that many participants considered them to be more or less the same thing. Expressions of Kriol identity (marketing a dish as Kriol, for instance) are not necessarily a dismissal of hegemonic nationalism in favour of pluralism but may be a reaffirmation of Kriol culture as the bedrock of a "real Belizean" identity in the face of dramatic demographic changes. Some of my research participants appeared to use both hegemonic and pluralistic models, switching from one to the other depending on the food involved. Calling a particular food "creole" on a menu may be an expression of hegemonic nationalism, multicultural pluralism or simply savvy tourism marketing. The same dish might be sold as "Kriol", "Belizean" or "local", depending on the political views and marketing strategies of the restaurant owner.

Fifty-seven per cent of my research participants identified themselves as Kriol. Ethnocentrism may account for their valuation of their food as being most Belizean; however, the other 43 per cent included most of the cultural groups recognized in Belize,[5] as well as second-generation immigrants from Guatemala, Honduras and the United States. Most of these non-Kriol participants also selected Kriol-associated food as being most Belizean.

THE CULINARY OTHER

When research participants grouped photos of food in whatever manner made sense to them, it became clear that cultural and national food categories are relevant culinary classifications for most Belizeans. Of the participants, 58.2

per cent created at least one food group with cultural or national labels, such as Belizean, American, Kriol or Spanish. Grouping food by meal (snack, breakfast, lunch, dinner, tea, etc.), by meal component (side dish, appetizer, sweet) and by type (bread, seafood, meat, etc.) was also common. The category of Spanish foods was used 31 per cent of the time, often side by side with groups such as "bread" and "breakfast", and usually comprised mainly corn foods (dishes with corn as a key ingredient). The free-list and Belize-continuum pile-sort data make it clear that Spanish people and food are a significant "other" to Placencia Kriol identity. This is not surprising, given the large influx of Spanish people (mostly from Guatemala, Honduras and El Salvador) and food into the community in the past ten or fifteen years.

Despite their smaller population, the Chinese have also become a culinary other, because of their high level of involvement in the food-services sector across the country. Twenty-nine per cent of my respondents created a "Chinese" food category when sorting food cards. In Placencia Village alone there are five restaurants and six grocery stores owned by Chinese families, all of which have opened in the past fifteen years. Smaller cultural groups that dwell in other parts of the country, such as Belizean East Indian (a food category for only 9 per cent of my free-list participants) and Mennonite (not mentioned by research participants), received little attention, showing that their food is relatively unknown in Placencia. Food items associated with North America, such as hot dogs and hamburgers, pizza, pancakes and pasta, were not completely ignored. Fifteen people (27 per cent) of the fifty-five pile-sort participants created an American (18.2 per cent) or American fast-food (7.3 per cent) category in their free sorting. One person created a "North American" category. Five people in the group (9.1 per cent) also created a "foreigner" category, which included the same foods associated with North America.

Styles of preparation and signature ingredients were used to mark the differences and similarities between culinary categories, at both the cultural and national level. Research participants explicitly associated the use of coconut milk and oil with Kriol and Garifuna people. "Garifuna . . . and Kriol culture I've seen it used a lot, Garifuna in their serre dishes and Kriol in making bread and their coconut rice." Participants also associated wheat bread and rice made with coconut milk with the Kriol.

Kriol bread, a soft-crusted coconut milk–based yeast bread – historically baked in a fire-hearth oven made out of a fifty-five-gallon drum or kerosene tin – brings together coconut and wheat flour and is clearly identified by name as a culturally "creole" food product. This reference to Kriol culture is often glossed, via hegemonic nationalism, as a reference to Belizeanness in general, and the use of coconut is associated with Belizean food on a national scale.

> Kriol bread – well, the name explains it all. The coconut part of it has made it Belizean, and I'm sure other parts, in Jamaica there's stuff like it. But yeah, every country has their own bread and it's the bread of Belize . . . Coconut rice, well, it's Belizean because of the coconut. Also in the Caribbean I'm sure they do that too, but the rice – the coconut in there adds a unique Belizean touch and changes the flavour completely from traditional Uncle Ben rice. . . . Tourists love it.

For some research participants this is explicitly opposed to the food prepared by the Mestizo populations of neighbouring nations such as Mexico, Guatemala and Honduras, where coconut is rarely used in cooking except in a few coastal Garifuna communities in the latter two countries. A Honduran immigrant clarified the difference, as she sees it, between Belizean and Honduran cooking styles. What I call the "corn/coconut divide" emerges clearly in her description of different ways of preparing and serving cowfoot soup, which is found in both Belize and Honduras: "In Honduras we mek dat, because yu find dat da Honduras but different way. Da Honduras no put coconut milk and then serve with corn tortilla. Right here dey put coconut milk, it serve with rice."[6] When asked why she placed coconut oil in the "most Belizean" category, she said: "Because Belizean style, di Garifuna, real Belizean-Belizean, always dem have coconut oil. [Researcher: So who cook with coconut oil?] Di one weh cook real-style Belize, Kriol people."[7] The same reason was given for placing coconut rice in the "most Belizean" category: "Because Belizean like eat di coconut."

This association of coconut with Kriol and, more generally, Belizean identity was also revealed in a free-list pile sort when a research participant placed the coconut rice card in a group along with chow mein and fried rice, which they called "Chinese restaurant". Once they realized that the card said "coconut rice" and not simply "rice", the participant immediately moved it to a pile that included rice and beans and other Kriol-associated foods. No research participants explicitly associated the Maya or the Spanish with the use of coconut, although many contemporary Maya do use coconut products. Coconut is identified as a key marker of Kriol, Garifuna and therefore Belizean identity.

Some participants considered the use of many different seasonings to be typical of Kriol food, as opposed to what they considered to be blander Spanish dishes. This formed the basis of assertions of culinary superiority. One Placencia Kriol woman said: "But if we Kriol mek dem, dey must tastier than di Spanish. [Researcher: Why dat?] Because we tek more care with di taste, might add more seasoning or some herbs or something. Even dough it someone else dish, we master it more."[8]

Because many participants applied a hegemonic model of nationalism that does not consider Spanish or Maya foods to be fully Belizean, the cultural boundary-crossing that some dishes have undertaken made it more difficult for them to decide just how Belizean they were. Tamales, dukunu or tamalitos (green corn tamales that often do not contain a filling), chimole or black dinna (a flavourful chicken or turkey soup made with black recado seasoning) and escabeche (a vinegary chicken soup flavoured with allspice and oregano) are examples of dishes and meals which some participants had difficulty associating with only one cultural group. This participant's reaction to tamales, which he placed in the "most Belizean" category, illustrates some of the difficulty around determining a single cultural origin for the dish: "Now this one funny, because a lot of people associate di tamale with the Maya people. As far as I know the tamales that first appeared here in Belize were made by the East Indian people. Again one brought here by the influence of the East Indian slaves that were brought here." Another participant argued that tamales, while perhaps being of Spanish origin, were perfected by the Kriol:

> Although other cultures perfect these dishes in a way, they [the Mestizo] authenticate it. . . . If you would really go into a Mestizo home and taste one of their homemade tamales and yu digest it, think of it. Go to a Kriol home and taste one of her real homemade tamales: the taste is of a higher quality, you know. It's just the Kriol people know how to handle their seasonings. Kriol people like their food well seasoned. But the Mestizo they are not a real big fan of seasoning. They want to taste the corn, not the seasoning.

The fact that chimole (black dinna) and *atole de maiz*, or caan lab (a thick corn masa drink or porridge), have both Spanish and Kriol names reflects their incorporation into Kriol foodways despite their acknowledged Spanish ancestry. My research participant who discussed the mixing of different cultural groups in Belize expressed the mixed identity of chimole in a particularly poetic manner:

> [Chimole/black dinna] is a – what di . . . borderline Belizeans – it comes from dem, you know. And you know, di borderline Belizeans, what we call di Mestizos – mix of Kriol and Spanish – most of their ancestors originated from somewhere across di border. Now and then they mix with Kriol, but they *are* Belizean, you know? You probably hear di poem weh say, "I think I see a new Belize." We can't separate dem, because we are all Belizean, you know?[9]

Dukunu, with their green corn and coconut milk ingredients, transcend the corn/coconut division. However, tamalitos, which are also made with green corn and look identical to dukunu, do not contain coconut milk and have a Spanish name, while the word *dukunu* has West African origins (a dish of that name is still eaten in Ghana). Which are more Belizean? It is not surprising that some confusion set in for research participants wedded to the hegemonic model, which draws a boundary between people with Spanish and people with African heritage. Pluralistic nationalism allows foods associated with all Belizean cultural groups to be defined as Belizean, avoiding the confusion of trying to apply hegemonic nationalism to a diverse and intertwined culinary situation.[10]

Adaptation, experimentation, cross-cultural borrowing, substitution and incorporation occur at the level of ingredients, dishes or entire meals and between all cultural groups in Belize. These activities blur and obscure the culinary dividing lines drawn by hegemonic nationalism and confuse its many advocates. American Kraft macaroni and cheese may substitute for coleslaw or potato salad in some rice-and-beans meals, Spanish corn tortillas may replace Kriol johnnycakes on a breakfast plate of fried fish, or white rice may be served with a Maya caldo instead of the traditional corn tortillas. Entire meals may even be "substituted". Many Maya households, for example, have adopted the Kriol Sunday dinner of rice and beans, stewed chicken and potato salad as a special celebration meal, like poch or tamales. Incorporation is another common strategy; many Kriol cooks are proud of their ability to learn about, incorporate and skilfully use spices and herbs from other cultural groups. No wonder proponents of hegemonic nationalism struggle to categorize a tamale in this invigorating and diverse society.

THE IMPORTANCE OF HOME COOKING

There is a way out that allowed research participants to apply a form of hegemonic nationalism to the content of the "most Belizean" food category even when the food in question was of non-Kriol origin. Enter the magic of home cooking. Applying Kriol culinary style to a non-Kriol dish Kriolizes it,[11] opening a pathway to being fully Belizean through the dish's transformation and incorporation into the dominant group's home cooking. By preparing these dishes at home and adapting them to their tastes, Kriol cooks, according to hegemonic nationalism, Kriolize and thus nationalize dishes such as escabeche and chimole that have acknowledged Spanish roots. This process is a gendered one, as women still do the bulk of the cooking in most Belizean Kriol households. As in many other societies, female home cooks are seen as repositories of culinary heritage who have the power to transmit and transform culinary traditions as they feed their families and teach their offspring how to prepare different dishes (see, among others, Avakian and Haber 2005; Di Giovine 2010; Moisio, Arnould and Price 2004).

The home is a crucial site for the adaptation and assimilation of introduced food items. Since the foods available and eaten in each home may be slightly different, each individual carries their own unique impression of what foodstuffs, ingredients and dishes are most or least Belizean. What is available also changes over time, and younger Belizeans may identify certain dishes as being "Belizean" which older Belizeans reject. The presence of a food item in Kriol (and for some Belizeans to a lesser degree, Garifuna) homes underlies many of the criteria used to determine the Belizean identity of a food. This is Kriol gastronationalism at work. If participants strongly associate the food item with Kriol foodways – that is, the production, preparation, distribution, consumption and disposal of food – they put it in the "most Belizean" category. My research participants placed flour tacos, recently introduced to Placencia by Spanish roadside vendors and not regularly prepared in Kriol homes, in the "most Belizean" pile only 28.6 per cent of the time. On the other hand, the chicken soup escabeche, which was likely brought to Belize by nineteenth-century Spanish immigrants from Mexico, is cooked in many Kriol households across the country. Because of this, even though most participants considered it to be of Spanish origin, they placed it in the "most Belizean" pile 61.9 per cent of the time and never put it in the "least Belizean" pile.

Research participant choices for the Belize-continuum pile sort made it clear that a number of criteria came into play when someone was trying to determine where to place a particular food. For most of my participants who subscribed to the hegemonic model of nationalism, if they considered the food to be Kriol, it immediately went into the "most Belizean" pile, while the food of foreign groups such as Chinese and North Americans were most often placed in the "least Belizean" group. If participants were not clear about which cultural group had originated a specific food item, they evaluated its Belizeanness based on other criteria, some of which were more important than others:

1. Is the dish cooked by Kriol or (to a lesser extent) Garifuna people in their homes?
2. Is the dish made from ingredients that are produced in Belize?
3. Does the dish/food item exist elsewhere (as far as the participant was aware) or is it only found in Belize?
4. Is the food a staple – that is, did the participant believe that it is found in most homes and eaten almost every day by most people in the country, including Kriol people?
5. Is it found consistently on the menus of Belizean restaurants?
6. Is the food believed by the participant to have been made or invented by ancestors, living or dead, who are considered Belizean?
7. Did the research participant grew up eating the food at home?

Some or all of these criteria may be used to make a decision about how Belizean a particular food item is. Even if the food was not strongly associated with Kriol or Garifuna cultural groups, the more of the other criteria it fulfilled, the more likely that it would still be placed in the "most Belizean" category.

Some criteria carried more weight than others. A food that research participants believed was made or invented by their Belizean ancestors (criterion 6) was more likely to end up in the "most Belizean" category than a food whose only claim to Belizean identity was that it is made from ingredients produced in Belize (criterion 2). For that reason a Belizean is more likely to place stew fish (a hearty soup with a long history in Belizean fishing culture) in the "most Belizean" category than a dish of blackened snapper over a rice pilaf with fresh pineapple salsa – made entirely of Belizean ingredients but totally disconnected from what is prepared in most Belizean homes.

Looking over these criteria, it is clear that home cooking is key to defining a dish as Belizean. Criteria 1, 4, 6 and 7 all refer to production and consumption of the food in one's home or the home of one's ancestors. These criteria are all closely tied to the private sphere and family. Criteria 2, 3 and 5 refer to the origin of the ingredients (are they grown or produced in Belize?), the uniqueness of the dish (is it found only in Belize?) and how common the dish is on restaurant menus. These criteria are oriented towards the public sphere and international comparison, although the private sphere sometimes plays an important role in the production and acquisition of ingredients, as will be discussed in more detail in chapter 7.

There are exceptions to the Kriol home-cooking pathway to Belizeanness. Seaweed, which over 90 per cent of my participants did not explicitly associate with a particular cultural group, was still considered by 97.3 per cent of my sample to be "most Belizean" because it is a product of Belize (criterion 2), is found consistently on the menus of Belizean restaurants (criterion 5), is considered to be unique to Belize (criterion 3) and is considered to have been discovered and used by fishermen ancestors (criterion 6). The criterion of its being made at home (particularly by Kriol and Garifuna people on the coast) (criterion 1) was not the only factor at play in determining the Belizeanness of this food.

A young Kriol man in his early twenties explained why he had placed certain foods in certain groups in his Belize-continuum pile sort. He used several criteria to determine where to place each food item.

> **Participant:** Again, dukunu is a Latin-originated dish. It comes from the Latin cuisine.
> **Researcher:** How do you know that?
> **Participant:** Well, most Spanish, dey eat a lotta corn every day, they consume a lot of corn. Yu go to Guatemala, Mexico, Honduras, you will find a lot of corn-made products – corn tortillas, dukunu, tamales – everything has to do with some sort of corn masa.

Researcher: So since it is made of corn masa it must be of Latin origin?

Participant: Yeah, must be a Latin ting. You notice I have di tamales in di Belizean category. . . . Made in Belize by di Spanish heritage, and it became a delicacy in Belize.

Researcher: Why is it not in the "intermediate Belizean" group with dukunu?

Participant: Because Belizean prefer to sit at home and mek di tamales. Di Belizean people decide, "We will mek tamales today." For funerals and wakes and big parties. You will not find dukunu in a party as often as you should. Usually [it's] di vendors, di Spanish street vendors that make and sell dukunu.

Researcher: So, more Belizean because non-Spanish Belizeans make them?

Participant: Yes, Belizean will sit and mek them, unlike di dukunu.

Here the research participant explained that dukunu is of Latin origin and that he knew this because it is made of corn, and the Spanish eat a lot of corn, which can be seen if you travel to Spanish countries such as Guatemala, Mexico or Honduras. If it is made of corn, it must be a Spanish thing. Given that the respondent did not consider Spanish food to be as Belizean as Kriol, why then were tamales in the "most Belizean" category?

Hegemonic nationalism shaped his food-sorting decisions. His reasoning reflected a belief that Spanish people and their foods are not as Belizean as other groups. His explanation for why he placed tamales, a corn-based food, in the "most Belizean" group shows how non-Spanish home cooking plays a gatekeeping role in determining how Belizean a food is. The research participant clearly distinguished between "Belizeans" making tamales at home in the private sphere and Spanish street vendors selling dukunu to the public. The fact that (non-Spanish) Belizeans make tamales at home (fulfilling criterion 1) was the reason for placing them in the "most Belizean" category. Dukunu went into the "intermediate Belizean" category because it is not found at parties or regularly made at home by non-Spanish Belizeans; instead it is made and sold by Spanish vendors on the street. Kriol home cooking and the private sphere play a gatekeeping role in defining the Belizeanness of this dish. Something made for sale in the public sphere, especially when it is made by Spanish people, is not as Belizean as a dish prepared at home by a Kriol person.

The same participant went on to discuss chimole, which he placed in the "most Belizean" category:

> **Participant:** Chimole is also another Belizean cuisine, but made by di Spanish culture who originated it in Belize.
>
> **Researcher:** So you are saying that chimole was invented in Belize by Spanish?
>
> **Participant:** Yeah. Di recado actually is made in Belize – di black recado. We actually mek our own recado. Di eggs is from Belize, the chicken is from Belize. Dat makes it Belizean cuisine.

Here the participant clearly stated that if the ingredients are made in Belize, the dish is Belizean (criterion 2). He also claimed that chimole, although invented by the Spanish, originated in Belize instead of being imported from elsewhere, and therefore belongs in the most Belizean category.

According to the same research participant, panades go in the "intermediate Belizean" category because they were not invented in Belize, unlike chimole. "Very good. Eaten by a lot of Belizeans. [Researcher: Why is it intermediate?] Because of its origin from di Spanish, Mexico and Guatemala, and brought over to Belize." The food that he considered to have been invented in Belize he categorized as more Belizean than panades, which he said were invented abroad and imported into the country. When it came to corn tacos,

> **Participant:** Belizeans, dey love it, but it's not an everyday delicacy.
>
> **Researcher:** What do you mean by that?
>
> **Participant:** Not an individual will buy it every day. Won't buy it everyday-everyday.
>
> **Researcher:** What mek it not 100 per cent Belizean?
>
> **Participant:** Because it originated from di Spanish cultures, because [in the "most Belizean" category] you are talking about Belizean-Belizean food, hardcore Belizean food.

Here the participant used criterion number 4 – whether the food is a staple eaten regularly by Belizeans – to help decide how to categorize corn tacos. The research participant acknowledged that Belizeans love corn tacos but, because they are not eaten every day and originated in Spanish cultures, they are not "hardcore [real] Belizean food" and therefore belong in the "intermediate Belizean" category. The same participant applied yet another criterion to his analysis of corn tortillas: "Same with di corn tortilla. Corn tortilla started, came from di Latin countries. Long wata beans and corn tortilla

Spanish delicacy [laughs]."[12] Criterion number 6 was used to determine how Belizean a food is. Since the research participant considered corn tortillas to have been invented elsewhere and then imported, they are not as Belizean as something that was invented within the country's borders.

KRIOLIZATION AND CULINARY STYLE

The participants who mentioned the cross-cultural nature of some foods often pointed out differences in the way that Kriol and Spanish or Kriol and Chinese people cook certain shared dishes. Around 15 per cent of my research participants (all Kriol) asserted that the Kriol way of cooking was superior in flavour. This claim of culinary superiority over other cultural groups – particularly Spanish, but at least one participant also asserted superiority over Garifuna cooking – also appeared in interviews and casual conversation with individuals who did not participate in the pile-sort exercises.

This may be an attempt to maintain dominance as the Kriol population continues to decline in relation to other cultural groups. With the proliferation of taco carts and stands serving Spanish corn foods and the appearance of new foods such as Salvadoran *pupusas* and Honduran *baleadas*, Spanish-speaking immigrants are increasingly dominating the fast-food and street-food arenas. Chinese sit-down restaurants are serving up quick and tasty food at prices that match or beat those of Belizean rice-and-beans joints, and North American venues are competing with local bars and restaurants that serve evening meals. Claiming that Kriol cooking is inherently superior in flavour allowed my Kriol research participants to assert their continued mastery in a food industry that is increasingly crowded with competitors and a society that is welcoming new waves of Central American, Chinese, European and North American immigrants.

In a clear case of hegemonic nationalism, this research participant pitted "we Belizean" (i.e., Kriol) against "Spanish", claiming that the style of cooking black dinna and cowfoot soup is what makes them Belizean instead of Spanish, even though the participant acknowledged that Spanish people do prepare it: "Black dinna, dah what Belizean mek, and dis cowfoot dish, da what Belizean mek. Spanish mek it sometime but dey no mek it like how we Belizean mek it, so we would call it wan Belizean dish."[13]

One Placencia Kriol participant who had done a free-list pile sort explained why she grouped flour tacos, chimole/black dinna, guacamole, garnaches, escabeche, dukunu, corn tortillas, atole de maiz/caan lab, burritos and panades together in one pile: "Wi mek dem too, but dem deh more Spanish dish. Kriol really end up di copy afterwards and mek wi food, but dat more from di Spanish side. If it Spanish-side Belizean or Spanish from Honduras – I don't know weh dese dishes. But if we Kriol mek dem, dey must tastier than di Spanish."[14]

MARGINALIZATION

The requirement of Kriolization prior to nationalization prevailed to some degree with regards to Garifuna-associated foods and even some Chinese food. For Kriol participants, Garifuna-associated dishes were included in the Belizean food circle with this explanation: "Well, the Garifuna are Belizean, so it is Belizean food." However, the Garifuna foods that were most readily recognized by Kriol participants were those which the Kriol cook as well, such as serre and bundiga, or Matilda foot.[15] It was usually the foods that my participants knew the best which were placed in the "most Belizean" category. Some foods such as darasa[16] were placed in the "least Belizean", "in-between Belizean" or "unknown" piles by non-Garifuna participants until it was revealed that they were associated with the Garifuna, at which point the participants wanted to put them in the "most Belizean" category.

Most research participants knew very little about the foodways of Belize's smallest cultural groups, the East Indians and Mennonites. Knowledge of and exposure to "Mennonite food" appears to be particularly low, even though, according to the 2010 census, more than eleven thousand Mennonites currently live in Belize. Mennonites were not mentioned by any of the participants, although they appeared as an ethnic group on the 2010 national census (even I did not think to include them until late in the research process). While Mennonite farms feed the country with foodstuffs like cheese, milk, meat, vegetables and baked goods, even the staples of rice and beans, few but the Mennonites themselves appear to have tried Mennonite home cooking in Belize. This is likely in great part because of the closed nature of most Mennonite communities. Experience with Mennonite home cooking is even less likely on the Placencia Peninsula, where only a couple of modern, electricity-using Mennonites live, than inland in Cayo and Toledo Districts. The Golden Corral Buffet restaurant in Spanish Lookout, Cayo District (a three-hour drive from Placencia), is the only place where other Belizeans can eat meals prepared by Mennonite cooks.

Participants agreed that Belizean East Indians are Belizean, but whether their food is was a matter of debate. Many people were unfamiliar with Belizean East Indian dishes such as tacari chicken,[17] as it is not usually cooked by Kriol people in Placencia. Unable to apply criteria based on home cooking or knowledge of the dishes themselves, the Placencia participants defaulted into one of two camps: One group claimed that if Belizeans of East Indian ancestry are Belizean then their food must also be Belizean. The other group decided that while the *people* are indeed Belizean, their unfamiliar food is not.

Why was Garifuna food so quickly accepted by everyone as Belizean (Garifuna people are Belizean, so therefore their food is too) while East Indian food was somehow detached from East Indian people and their Belizean identity? The answer returns again to the importance of home cooking as a way to gain familiarity with "outsider" foods. A number of dishes are prepared by both the Kriol and Garifuna, such as serre, Matilda foot/bundiga and fufu/hudut.[18] The fact that these dishes are prepared at home by the Kriol legitimizes them as Belizean. These foods are considered by some to be representative of African heritage and by others to reflect Caribbean colonial history. (See Mintz and Price [1992] for a review of the broader debate.) They unite the Garifuna, who arrived in Belize in the early 1800s, with the already established Kriol population. This is an uneasy connection in Placencia, which has a tension-filled history of racialized discrimination against the Garifuna in neighbouring Seine Bight Village. Similarities between Kriol and Garifuna cooking, such as the combination of coconut with ground foods and seafood in dishes like serre, help make Garifuna food familiar to the Kriol, as did the presence of Garifuna servants in a few better-off Kriol homes in Placencia prior to the 1980s. This may also help account for the quick assertion of the Belizeanness of Garifuna foods.

East Indian food fails criteria 1, 4, 5 and 7 for evaluating Belizeanness. Only a handful of people knew of ancestors who had prepared any of their foods, so for most participants East Indian food also failed criterion 6. Since most participants were not East Indian Belizeans and were completely unfamiliar with Belizean East Indian food, they were unable to fully evaluate the foods using criterion 2 (whether the dish is made from ingredients that are produced in Belize) or 3 (whether the dish/food item exists elsewhere or is found only in Belize). By most of the criteria participants used to evaluate Belizeanness, East Indian food is not Belizean.

This conclusion caused a lot of confusion for some respondents because, according to most measures of Belizean identity, East Indian *people* are Belizean. East Indian people have been in the country for more than a century (since the 1870s); they arrived in Belize as a result of British colonialism, just like the Kriol; most speak Kriol – Belize's lingua franca and an important marker of Belizean identity – as a first language; and they have intermarried extensively with other groups, including the Kriol, for generations. Hence the dramatic division over this small group's culinary offerings. If the same research exercises were conducted in Belize's Toledo District, where there is an established East Indian population and tacari chicken and cohune cabbage regularly appear on restaurant blackboards, these foods would likely be more firmly placed in the "most Belizean" group.

CULINARY GIANTS: CHINESE AND (NORTH) AMERICAN FOOD

The Chinese and Americans (often glossed in Belize to include Canadians) represent the two most significant national "other" categories in free-list pile sorts of foods found in Belize. In the free-list pile sorting, where participants sorted food cards into whatever groups made sense to them, food groups labelled "America" and "North America" were the most common national food category (27 per cent) after the Chinese (29 per cent). The other national food groups listed appeared much less frequently: Italian (3.6 per cent), Mexican (7.3 per cent) and Indian (1.8 per cent).

The first Chinese people to come to Belize were several hundred labourers brought to the colony in the 1880s (Simmons 2001). Some merchant families moved to Belize from other parts of Central America at the end of the nineteenth and beginning of the twentieth centuries. Descendants of those few early Chinese immigrants opened several restaurants in Belize City and other parts of the country, but most communities did not boast a Chinese restaurant and Chinese-owned grocery stores were unheard of in the 1970s. Starting in the early 1990s, waves of immigrants from Taiwan, Hong Kong[19] and mainland China began to arrive in Belize, prompting panic and resentment of Chinese wealth and business success. Newspaper headlines from the mid-1990s describe a "Chinese invasion". In Belize City, gang violence against Chinese-owned businesses grabbed national attention, as did the proliferation of Chinese-owned "dolla chicken" fried-chicken joints in Belize City and other town centres. Immigration, both legal and otherwise, continues today, but while some resentment persists, Belizeans seem by and large to have accepted the reality of Chinese groceries and restaurants popping up like mushrooms in every sizeable village and town across the country.

Many research participants in Placencia felt that all Chinese food – a category regularly expanded to include anything perceived to be of Asian origin – is categorically foreign and not Belizean. However, a significant minority argued otherwise. Chinese-produced fried chicken, fried rice (called fry rice by most Belizeans) and chow mein are commonly and regularly eaten by many Belizeans. Because of this and because Kriol people sometimes make their own "fry rice" and chow mein at home, using Belizean-produced ingredients, some participants argued that several Chinese foods have now become Belizean through assimilation into everyday society. This would explain why 35.7 per cent of my research participants placed chow mein and/or fried rice in the "intermediate Belizean" category. Only one person put fried rice in the "most Belizean" category, indicating that these foods have been only partially assimilated. Some participants noted that Chinese-associated dishes such as chow mein are cooked in Belizean homes and, moreover, that they are being adapted to Belizean Kriol tastes:

> **Participant:** And den dis again [chow mein], dis one chiney food, but this [picture] look more Kriol-style.
>
> **Researcher:** What mek it so?
>
> **Participant:** Well, di chiney one wouldn't have all des vegetables, wouldn't have all des colours, just fast. . . . When we mek a chow mein, we woulda put everything in it. Weh woulda build up di taste and di looks, yu know . . . more our style of food. Even dis fry rice, yeah, dat more a chiney food, but yu could see da no chiney mek it. Dah more Belizean style.
>
> **Researcher:** What mek it so? Tell me what mek you tink dat.

Participant: Because, well, di way how it look. Chiney have a way of using more just cabbage and celery and plain stuff, dat if yu see a green pepper in it or di carrots you could pick out di colour. Dis one just have a little more . . . I don't know . . . if I mek a fry rice I would have a lot more veggies in it than what dis have, but it still no look like a chiney fry rice.[20]

In several decades these dishes will be further Kriolized, thus rendering them more Belizean. With the passage of enough time, assimilation may take place while the Chinese roots of the dish continue to be acknowledged, just as has occurred with escabeche and chimole/black dinna, which are now well ensconced in the culinary repertoire of many Kriol cooks and considered Belizean despite their Spanish ancestry.

Americans have been migrating to Belize since the American Revolution, with a noticeable spike after the Civil War, but, as with the Chinese, the largest wave of immigration has occurred from the early 1990s into the present day (Simmons 2001). This migration has been driven by tourism and the government's retirement programme. While the Chinese have opened restaurants and grocery stores across the country, Americans have tended to congregate in tourist destinations such as Caye Caulker, Ambergris Caye, San Ignacio Town and Placencia Peninsula. Some American immigrants have opened restaurants and bars and, as mentioned in the previous chapter, American consumers have influenced the offerings in the (often Chinese-owned) grocery stores. I included in my pile-sort cards a number of food items commonly found in Belize and typically associated with the United States, including macaroni and cheese, pizza, hamburgers, hot dogs, spaghetti and meatballs, and pancakes. Like Chinese-associated foods, some items were more assimilated into Belizean culture than others.

In the Belize-continuum pile sort slightly over 90 per cent of the participants placed pancakes in the "least Belizean" category. In both pile sorts participants described them as not Belizean and grouped them with other non-Belizean food items. Explanations ranged from succinct – "Pancakes. American" – to more detailed: "This is more Western food or fast food, like from the United – you know, like hot dogs, mac 'n' cheese. Actually I can't even say just North American, 'cause it's not just there anymore, but more processed. The ham is processed, the pancakes are probably fluffy from a box – stuff that is more processed or more American meals. If you are going [to do] cultural standards right, these are more American meals." A woman who grew up in the then famous American-Kriol Mom's Restaurant in Belize City explained, "Pancakes: that's European or American in background and really not a lot of them here."

Despite the high level of consensus that pancakes are not Belizean, most Belizean-owned restaurants in Placencia offer them as a breakfast item along with local staples such as fry jacks and tortillas. One foreign-owned diner-style venue quickly become known for its tall stacks of pancakes covered with Belizean raw sugar, tropical fruit and imported American canned whipped cream. Pancake mix is found in the baking aisle of local grocery stores. Yet you hardly ever find pancakes in restaurants in non-touristy areas of Belize, and only one research participant mentioned making them at home. Even though she placed them in the "intermediate Belizean" pile, unlike 90 per cent of my participants, she still called them American. "Pancakes. Dis da American . . . Belizean like dat too, so . . . Well den, dat could go inna any one of the three dem, because da no only we Belizean people mek pancake. Because we usually mek it. I mek it a lot, because dat one over dey [gestures towards girlfriend] like when I mek pancake. But when I mek pancake, I mek it from scratch. Pancakes with egg and bacon."[21]

Some research participants clearly viewed pancakes as a foreign import that existed in the country more to appease American visitors than because of Belizean interest: "It's an international ting that got introduced to Belize, but it's not popular da Belize. They eat it; it's been introduced here by foreigners [and] it's all over the world. Mostly American call for pancakes. But it's 'least Belizean'."

Pancakes were the "American" food item in the pile sort least associated with Belizean identity. Only 64.3 per cent of research participants declared cornflakes to be "least Belizean", even though they were invented in the United States, likely because they have been available in some dry goods stores in Belize, and thus consumed in some Belizean homes, for more than thirty years. Over a quarter (26.2 per cent) identified cornflakes as being "intermediate Belizean", and a significant 9.5 per cent of participants declared cornflakes to be "most Belizean".

One of my research participants, a woman in her fifties, remembered eating cornflakes when she was growing up, as a treat. This woman placed pancakes in the "least Belizean" category but put cornflakes in the "most Belizean" group, stating:

> Participant: We used to get cornflakes. I loved it.
>
> Researcher: So you grew up with that?
>
> Participant: Not from a very early age, but I would say I started having that when I was about seven and liked it ever since. Actually it was one of the first cereals we would get in Belize, here in Placencia. Needless to say it didn't last very long. My mom had a bunch of kids and we used to go through that like crazy.

This same participant, who had worked in restaurants and resorts across the peninsula, had this to say about pancakes, which she did not consider to be Belizean:

> Participant: [shakes her head] That's not really Belizean either.
>
> Researcher: What would you consider it to be, then?
>
> Participant: I'd have to say international now. No matter where I work you have to have pancakes, do pancakes. Whether it's resorts or restaurants here, pancakes are done everywhere now. I mean, it's a North American or European thing, but everything change up because of tourism.

The same criteria that research participants used to evaluate the Belizeanness of different cultural groups within the country were also applied to Chinese and North American foods. In the case above, whether the participant grew up eating a food item in her home (criterion 7) or the food is a staple in Belizean homes (criterion 4) seems to have influenced whether she considered a particular dish to be Belizean or not. Whether a person likes a food or not may also influence how Belizean they consider it to be, if its identity is not clear as determined by other, less personal, criteria.

Participants often identified American foods as either being partially assimilated into Belizean food culture – that is, they were eaten by Belizeans but not every day – or as "universal" or "international" foods that "everyone" eats, though their American/North American/European heritage was usually acknowledged. One participant in his early twenties placed most "American" foods in the "least Belizean" pile and explained his decisions (based on criterion 4) as follows:

> [burger] Because burger wasn't originated in Belize and it's a worldwide meal. [hot dog] Same with di hot dog and pancake. It di ya [here], we eat it a lot, but it no something – da no wan main Belizean staple. [cornflakes] Mainly a break-

fast ting. Lotta Belizean eat it too, but it's not a Belizean food. Because it's not a Belizean staple. They are not going to eat dat every day.[22]

Yet another research participant, also Kriol and from Placencia but in her early fifties, placed cornflakes and pancakes in the "intermediate Belizean" category, using the same criteria to argue that since everyone eats them in Belize, they belong at the very least in the intermediate category, despite their acknowledged non-Belizean origin.

> **Participant:** [cornflakes] *Da* cereal people eat fi breakfast all over.[23]
> **Researcher:** What makes it Belizean enough to be in this group?
> **Participant:** Everybody eat it whether it Belizean or not. [pancakes] Everybody eat pancakes. All over.

Explicitly acknowledging this uneven process of assimilation, one Placencia-born Belizean in her thirties placed cornflakes in the "intermediate Belizean" pile and described them as being one of a number of foods that represented a "generation gap" in eating: introduced dishes and ingredients that had become more common in homes in recent years:

> **Participant:** That's American to me.
> **Researcher:** Why did you put it in the "intermediate Belizean" pile?
> **Participant:** Because I think it's also a generation gap again. Its more introduce to . . . A lot of people are eating cereal now, than before. When I was a kid, we never had cereal. I so don't recall eating cereal. We used to have, like, bread and cheese, egg and bread, fry jack and egg, sometimes fried fish or boiled fish. Cereal was so not in our diet. Sometimes oatmeal.

Another participant, also in her thirties, placed cornflakes in the "least Belizean" pile along with pizza, hot dogs, macaroni and cheese, burgers, fries and other "American" foods, based again on her own experiences in her childhood home:

> Hmm, I don't know about cornflakes. Cornflakes – I hate di idea of cornflakes fi breakfast, serious. I mean, when yu deh pon wan diet it work, but I mean, again it di same ting. I guess we grow up with *breakfast*. Yu no eat cornflakes fi breakfast [not in my house, she says about growing up]. Six pikney yu can't give dem cornflakes fi eat! It falls under di American idea of breakfast, cereal.[24]

In the free-list sorting exercise food items were often grouped together under the category of "foreign", "American" or "American fast food". As one participant described their category, "Ham, mac 'n' cheese, spaghetti and meatballs, pizza, hot dog, burger, ketchup, pack bread, pancakes, cornflakes, peanut butter – that's more American, American comfort food. Pizza, pasta, hot dogs and burgers and stuff I would eat, but it's in a different category: cornflakes and imported comfort food." Along with Chinese food, foods of American/North American origin formed an important category in both free-list and Belize-continuum pile sorting. As with Chinese dishes, the process of assimilation was again centred on the presence, production and consumption of these foods within the home. The appearance of foods such as pancakes and chow mein in some restaurants in Belize does not qualify them as "Belizean" foods. Criterion 5 by itself is not sufficient to establish full Belizean status. It is not until born Belizeans are cooking and eating such dishes at home that a patina of Belizeanness can begin to overlay their foreign ancestry.

DISCUSSION

DeSoucey (2010, 432) explains that gastronationalism "signals the use of food production, distribution, and consumption to demarcate and sustain the emotive power of national attachment, as well as the use of nationalist sentiments to produce and market food". But how does gastronationalism relate to ethnic identity in the context of a culturally diverse nation like Belize? Which groups' foods will be marketed by using nationalist sentiments? Which foods function to "demarcate and sustain" nationalist sentiment in a given country? How do we decide on the content of a national cuisine? In Belize, identity politics are expressed not only on the street but also in the home, and Kriol home cooking plays an important role in determining what foods represent the nation. The hegemonic model of nationalism shapes the contents of the "Belizean food" category, acting to exclude certain foods and, by extension, cultural groups while reifying others as "most Belizean".

There is no well-consolidated official culinary narrative in Belize. No restaurant associations, famous chefs or culinary bodies have bothered to publish anything substantial on the subject of a Belizean cuisine, and the

Government of Belize has other fish to fry. The BTB, the public arm of the Ministry of Tourism, comes closest to taking a pluralistic nationalist stance, positively representing difference without reifying cuisines along ethnic boundaries or blending everything together into a synthetic mashup. The BTB briefly maintained a website (from spring 2011 until early 2012) promoting the country's foodways. Belize's unique history and cultural diversity were celebrated on a home page that declared: "As the Caribbean gateway to Central America, Belize is a treasury of tastes, specialties, styles and traditions from cultures all over the world. And when all of these incredibly diverse and delicious influences comingle in the kitchen, your palate is rewarded with uniquely delectable dishes. For the first time, all the sumptuous tastes of Belize have been brought together in one place" (BTB 2011). Though this semi-official pluralistic nationalist model may be attractive to tourists, my research indicates that Belizean food does indeed have a dominant flavour. The most powerful groups usually have a disproportionate influence on what foods become part of national cuisine, as suggested by Appadurai (1988) and documented by Trubek (2000) and Goody (1982) in their respective analyses of French and Chinese cuisines.

If hegemonic nationalism is indeed the dominant form of nationalism in Belize, as Medina claims, then the composition of the "Belizean food" category should reflect most powerfully the cooking of Belizean Kriol people. This conclusion is supported by my research data. Certain foodstuffs, dishes and even meals are shared among different cultural groups, forming the broth of what both Wilk (2006) and Houston (2005) call a "lumpy stew" of Caribbean culinary expression. Dishes such as tamales that are commonly prepared by a number of cultural groups can confuse Belizeans who apply a hegemonic nationalist model to food categories, as their cultural affiliation is not so clear-cut, but for many people the flavour is still dominated by Kriol home cooking, which determines which seasonings go into the shared national broth.

Wilk (2006) argues that the future for Belizean food sovereignty as the nation evolves in its first decades of independence may lie in the diversity and sustainability of home cooking. However, in Belize today that diversity is not fully expressed in the "national food" category. Kriol home cooking usually determines what is considered Belizean food and what is not. Even Garifuna home cooking, which most research participants considered Belizean, is often explained as being Belizean not only because Garifuna people are Belizean but because of similarities with Kriol food practices.

As you can see in figure 3, the majority of my research participants, whether they are Kriol or not, consider the label "Belizean food" to refer to a range of foodstuffs, dishes, meals and preparation styles that include most Kriol and Garifuna dishes as well as certain Spanish foods that have been assimilated into Kriol foodways. This clustering of Kriol and Garifuna foods in the "Belizean food" category reflects Medina's description of a racialized hegemonic nationalism.

As can be seen in figure 3, some culinary categories such as "Maya" and "Spanish" are fuzzy sets that overlap. The Spanish foods included under the Belizean food category tend to be those that have been adopted into the Kriol culinary repertoire; that is to say, Kriol people cook these dishes at home while explicitly acknowledging their Spanish origins. As one Kriol female participant explained, "Most of the food weh you will pick up right now are Mestizo Belizean, a mixture of Spanish and creole, but they are Belizean."

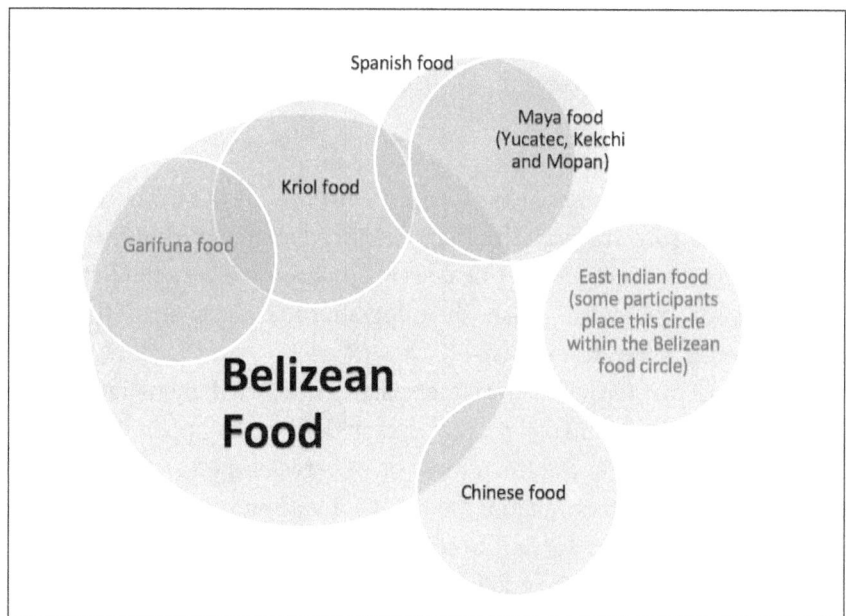

Figure 3. Venn diagram of overlapping cultural and Belizean food categories, the results of two Placencia-area food pile–sorting exercises conducted with fifty-five and forty-two people

In another fuzzy set, the majority of participants considered Maya and Spanish foodways to be very similar, with much overlap based on their shared consumption of corn as a staple. Most research participants did not include Maya food items in the "most Belizean" group alongside Kriol and Garifuna cooking. The Spanish and Maya are associated with the consumption of corn, especially in the form of corn tortillas. One Belizean, whose mother is Kriol and whose father is Maya, clearly illustrated this in his free sorting of food items found in Belize. He went so far as to include cornflakes in a group he described as Maya/Spanish, merely because they were corn.

> Den ya come off to me mostly, as I would even say as indigenous food. Di corn, di corn inna most of dese foods and di guacamole and di black dinna come off as Mayan, Indian-ish, Spanish-ish. . . . Ah, how to put it to you – it's like . . . Mayan-type foods dey really have. And when I say Mayan, I really think about Mexicans as well because di guacamoles you will find da Mexico. Alla dem tings does come from dose people. We know dey eat a lotta corn, although we may tek it and mek our own tings like di panades here. Di guacamole now, again di avocadoes and stuff, dose are like again food yu find Mexicans eat it a lot, Mayans eat it a lot. Di only reason why I was thinking alla dem tings – everybody eat dem but one set of people definitely deal with dem: da Mayan Spanish people. I throw in di cornflakes simply because ih corn. Tamalitos and so, definitely Mayan foods.[25]

Despite this man's personal association with the Maya culture through his father and paternal grandmother, who lived and cooked in the family home when he was growing up, he does not distinguish between Maya and Spanish foods, but rather glosses them together as coming out of the same general "indigenous" traditions.

While most participants in my Placencia-area research demonstrated some level of hegemonic nationalist perspectives in their explanations of why they placed certain foods in the least, most or in-between Belizean categories, a small minority (which included both Kriol and non-Kriol participants) justified some of their sorting decisions by using the pluralistic model. These exceptional participants, who made up less than 20 per cent of my research sample, argued that all Maya foods are Belizean because the Maya peoples were here first and were therefore the most Belizean of all, or they included the Maya as Belizean based on the pluralistic model of nationalism which celebrates cultural diversity. Explaining why he put caldo (a Maya soup) with corn tortillas in the "most Belizean" pile, one person stated, "That sound Maya, and the Maya mi di first settlers inna Belize. I mean the first people ya, so."[26] Several people claimed that any Maya food would be automatically Belizean because the Maya people are Belizean: "Okay, it's Belizean, because the Maya are Belizean," stated one participant. An older female Kriol participant from Placencia stood out from other local Kriol women when she said that the Maya foods poch and caldo belonged in the "most Belizean" pile because "Dat's a Mayan food also, so that's Belizean, di same ting. Dat's local chicken and di local corn dey mek di tortilla with." This woman had raised two Maya godchildren and also had hired Maya women to help cook in her restaurant. Through them she had learned about Maya food and culture. In my interviews with her she expressed a strong sense of Belize as a pluralistic melting pot of cultures, where different ethnic groups had their own cultures but intermarried and mingled and everyone was Belizean. She was an exception to the hegemonic nationalism expressed by most other Placencia Kriol women and men.

Most research participants, whether Kriol or not, did not include Maya food items in the "most Belizean" group. Even the two participants who identified themselves as Maya did not place all Maya-associated foods in the "most Belizean" pile during the Belizean-continuum pile sort. A young Belizean Kekchi Maya woman had this to say about why she placed two Maya foods in the "intermediate Belizean" category:

> **Participant:** 'Cause caldo with corn tortillas dat da lone like di mayas food and di Spanish one. Real Belizean people, dey no really really like fi eat dat. Dey no mek dat den. Dey eat it but dey no mek it.
>
> **Researcher:** Who da di real Belizean people?
>
> **Participant:** Di people who say dey born Belizean. Some Maya people come from across. Da no really Belizean food because you have Guatemala Maya people, because da Guatemala you could find dis dishes. [regarding poch] Dat da like – I don't know how fi say dat. Because di mostly di Maya people like dat.[27]

Non-Maya Placencia participants for the most part were unaware of common Maya foods such as poch and jippy jappa, despite the growing number of Maya people working in the local tourism industry. This lack of familiarity was a strong contributing factor to their exclusion from the category of Belizean, but even when they were informed that these were Maya foods, most participants still did not place them in the "most Belizean" pile, but rather in the "in-between" or even "least Belizean" group. One research participant accidentally placed a food that he considered to be Maya in the "most Belizean" pile, and then when he realized his mistake, moved it. His thought process is revealing of the way that hegemonic nationalism marginalizes less powerful groups like the Maya. "I put that [caan lab, or porridge] as most Belizean? That sounds like Maya, right? Can I put that back into the pile of least Belizean? [Researcher: Yes.] I've never heard of that. Yeah, it's probably more Maya or more, a small . . . most people in Belize, you ask them about that . . . flour lab you hear more about than corn lab. I don't know how that one slip past my radar."

TOURISM AND CULTURAL FOOD MARKETING

What do the prevalence of the hegemonic nationalism model and the dominance of Kriol home cooking imply for food marketing in the tourism industry? During this period of rising ethnic awareness and shifting demographics (mid-1980s until today), tourism has grown exponentially to become the country's number-one industry (Wilk 1999). Some towns and villages, including Placencia, have experienced unprecedented growth and turned into international tourism zones boasting a wide variety of restaurants, hotels, resorts and tour operations. High concentrations of First and Third World immigrants and foreign investors join Belizeans to work in the tourism industry in these locations. The desires and demands of tourists and these new immigrant groups are visibly reflected in the food sector. Some restaurants cater exclusively to tourists and northern immigrants, and most at least keep them in mind; as a result, dishes like chicken Parmesan and grilled cheese sandwiches can be found on some menus. Grocery stores carry exotic foods like pickled beets and imported Camembert cheese. Even the street vendors and cool spots serving tacos and hot dogs get business from budget travellers. In the menus and on the plates of Placencia, identity, ethnicity, authenticity and the exotic other come together in a commercialized cross-cultural culinary arena.

Explicit promotion of foods in Belize on an ethnic and/or national basis is a relatively recent, mostly post-colonial phenomenon, part of the processes of nation building and tourism marketing that have been taking place immediately preceding and since independence. According to Wilk, the idea of Belizean food as a culinary category within the country arose only in the early 1990s, when a growing Belizean (mostly Kriol) community in the United States and increasing exposure to the outside world led more and more Belizeans to identify local foodways as distinct from those from other parts of the globe (Wilk 2006). The first self-styled Belizean restaurant in the United States opened in New York City at the end of the 1970s as plans for independence were being finalized. This new gastronationalism was later carried back home: the first place to advertise "Belizean food" in Belize itself was a restaurant opened by returned Belizean Kriol owners in 1990, which served a strongly Kriol-flavoured menu (Wilk 2006).

In Placencia Village, a historically Kriol community that now hosts a diverse array of people, the majority of locally owned restaurants at least occasionally market Kriol food using a cultural angle, and some do so on a regular basis. The most common practice is simply to place the adjective *creole* (the most common spelling in Belize) before the name of a dish. A review of hundreds of chalkboard specials and menus from restaurants in Stann Creek, Belize, Toledo and Cayo Districts suggests that the fewer adjectives used, the more likely that the venue is not catering to tourists. In less tourist-oriented communities and even at cool spots and other eateries in Placencia that do not cater to tourists, cultural marketing is usually at a minimum, although occasional references to the nationalist "Belizean food" category may still be found. Businesses owned by non-Belizeans tend to avoid cultural marketing, as they have no "authentic" claims to those identities. All-inclusive resorts on the peninsula are the exception, having moved to capitalize on their guests' interest in local food by opening on-site "Belizean" restaurants. At least one of those resort restaurants has also advertised "creole" and "Garifuna" nights with entertainment, where the supper special is a dish thought to be typical of the culture.

It is interesting to see the shift of some businesses to culturally framed marketing for Kriol food, given that the same dishes, if they were called anything other than "dinna", have been labelled as "Belizean food" for more than twenty years. In Placencia itself the same dishes may be marketed as Kriol, local or Belizean, sometimes on the same menu or chalkboard.

Motivations for using culturally framed marketing strategies are various. Groups such as the Garifuna have been marketing food to visitors on a cultural basis for longer than the Kriol. North of Placencia, in the Garifuna community of Hopkins, "cultural foods" are a common menu item, and many locally owned venues specialize in signature dishes representing Garifuna foodways. Television channels like the Food Network and food travel shows expose many Belizeans to the northern concept of "ethnic food" and the ubiquity of cultural food marketing in other parts of the world. The Food Network show *Diners, Drive-Ins and Dives* even featured a Chicago Belizean Garifuna restaurant in one of its episodes, bringing cultural and national pride home to viewers in Belize.

Placencia has a long and proud identity as a Kriol community, so it is not surprising that when other cultural groups began to move into the area as part of tourism growth, the original Kriol inhabitants would begin to distinguish and promote their food as a distinct culinary category. In the context of Spanish and Maya burrito stands and North American and European fine dining, Kriol-owned restaurants and cool spots had to find a way to assert their identity and compete.

SUPPLY AND DEMAND, OR THE CURSE OF HEGEMONY

Regardless of whether food is marketed on a national basis as Belizean or culturally framed as Kriol, serious reductionism exists in the range of dishes available in many Belizean-owned restaurants. Most of my research participants did not consider the category "Belizean food" to encompass all the dishes of the Belizean population, reflecting instead a hegemonic nationalism focused on Kriol and (to a lesser extent) Garifuna cuisine. Even within the already reduced category of "hegemonic Belizean", what is served in many restaurants across Belize excludes many Garifuna and Kriol dishes and centres around a predictable rotation of rice-and-beans plates accompanied by stewed meats or fried seafood, fried plantain and coleslaw or potato salad, along with the occasional conch or cowfoot soup special and a few Spanish-associated additions such as escabeche and chimole. These are the "rice-and-beans joints" of Belize, good places to buy a hearty plate of what was once the Kriol Sunday dinner and is now Belize's unofficial national dish – rice and beans and stewed chicken with plantain and potato salad – but not great for tourists or Belizeans looking for exciting and unusual ingredients and meals.

Thanks to the curse of hegemonic nationalism that prioritizes Kriol and to a lesser degree Garifuna food over other cultural groups, the foodways of entire groups are eliminated from the menu. Caldo and corn tortillas, tacari chicken, curried cohune cabbage, poch, black bean and chaya tamales, black corn porridge with allspice, chu'uk kwa and many other hidden delicacies are denied the limelight that they deserve. Ignorance of the full breadth of Belizean foodways and a hegemonic nationalist perspective keep these foods off the national plate, relegating them to regional specialties or secrets known only to members of a particular cultural group and dimming the prospect for food-focused tourism in Belize.

What is advertised on a cultural basis as "creole" food in Placencia is a limited menu compared to the full range of traditional Kriol home cooking. The term *creole*, as found on Placencia menus, is not used to refer to all the foods which participants identified as being Kriol in their sorting exercises. Instead it typically describes just two modes of food preparation: meats or seafood that are either cooked in a tomato-based sauce with onion and sweet pepper and coconut oil (sometimes without the tomato) or stewed in a recado and vinegar–based sauce.

Most restaurants completely ignore traditional local Kriol and Garifuna delicacies such as steamed, baked, fresh corned or hashed fish; Matilda foot/bundiga;[28] fufu/hudut;[29] and a wide array of sweets ranging from jellies and jams to cassava cake and potato pound to coconut trifle, pies and tarts and whole wild fruits stewed down with sugar and allspice. Rice and beans and beans and rice remain the mainstay of many menus and specials boards, while serre, boil-up and stew fish, traditional hearty fisherman dishes, are relegated, at best, to an occasional appearance. More esoteric Kriol or Garifuna meals – boiled fresh corned barracuda topped with coconut oil and pepper sauce and served with hot johnnycakes, hudut, serre, and wiliks/wilks (whelk) or land crab soup – are difficult or impossible to find outside of people's homes. Treats like the fried swim bladder of a barracuda, the gills of a hogfish or the much-appreciated roe of spawning snapper are consumed only at home and never served in restaurants.[30]

At the same time, most local restaurant owners in Placencia are quick to incorporate foods which they do not consider to be Belizean in order to boost revenue. One restaurant advertising "creole food" has a full page of burritos and burgers on its menu, and many restaurants offering local food also serve nachos, fajitas and sandwiches for the less adventurous guest.

Another reason for this reductionism, which I address in more detail in the next chapter, is economic. Rice and beans and chicken are cheap and reliable staples, shipped in weekly from (often Mennonite) farms in Cayo District to Chinese-owned grocery stores across the peninsula. Meanwhile, for a number of reasons, traditional local ingredients such as fish and coconuts have become increasingly expensive and difficult to source. Hurricane Iris and the disease lethal yellowing decimated the local coconut population, while demand for drinking coconuts and coconut water on the peninsula prevents many nuts from reaching full maturity, the only stage at which they can be transformed into coconut milk and oil – key ingredients of Placencia foodways. Focusing on rice, beans and chicken ensures a higher profit margin and more reliable product supply for a restaurant.

These reduced "restaurant creole" and "hegemonic Belizean" menus help to perpetuate the myth that the only thing Belizeans eat is rice, beans and chicken. A large number of delicious dishes are missing from most tourists' culinary experiences in Belize simply because they are not readily available for sale. The continued success of hegemonic and Kriol nationalism in Belize has, sadly, left our gastronational expression often lacking in the cultural diversity for which we are famous and of which we should be proud. Is Kriol home cooking's role as a stringent gatekeeper preventing us from developing a fully representative national cuisine? How can we change this? We need to better understand how home cooking enters the public realm where it can contribute to cuisine development, as well as the role of professional cooking in culinary exploration and innovation.

7
BUILDING A BELIZEAN CUISINE

CUISINES DEVELOP, EVOLVE, CHANGE AND SPREAD THANKS TO the actions of those who cook. As discussed earlier, the distinction between lowly "cooks" – those who cook informally for friends, family and other loved ones – and revered "chefs" – who prepare food as a profession after specialized training on the job and/or through culinary school – is highly gendered and predicated on a public/private-sphere dichotomy that originated with nineteenth-century modernist theory (Horwitz 1982; Weintraub and Kuma 1997). This dichotomy privileges work (including cooking) done in the public sphere as more valuable than work performed in the private sphere of the home (Harris and Giuffre 2015; Landes 1998; Neuhaus 2003). Home cooking is feminized and hidden in the private sphere, where it exists in implicit contrast with professional cooking, which in the Western half of the world is tied to the rules and regulations, practices and ideologies of well-codified masculinized French professional cuisine performed in public (Avakian and Haber 2005; Harris and Giuffre 2015; Moisio, Arnould and Price 2004; Swenson 2013; Trubek 2000; Whitaker 2005). Home cooking is defined as a labour of love, a nurturing act of feeding one's family, which simultaneously provides a powerful arena for both experimenting with and transmitting culinary heritage from one generation to another (Di Giovine 2010; Moisio, Arnould and Price 2004). Because women are so strongly associated with home cooking, female chefs are still regularly viewed as imposters in professional kitchens. According to Deborah Harris and Pattie Giuffre (2015, 47–48), in their book on gender inequality in the restaurant industry, "Not only are men and women chefs written about in very different ways but these ways reinforce the home versus haute divisions in professional cooking as men chefs are described as creators who master the kitchen, innovate cuisine, and build empires while women chefs are depicted as being food producers who re-create traditional or homey dishes and are not highly invested in their careers unless guided by a man."

Despite this derisive attitude towards homemade food in the professional kitchen, home and professional cooking are deeply intertwined and both play a fundamental role in cuisine creation (Ferguson 2004; Harris and Giuffre 2015). Like the public and private spheres, home cooking and professional cooking have always been mutually constituted, and ideas, dishes, preparation techniques and ingredients are continually shared between the two culinary genres. While an enthusiast might buy famed Chef Adrià's cookbook and try out some molecular gastronomy at home, few people would define a dish such as Apple Caviar with Banana Foam as home cooking, regardless of where, by whom and for whom it was prepared. But in the United States macaroni and cheese may be home cooking or professional cuisine, depending on the complexity of the recipe, the ingredients (sodium citrate as an emulsifier!), the presentation and the creativity involved. Professional cooking builds on, elaborates and transforms the everyday food preparation of the home. Without home cooking, professional chefs would have nowhere to start, and cultural and national cuisines would not exist. In order to understand and examine the way that cuisines develop, we must start in the home. As we saw in the last chapter, Kriol households play a gatekeeping role in defining Belizean cuisine, and in every Belizean home experimentation, the adaptation and substitution of new ingredients, dishes and meals contribute to the development and evolution of cultural and national cuisines.

But home cooking does not dwell in just the private sphere. In order to understand how a national cuisine might develop we must explore how home cooking interacts with the public sector of restaurant food and professional cooking, where client demand helps to drive culinary innovation and evolution. Exploring the complex connections between private and public, between home and professional cooking, might help us understand why there is less variety among Belizean dishes in Placencia restaurants than in Placencia homes and what must happen for a truly representative national cuisine to develop.

The concept of public and private spheres dates back to at least the seventeenth century. Considered one of the "grand dichotomies of Western thought", it is one of several binary oppositions that underlie modern Western inquiry (Weintraub and Kuma 1997). In reality it is a continuum, one that is useful for explaining how home cooking is treated when it enters the market economy. This transition from private to public space is essential for the development of a recognized cuisine. Individuals draw from and experiment with home cooking, often from different cultural and regional foodways, until these private-sphere innovations go public in restaurants, cool spots and bars, or even as part of a tour package. There, with continuing creativity and ongoing dialogue between home and professional cooking, the techniques, ingredients, flavour combinations and dishes may be eventually systematized into a cuisine, become the topic of food writing and media exposure, and be discussed, evaluated and ultimately compared with other cuisines. The new, professionalized cuisine then reaches home kitchens across the country, inspiring a fresh round of creative experimentation. French cuisine, for example, is not merely prepared in French homes and restaurants across the nation and around the world but is debated, written about, celebrated and displayed in a very public manner on the local, regional, national and global levels. It is this public discussion and the codification of systems of culinary technique, flavour profiles, recipes and dishes (which typically occurs in professional kitchens) that ultimately establishes the somewhat fuzzy parameters of any cuisine (Goody 1982; Iyora-Diaz 2012; Trubek 2000). Can this be happening yet in such a young country as Belize?

HOME COOKING OUTSIDE THE HOME

I broadly define *home cooking* as cooking that is meant to feed people with whom you have (or hope to have) a personal connection that goes beyond the economic. Home cooking is about establishing and maintaining relationships: family connections, romantic partnerships, friendships, acquaintanceships (Avakian and Haber 2005; Di Giovine 2010; Halloran 2016). In Placencia (and across Belize and the Caribbean), home cooking enters the market economy, the public sphere and professional kitchens through a variety of paths, challenging the public/private dichotomy and complicating the discourse of family, reciprocity, emotional bonding and gift-giving associated with the home and "di yaad" (Houston 2005; Spang 2013).

Why does it matter whether home cooking enters the public sphere? It is the food that reaches public spaces which receives the most attention from visitors, many of whom will not experience a Belizean family meal in a private home. It is the food available in public spaces – restaurants, bars, cool spots, even sold out of a five-gallon pigtail bucket – that is written about in official tourism publications such as *Destination Belize* magazine and discussed on most websites and blogs about Belize. It is the food in public spaces that is evaluated in events like the annual Taste of Belize cooking competition. It is this publicly accessible food that the shows *Bizarre Food* and *Booze Traveler* showcased in their Belize episodes. While some foodie journalists and itinerant culinary anthropologists may get excited about esoteric dishes or ingredients that rarely appear on menus, we are a tiny minority among the forces shaping perceptions of Belizean food. For a representative Belizean cuisine to develop or for a cultural cuisine to be recognized as such, sufficient public attention and discourse must come into play. Let us examine how that happens in Placencia Village.

One important way that home cooking reaches the public in Placencia is through entrepreneurial women who are seeking to generate income for themselves and their families. For many decades women in Placencia Village have engaged in money-making activities that could be fit into a domestic work schedule of child care, cooking and cleaning. Sewing, doing laundry for others, making coconut oil and guava jelly, and baking Kriol bread, bun and other treats for sale were common activities for stay-at-home mothers. These activities are not restricted to Placencia Village, Belize. Around the world such informal microenterprises are common survival strategies (among many others, see Browne 2004; Houston 2005; Tinker 2003). Today many women, especially those aged forty and older, still spend much more time in and around their homes than their male counterparts. They may now bake in a gas oven instead of a fire hearth and wash laundry in a machine instead of by hand, but the goal of obtaining extra income is the same. Women accomplish this by reaching out from the private sphere and engaging in the market economy of "di street".

In Placencia today several women regularly bake Kriol bread, bun and cakes to sell to the public. Some women set up a table in their yard at the side of the street and sell from there, while others send a young relative around the village with a Tupperware container. Several women have arranged to sell in a grocery store. One sends her niece or nephew to the shop every week with a box of bread and bun, and the same lady also makes guava jelly

Figure 4. A typical Kriol home in Placencia Village

at home, which is sold in several stores in the community. These women have an ongoing side business in baked goods, but many other households occasionally enter the market this way when finances are tight. Homemade products sold out of containers on the street in Placencia include ready-to-eat johnnycakes stuffed with beans and slices of processed cheese, chicken wings, panades, lobster and conch fritters, doughnuts, tamales, green mangoes and golden plums peeled and ready to eat with salt and chile, and a wide variety of sweets, including coconut and lime tarts, bread pudding, sweet potato pound, cassava cake and various kinds of fudge. Almost all the cooks behind these street snacks are women.

Both cooks and food move between the public and private culinary spheres. A home space may be transformed into a commercial one, bringing the public street into the private yard. A Kriol woman in her mid-seventies recounted to me her many years of cooking food at home to sell to the wider village. While raising ten children she baked Kriol bread to sell, and in the early 1970s she began preparing tamales every Saturday after a friend taught her how to make them. At one point in her long career she had picnic tables set up in her yard and would serve a fire-hearth-prepared lunch to tourists who wanted to try local food. By opening her yard to visitors she transformed this semi-private family space into a more public, tourism-oriented arena. Entering the public commercial sphere and engaging with the tourist market also changed her dishes. She used her host gaze and consciously adjusted the food to accommodate her perception of what tourists were looking for. She would stuff and bake fish fillets for tourists on the fire hearth as a boneless (and therefore presumably tourist-friendly) alternative to whole baked fish, which is preferred on Belizean tables.

Today she no longer caters to tourists but continues to make a wide array of home-cooked food that is considered among the best in the village. Several of her sons sell her products around the village for a share of the profit. Her loyal customers, many of whom are related in some way, buy whatever she has for sale, knowing it will be good. These days she rarely leaves her home, even to walk down to the shop, preferring to send one of the many family members living in her crowded yard. She uses a fire hearth fuelled by coconut husks for much of her cooking and baking, a "traditional" cheap but time-consuming method that Belizeans believe imparts a delicious flavour to all food.[1]

Entrepreneurs such as Ms B. are important because they produce labour-intensive ingredients like coconut oil and dishes such as tamales, which most families do not make regularly, and they help maintain culinary traditions passed down from generation to generation. They bring into the public sphere food items – such as green mango with salt or cassava cake – that are rarely found in sit-down restaurants, and some experiment with new cooking techniques, ingredients and recipes.

Belizeans in Placencia and elsewhere in the country often associate these productive activities with poverty. For many households they are a survival strategy which may be shameful in Belize's modern consumer-oriented society. During the "slow season" – that part of the year when few tourists are around and many households are tightening their belts – there is a noticeable spike in food vending, particularly of small, cheap snacks that locals can still afford. Children may be reluctant to go sell food on the street when everyone knows that the household is struggling to make ends meet. Exceptions include cases where food preparation has become a significant income generator, in which case the household might build a cool spot

Figure 5. Ms Buela's grand-niece grating coconuts to make coconut oil

in their yard or even open a restaurant. Having a storefront legitimizes the business, transforming it from a temporary survival strategy to proud entrepreneurship.

Radiance Williams,[2] a local Kriol woman in her fifties whom I interviewed, recounted her adventures of taking her home-cooking skills public when she worked at resort restaurants in the 1970s and 1980s. She learned new techniques and recipes in the resort kitchens which she then experimented with at home, a clear demonstration of the give-and-take between home cooking and professional cuisine. During her adventurous life she worked in two resort kitchens and several restaurants and also spent time with a British soldier-husband in England and around Europe, where she learned British and continental cooking. Nine years ago Ms Radiance left her restaurant jobs and opened her own takeout cool spot with a picnic table attached to her house, so she could be at home for her daughter as she entered her teenage years. Her private yard was thus transformed into a public space: two tables on her veranda and a brisk takeout business yield her a steady income.

NEGOTIATION AND COMMODITIZATION

Clearly there are different ways of taking home cooking to the public and turning it into a commodity. How does the home-cook-turned-entrepreneur negotiate this transformation of a "free" meal laden with emotion and reflective of interpersonal relationships into a commodity for sale, especially in a community where at least half of her or his customers are likely to be family and friends? Marcel Mauss's (1950) seminal work reminds us that a gift implies the notion of credit and that barter arose from a system of gifts given and received on credit. In Belize, exchanges of favours and gifts is called "hand wash hand" and a robust gift/barter system coexists alongside a dynamic cash economy; food is a common gift, barter item and market product.

In Placencia Village, there are at least seven year-round Kriol home-cook entrepreneurs selling meals and food products out of their home, on the street after having cooked it at home or out of a cool spot located in their yard. Straddling the public/private divide is just part of the job, and engaging in a balancing act between personal relationships and commercial transactions is something that many small-scale Belizean entrepreneurs enact every day.

Ms Radiance's cool spot is attached to her home and she does her commercial cooking in her home kitchen. She conducts commercial and non-commercial food transactions on a regular basis. Kinship ties and reciprocity networks are in evidence in this space that is part street and part home, part commercial venue and part home kitchen (Houston 2005). Ms Radiance sends food and bread over to her aunt, who is bedridden in a nearby house, and one of her elderly uncles comes up the wooden stairs, Tupperware in hand, to pick up a meal for later or sits down at her table and is fed. Neither relative expects or is expected to pay for the food. At the same time paying customers come and go, picking up Styrofoam containers of split peas and pigtail or lasagne with a side salad, or sitting down to eat at a table alongside other paying and non-paying consumers. Regular customers get credit if they forget their cash or if Ms Radiance does not have change. Since these are local villagers she knows she will see again, she expects that eventually she will get her money.

A former business partner and I participated in reciprocity exchanges with Ms Radiance. She was looking for coconuts and we were making a trip to the islands that allowed us to pick a sack for her. In return she gave us homemade Kriol bread free of charge – bread made with the same coconuts we had given her. We ate some at home and used the rest on tours that took us to the islands where the coconuts grew. The fact that my then partner was a distant cousin of hers, a kinship tie that both referred to on occasion, increased the appropriateness of the mutual support and reciprocity. She also sells the bread that she gave us, so it is the context of the exchange, not the actual food item, that determines whether it is public or private, commodity or gift.

This kind of reciprocity reflects the Kriol saying "hand wash hand". By exchanging raw and processed food items gathered from the wild, we avoided the cash economy and subsidized both of our businesses while building personal networks and a sense of community through gift exchange (Mauss 1950). In the space between cash and non-cash economies, reciprocity and market exchange, there is room for negotiation, for mutual support and for using the home to subsidize commercial ventures. At times this can make the difference between success or failure for a small-business venture. It can also be dangerous to depend too much on family ties and reciprocal exchanges. If they become unbalanced or if one person fails to do their share, small-business owners may find their profits falling. The objectives of network-building and profit-making can clash spectacularly in a homegrown business. One woman complained to me that she had to quit working with her husband in a joint restaurant venture, because he would always give beer and food to his friends for free. While this was a great way for him to build personal networks and boost the restaurant's reputation, it was a lousy way to make a profit and sustain the household. She ended up opening her own taco stand instead, keeping the money to maintain their household, while her husband got a job in construction.

Since her food is prepared and stored in a home kitchen, Ms Radiance and her family eat any leftovers from the day's lunch special. Thus home cooking and commercial cooking efficiently coexist in the same location, reducing overhead costs and labour for Ms Radiance, subsidizing family meals, and simplifying food prep and clean-up. Ms Radiance also achieves her goal of spending more time with her daughter without sacrificing income. Even though her food was described by many of my research participants as prepared with love and "what yu ma woulda cook" – the epitome of

Figure 6. Ms Radiance's blackboard, listing her daily lunch specials

non-commercial home cooking – most customers arrive cash in hand to pay for their meal. Hearty portions for a good price, filling dishes and a tasty mix of seasonings combine to make what many in the village consider some of the best Kriol food available for sale. At the same time, if a customer wants something different, Ms Radiance makes an effort to serve two lunch specials every day, one that is Kriol home cooking and one that is foreign-influenced. She experiments with new dishes in her kitchen, drawing from cookbooks and her broad exposure to professional kitchens and cooking across Europe. If she deems her creations successful she will put them on the lunch menu, but there are some limits to what she can serve. Her dishes must stay within the economic boundaries of her lunch spot: she cannot charge more than BZ$10 to BZ$12 a plate if she wants to retain her mostly Belizean customer base and stay competitive with other lunch specials in the village. Wilk (2006) defines home cooking as being economy minded, and this need constrains some forms of experimentation. The rare and expensive ingredients, high-tech kitchen tools and extremely labour-intensive techniques associated with high-end professional chefs are too costly for a home-cooking operation like Radiance's cool spot.

TOUR FOOD

Street vending, cool spots and casual restaurants are not the only way that home cooking enters the public sphere. In Placencia, Belizean-owned tour operations and guides often serve their guests home-cooked food. This is an excellent way for small tour operators to simultaneously cut costs and form a personal connection with their guests. It is also another arena for raising consciousness about differences and similarities between Belizean and foreign home cooking, as guests and guides often converse about what they are eating when they share a meal on tour. Many tour operators serve rice and beans that a Placencia-born female cook prepared at home or at her cool spot. With small tour operations it is common that this person be a member of the immediate family. The rice and beans are usually accompanied by freshly barbecued chicken and sometimes served with potato salad or potatoes, thinly sliced and covered with Cheez Whiz, cooked in foil packets on the grill. One immigrant tour operator serves a meal prepared by a local Kriol cook that includes fried chicken. A Canadian couple in their late fifties, repeat visitors to the Placencia area, described their experiences with Belizean food on tours:

> **B (husband):** One of J's problems with the meals is she doesn't like beans and rice.
> **J (wife):** Yes, or rice and beans.
> **B:** And that comes with a lot of meals in most places.
> **J:** And I also don't find them very good when I find them. I understand it's

> basic food, but it's such a focus of the meals. So last year we went on a lot of trips where we were very active. So you would come out, the food would be provided and it would be a chicken leg, stewed, which I don't like, and a huge amount of beans and rice – carbohydrates – which I understand culturally why that is, but for me it's not. The best food I had – and for me that's why I like going out with K on *Callaloo* [a sailboat used for snorkel tours], because M by Kelly's does the lunches for him, and I think I would call her the best cook that I have had food-wise in Placencia.
>
> **B:** The food is very good.
>
> **J:** She does a fried chicken that I've never had. I'm still trying to figure it out. Of course, she won't share anything. She also uses, I think, curry in the batter that she puts on it, and the chicken is cooked perfectly. For me that's the favourite food, so we go out on that trip a lot, [to] get that lunch.

Another visitor told me that he gave his fly-fishing guide an extra tip specifically for the guide's wife, who had cooked all the food for their lunches. He said they were big and delicious and favourably compared the meals to his experiences with fly fishing in Canada, where on guided tours cold sandwiches were the norm. Sea tours that include freshly caught and grilled seafood as part of the excursion are particularly popular.

Unlike independent Belizean-owned tour-operator shops, foreign-owned resorts with tour operations have professional kitchens on-site. Despite this, the tour food at some of the resorts is not spectacular. One of my informants had experience tour guiding with a high-end American-owned resort. He commented repeatedly about the lunch that the resort provided, which consisted of cookies, fruit and sandwiches of cold cuts. According to him, it was not a proper lunch for going to sea, where people get out of the water hungry and want a filling meal. When more than one boat was at the same island, he noted that the guests always looked hungrily at the barbecued chicken the other tour operators made for their guests. One time a guest even asked the man grilling chicken for another tour operator if he could have a piece. My informant said he felt bad seeing that happen and thought the resort should provide a better lunch on tours, especially given the high-end nature of the hotel. He personally would beg for chicken because he did not want to eat the cold sandwich. Another foreign-owned resort on the peninsula switched from serving sandwiches to making fresh barbecue when they saw that their guests clearly preferred a hot meal on trips.

Cooking on tour is an excellent way to form personal connections, one of the objectives of home cooking. While the cooked meal forms part of a commercial product (the tour), it is still home cooking. Economy and taste must balance, and food is used to forge personal connections with and memorable experiences for the guests. Often guests ask what seasonings are used or want the recipe for the pineapple coleslaw, thus starting personal conversations about food experiences and preferences that move away from the commoditized nature of the meal.

Belizean guides (often male) who serve bread baked by their mothers and rice and beans that their wives have made, or who cook up seafood they have caught, symbolically extend their kinship and friendship networks, their way of life, to temporarily include the tourist. The homemade food, the links to a broader kinship network hinted at by the guava jelly or coconut bread on the table, and the conversation around the table imitate an idealized home meal. By consuming food that the guides or their family have cooked and that Belizeans would normally eat at home, tourists feel part of something larger than the tour. They consume and to some degree participate in Belizean culture and identity as they eat their lunch. They send their compliments to the mother who made the delicious coconut bread or praise the guide who caught the big lobster. This dining experience fulfils tourist imaginaries of intimately engaging with the other. The most successful tour will seamlessly combine public and private, allowing visitors to purchase a commercial product from the public, tourist-oriented sphere that will provide them with an intimate private-sphere experience which they may call "authentic" (Hughes 1995; Quan and Wang 2004; Sidali, Kastenholz and Bianchi 2015).

The content of these meals is shaped by a variety of factors. Economy is important, especially for small tour operators. Tour companies will not serve something that is too expensive. While the food should be good and filling, guests do not expect five-star dining on a snorkel tour. For small group tours, catching fresh seafood ourselves reduces tour expenses while at the same time providing visitors with an "authentic" experience of how Belizeans spend a day on the islands.

This authenticity is adapted to business needs and visitor expectations. Some people may consider the culinary code-switching to be partially staged, that is, altered from how things would be done if the day at sea were not a tour catering to tourists (MacCannell 1973). There is no time on a day tour to cook up stew fish or serre, which fishermen often eat on the cayes at the end of a long workday, so seafood is simply grilled. It may be grilled with olive oil because visitors cannot always digest and do not always like coconut oil, which is more reflective of the culinary heritage of Placencia. And guests are typically served lobster tail only, while Placencia locals would also eat the head. A pineapple and cilantro coleslaw with olive oil and lime dressing may taste like the Caribbean to visitors, but most Belizeans would argue that coleslaw should include grated carrot and not involve olive oil (a relatively recent import) in the dressing. Here again the preferences of visitors (along with the time constraints of a day trip) shape the menu and result in experimentation and innovation with local dishes as they are altered to appeal to the palates of North American guests. Tour operators and guides use their host gaze to evaluate their customer base, creating an emic tourism typology that, combined with economic considerations, helps them decide what culinary experiences to offer their guests on tour.

A tour guide who does inland tours explained that cooking for tourists who had gone on tour with him was a post-tour activity that he would save for people he felt a personal connection with. For him, home cooking takes the interaction out of a commercialized, commoditized "host" and "guest" exchange and into the informal arena of potential friendship or romance.

> **Researcher:** You ever do any cooking as part of your tour guiding over the years?
>
> **Respondent:** Well, yeah. Hell, yeah. Of course. [laughs]
>
> . . .
>
> **Respondent:** Yu know, cool people. You don't always meet cool people on their trips. When you meet them, you want to hang with them for as long as possible, so I would invite them over for dinner and cook it up.
>
> **Researcher:** And impress them too, right?
>
> **Respondent:** Well, yeah. [laughs] . . . You know Erin, Erin P? Well, her brother came down and he didn't like seafood. He keep saying the only time he is going to eat fish, he is going to eat fish from me again. It's stuff like that. They aren't making that shit up. They're serious, and that makes me want to do more and cook more, you know?

The positive response of guests to local Belizean home cooking encourages this tour guide and others to feel good about and have pride in their food and culinary skills. In this way tourism fosters awareness and culinary pride in tourism destinations like Placencia Village. It is not surprising that tourism zones in Belize are the areas where culturally framed food marketing is most likely to be seen. It is in these arenas that chefs and home cooks are more likely to be exposed to and inspired by foodways and culinary imaginaries from different parts of the world (Salazar and Graburn 2014; Wilk 1999). As Sammells (2014, 2017) explains in her work in Bolivia, exposure to tourism as a "cultural practice" influences the way in which individuals think about and express their culinary heritage. The resulting culinary pride and experimentation are essential prerequisites to creating an innovative national cuisine.

These are just a couple of examples of how home cooking can enter the public sphere to be consumed, experienced, discussed and evaluated by people outside of a particular household. Here, in the public sector of a tourism zone, comparative feedback from visitors and well-travelled Belizeans and the circulation of imported culinary imaginaries build awareness of what ingredients, flavours, techniques and dishes comprise Belizean foodways, by encouraging self-reflection and facilitating comparison with outsider cuisines (Wilk 1995, 1999). The ongoing sharing between home cooking in the commercial sector and home cooking in the private sphere ensures that Belizean home cooks of different cultural backgrounds, especially those who offer their food to the wide audience of consumers present in a tourism zone, will (within the constraints of economy) continue to learn and experiment with new recipes, ingredients and ideas, contributing to the evolution and development of local culinary practices that shape what is ultimately known as Belizean food.

PROFESSIONAL COOKING

If home cooking, whether it occurs in a private or public space, is cooking for people with whom you have or hope to have a personal connection, what is professional cooking? What role does professional cooking play in influencing and shaping foodways and encouraging cuisine development? In the Western world we look to France for the answer. In her thorough analysis of the subject, Trubek (2000) discusses how French haute cuisine, the food of the noble classes, was the foundation of professional culinary practices that have shaped restaurant cooking the world over. The French codified and standardized the techniques, practices and recipes of haute cuisine, which forms the foundation of Western professional cuisine now found in higher-end restaurants around the world. The basic techniques, practices, terminology and mores of the Western culinary profession are derived from the publications of French culinary masters such as Carême and Escoffier (Ferguson 2004; Trubek 2000).

As Jack Goody (1982) describes, a similar process of haute and professional cuisine development took place in the royal courts of imperial China and spread to other countries across Asia. However, professional cooking derived from the French tradition or some variant is what is found in most high-end restaurants in Belize. Western professional cooking derives from a basis of French haute cuisine, which is inspired in part by peasant food (Trubek 2000). The great difference from home cooking is that haute cuisine developed in a context where economy was not a factor and creativity was in high demand. In the upper echelons of the bored nobility of France, jaded palates and eyes were always on the lookout for dishes that pushed the boundaries of creativity in both flavour and presentation. Ostentation was the name of the game among French aristocrats, and the use of costly, rare and imported ingredients was encouraged as a way to distinguish the cuisine of the wealthy and powerful from the food of the peasantry (Ferguson 2004; Spang 2000). Creativity was not constrained by budgetary considerations and innovation was not only encouraged but demanded. Feasts were a source of entertainment as much as sustenance; the visual appeal of each dish was as important as taste, smell and theatrical performance (Strong 2002).

Mintz (1989) defines haute cuisine as the foods of an elite that distinguish their dishes from the food of the masses. Haute cuisine involves cooking and serving rare, exotic, expensive ingredients that are sometimes protected by sumptuary distinctions. It demonstrates exclusivity by supplying things out of season, from far-off locations, and the best of what is available. It is prepared elaborately with complex equipment and techniques and evaluated in part by the number of person-hours and quantity of accumulated skills and training invested in each bite of food. Today, in a school like the Culinary Institute of America, this system is taught with the goal of producing graduates who have a firm foundation in the "culinary arts", "classic [French] training", "quality" and "innovation" (Culinary Institute of America 2014). This is Western professional cooking.³

PROFESSIONAL CUISINE MEETS HOME COOKING IN PLACENCIA

When Wilk wrote about Belizean food in 2006, he asked, "So why hasn't Belizean food gone to that higher level? Why aren't there high-end Belizean restaurants figuring out ways to use unique local ingredients and combinations to please sophisticated foreign palates?" (187). He believed the reason was that most professional chefs working in high-end restaurants in Belize were foreigners or had been trained by foreigners who knew and cared little about Belizean food. More than a decade after he bewailed the lack of a national cuisine, foreign chefs and their trainees still dominate the professional culinary scene on Placencia Peninsula. Belize's foodscape has expanded dramatically and some Belizean chefs are now innovating with Belizean ingredients and flavour profiles, but these exceptional chefs and restaurants are still a minority. On Placencia Peninsula professional "international hotel cuisine" and "classic" (French-derived) culinary training are strongly associated with foreign (male) chefs, restaurant owners and clientele.

Of course, not all food that enters the commercial sphere is the product of professional culinary arts. Many of the forty-odd restaurants, bars and cool spots on Placencia Peninsula serve homestyle cooking to their guests. In Placencia many of my research participants (tourists and residents, foreigners as well as Belizeans) identified categorical differences between restaurants owned by Belizeans and restaurants owned by North Americans and Europeans. This latter group includes resort restaurants, as most are foreign-owned. The main difference between most foreign-owned and Belizean-owned restaurants is the distinction between a trend-aware professional culinary approach and an approach rooted in home cooking. Most of the internationally oriented spots attempt to ride the coattails of cosmopolitan "global" trends that have often trickled down from famous restaurants in North America and Europe. Not all foreign-owned establishments are dishing up high-end professional cuisine and not all Belizean-owned restaurants serve homestyle food, but most professionally trained chefs work at foreign-owned restaurants. Differences in how foreign- and Belizean-owned restaurants operate also reflect the degree to which each business is tied to private spaces, family ties, and kinship and friendship networks.

Sammells (2014, 143) describes what she calls an "idealized division":

> local food ways are often associated with the labor of unpaid (or underpaid) anonymous women cooking at home or in liminally public spaces such as street markets. Cosmopolitan cuisines, in contrast, suggest food ways that are perceived to cross international boundaries. These are produced by professionally trained chefs, largely men, who are paid and respected as individuals for their skills. Such cosmopolitan food ways are often presented and consumed in elite public spaces such as upper-end restaurants and public banquets rather than in private homes.

This dichotomy is constantly breached as home cooks experiment with new ingredients in their "traditional" dishes, incorporating cosmopolitan foodstuffs into their local food, or establish food businesses in the public sphere. Regardless, it reflects common beliefs in the existence of different levels – local versus international, public versus private – of cooking and food. How do these beliefs affect culinary innovation, experimentation and, ultimately, the development of Belizean cuisine?

While all good kitchen managers on the peninsula know that they have to get along with their produce vendor, some businesses rely much more heavily on a foundation of family connections, friendship ties and reciprocity networks than others. These businesses tend to be Belizean-owned. Reciprocity networks of kin and friends are often utilized by Belizean entrepreneurs to give themselves an edge in this highly competitive arena. In a country of four hundred thousand people, personal contacts, kinship networks and informal reciprocity networks based on "favours" are invaluable. The private sphere provides supplies, support and connections that subsidize public-sphere commercial activities. Insider information plays an important role in knowing how and where to obtain certain ingredients. Foreign-owned restaurants are usually based on a business model that is much more firmly situated in the public, commoditized space of the capitalist marketplace, either because there is less need to economize through reciprocal networks and/or because the owners do not have the family and friendship connections necessary to do so.

One common way in which Belizean-owned venues use kinship and friendship connections to support their businesses is in sourcing ingredients, as Ms Radiance does at her cool spot. Belizean-owned businesses are likely to have friendship or kinship ties with purveyors, fishermen, hunters and farmers, allowing them to obtain hard-to-find ingredients, discounts and sometimes free merchandise. One Belizean-owned restaurant in Placencia got an ice chest full of free shrimp from a cousin who works at a shrimp farm. The same venue regularly catches some of its own seafood, unlike foreign-owned restaurants. Another restaurant buys gibnuts from the Belize River Valley, from hunter friends who live there. Cool spots are even more likely than sit-down restaurants to rely on these personal networks to obtain labour and products. Connections like these can give Belizean-owned restaurants a chance to obtain rare or seasonal ingredients of which foreign-owned and operated venues may not even be aware, all while reducing overhead costs.

Recently some foreign restaurateurs have developed their own personal networks, sometimes with Belizeans but also with a growing community of mainly white North American and European immigrants who are farming or have established import businesses. Savvy foreign business owners may also rely on the connections of Belizean employees to get them the freshest fish or best produce. These connections are distinct, however, as they are cash-based and rarely involve kinship ties, an important factor in Belizean public interaction and business.

THE MORAL ECONOMY OF FOOD

Kinship brings with it a host of obligations (not always followed but still powerful), and that includes giving a family member a good deal. This responsibility shapes the menu of many Belizean-owned restaurants, as in our example of Ms Radiance's cool spot. The food served at Belizean-owned establishments reflects the necessity of catering to different consumers. In a given restaurant, "foreigner-" and Belizean-oriented menu items, pricing and marketing often coexist simultaneously. Profitability is not the only reason for a diversely priced menu in Placencia restaurants. Many Belizeans feel a moral obligation to offer at least some meals at a price that most Belizeans can afford, while at the same time serving dishes that cater to foreign visitors and immigrants. This moral obligation can constrain menu options but also permits business owners to maintain a positive reputation in their community. With the average annual income across the country hovering around US$8,000 a year, most Belizeans have much less disposable income than many of the tourists and immigrants who come from North America and Europe.

This obligation derives in part from the personal connection that home cooking establishes between the producer and consumer. In a small community like Placencia, locals who own a restaurant ignore the financial constraints of friends and family at their peril. Restaurants that clearly do not cater to Belizeans (for example, by serving only high-priced foreign dishes and nothing that the average Belizean can afford) are less likely to be recommended by them. Some Belizeans would consider this an outright betrayal if perpetrated by a Belizean business owner. On a given Belizean-owned restaurant menu, some dishes are more strongly associated with the home and the private sphere and those dishes tend to be cheaper. Belizean home cooking, when brought into the commercial sphere, balances economy and taste not only for the business but also for the intended (Belizean) consumer.

Belizean-owned establishments like Ms Radiance's serve daily lunch specials for BZ$10–$12. These are popular with working Belizeans on lunch break from their jobs for what is Belize's biggest meal of the day. Having midday specials that cater to Belizean tastes and income makes sense for Belizean-owned restaurants, which depend on a variety of clientele to make a living. One owner told me that he did not really make any money on his lunch special but he "had to have it" so that Belizeans (often relatives and friends) could afford a midday meal at his place. There are also more expensive dishes (BZ$20 and up) on the menus of Belizean-owned restaurants on the peninsula. These pricier meals are aimed at foreigners and normally served at supper time, the largest meal of the day for the mostly North American tourists and immigrants. Less well-off (often Belizean) customers order them only for special occasions.

This moral imperative is particularly powerful as regards staple meals that are strongly associated with the home. Belizeans expect them to be much cheaper than other dishes. This was forcefully illustrated to me one day when a Kriol informant from Placencia and I made a trip to the village of Hopkins, a Garifuna community also affected by tourism, a forty-five minute drive north of Placencia Peninsula. We stopped at a restaurant only to find that a standard plate of rice and beans with stewed chicken and potato salad was being sold for BZ$25. My informant was astounded – and incensed. He grilled the waitress who had come outside to greet us. She tried to defend the price by saying that the restaurant "wasn't for locals". My informant rejected this argument, stating that this was not fancy food, that this was local food and that it was supposed to be cheap. He informed her that nowhere in Placencia would anyone charge so much for a plate of rice and beans and stew chicken. (We did not eat at the restaurant, settling for Chinese fried chicken instead.)

Upon our return to Placencia, my informant recounted this event several times to other Placencia Kriol friends, stating that he could not believe that a restaurant would dare to charge such an outrageous price for local food. Sitting down at Ms Brenda's cool spot, he said to a Placencia fisherman, "Dat da fi we *local* food family . . . I could understand if ih mi piece of fillet or lobster or something, but ih fi we local food!"[4] A man listening in said, "Di easiest food fi cook" (the easiest food to cook). The fisherman said that he had eaten at the place in question, that it catered to fly fishermen and other tourists from a nearby resort. He noted that he had once been charged "tourist prices" when eating there with some fly-fishing clientele and that it was not until the owner of the restaurant (a friend of his) intervened that he got a local price. My informant repeated emphatically, "Our local food never cost that much!"

What does this exchange say about tourism and cooking? My informant associated local Belizean food with affordability and understood that tourist favourites could be pricier, but not a plate of cheap staples like rice, beans and chicken. Certain local Belizean dishes are protected by the moral imperative of home cooking: filling, tasty food that *must* be economical.

These ethical considerations bring with them important implications for culinary innovation and experimentation and the active development of a representative Belizean cuisine. Restaurant and cool-spot owners, who work with a thin profit margin and cater to working and middle-class Belizean consumers, are often fearful of taking risks with new and different dishes if what they serve now is paying the bills. This is often accompanied by a "why fix it if it isn't broken?" attitude – if the venue is making a profit, why waste time and money on culinary experimentation? When business owners obtain prized and rare ingredients through their social networks, they will be featured in a special, but "restaurant Kriol" dishes like rice and beans with chicken are sales tax–exempt staples that are available year-round in every grocery store. While not particularly exciting or innovative, they are popular, filling and dependable fodder for a Belizean-priced meal.

Foreign-operated establishments face the same challenge of how to make a profit, because the busiest part of the tourism season lasts only about five months of the year. Few appear to feel a public responsibility as regards pricing. There is only one foreign-owned establishment on the peninsula that has a BZ$10 lunch special. It is an American-owned bar catering to foreign immigrants and tourists. The lunch special is almost always Euro-American comfort food, also known as "home cooking" – meatloaf, chicken Parmesan sandwich, braised cabbage and beef. Other foreign-owned venues charge more for their lunches and leave the ten-dollar specials and moral obligations to the Belizean-owned restaurants. Fewer Belizeans can afford to dine at these locales, particularly the higher-end restaurants, except for special occasions. Slow-season customers tend to be First World immigrants or part-time residents and foreigners in town on business, people who have more disposable income and do not want to eat "restaurant Belizean" every time they dine out.

Most of the higher-end foreign-owned restaurants are influenced to some degree by international trends of modern high cuisine and professional culinary and hospitality training. With no dedicated culinary school and the relatively recent arrival of fine dining in Belize, many investors in the resorts and high-end restaurants catering to the tourism industry do not consider the country (and, by extension, Belizeans) a good source of such training and knowledge. Instead of training talented Belizean cooks, they seek their chefs abroad. A well-known restaurant consultant in the area could name only one Belizean on the peninsula with any formal culinary training, and that was a male pastry chef who had taken classes with the BTB. Otherwise, those working on the peninsula today with a serious foundation in "classic" (French-derived) professional cooking techniques, practices and recipes are all foreigners from First World countries. There are at any given time four to five foreign, almost always white and male, classically trained executive chefs on Placencia Peninsula (for Bolivia, see Sammells 2014). Some of them have worked all over Belize at resorts and higher-end foreign-owned restaurants or have moved from one resort to another on the peninsula. Short-term foreign consultant chefs are jetted in when a resort or restaurant decides extra assistance is needed.

Despite the lack of a culinary school, an increasing number of Belizeans have gained some hands-on training of a classical nature while working in resorts, hotels and tourist-oriented restaurants. Chef Rob Pronk, originally of the Netherlands and now based in Hopkins Village, has been encouraging culinary exploration in Belize since 1999, even starring in the country's first cooking show. Many Belizeans have worked with him and other classically trained foreign chefs, gaining valuable experience not otherwise available in-country. As a result there are now a couple of Belizeans in executive chef positions at foreign-owned, higher-end restaurants on the peninsula. One such venue is owned and managed by Culinary Institute of America graduates. It brought in a Cordon Bleu–trained foreign consultant chef for a brief time in 2013 to help upgrade the menu, and now has a Belizean Mestizo male executive chef who has worked in several resorts on the peninsula, where he picked up some "classic" techniques and knowledge. He has not had any formal training, either at a culinary institute or through apprenticeship, and has not worked in restaurants outside of Belize. Another high-end (by Placencia standards) spot promoted its Belizean sous-chef to the executive chef position when the foreign executive chef quit.

Professional cuisine on Placencia Peninsula is not just about how the chef was trained, as not all the chefs at the fancier restaurants have formal culinary education. The handful of relatively expensive restaurants on the peninsula aspire to a European and North American–centric cosmopolitan culinary identity. Their menus are inspired by food trends and practices developed in the kitchens of famous restaurants in North America and Europe and showcased worldwide on food television and the Internet. The result is an international culinary trickle-down effect from Michelin-starred destination restaurants and famous chefs to tourist destinations around the world. Those famous restaurants are run by chefs who have learned (whether formally or informally) and use the French system of professional cooking (Sammells 2017). The language used to describe dishes on restaurant web pages and menus hints at this professional training and international exposure. On Placencia-area menus, terms such as *braised, seared, blackened, au gratin, aïoli, vinaigrette, croquette, béchamel, sautéed* and *crusted* not only describe certain

Figure 7. Evening specials board at a Placencia restaurant owned by graduates of the Culinary Institute of America

cooking techniques but also demonstrate French professional culinary capital, drawing the eye of foreign immigrants, tourists and well-travelled Belizeans.

Some adjectives such as *seared*, *blackened*, *crusted* and *sautéed* are also found on the more foreign-oriented dinner menus of full-service Belizean-owned restaurants. Belizean homestyle dishes, which dominate the lunch menus and specials boards of these same restaurants, are described using plain English words such as *fried*, *stewed*, *steamed* and *baked*. Belizean Kriol cooking has its own repertoire of culinary terms as well. Some are unique to Belize, like *fry bake* (dry frying) and *tun* (turned, or half-ripened) plantain or coconut. Also, some terms do not mean the same thing that they do to chefs with French training. "Steamed fish", for example, is prepared in a way that a professional chef might call poaching. These preparation techniques and terms rarely appear on the menus of the peninsula's most expensive restaurants. The subtleties of Belizean cooking are thus unknown to most foreign immigrants and often ignored by the most expensive restaurants where professional cooking is practised.

While some foundation in the systems, techniques, key recipes and flavour combinations of international professional cuisine shape higher-end foreign-owned restaurants on Placencia Peninsula, a few enthusiastic Belizean restaurateurs are looking for ways to innovate in the face of increasing competition for customers. The foreign owner of one relatively expensive venue in Placencia expressed concern about growing competition from a Belizean-owned restaurant. The locale, not known for fine dining, started using the same square white plates that several foreign-owned higher-end establishments utilized. This Belizean restaurant also began to standardize its sauce making, increasing the efficiency and consistency of the dishes coming out of its kitchen. With the Internet and the Food Network readily available and new high-end restaurants opening down the street, it is becoming easier for everyone to learn something about professional cuisine.

A SECOND-CLASS CUISINE

Foreign-owned restaurants that do higher-end professional cooking tend to shy away from Belizean culinary terminology and techniques and anything that seems too much like Belizean food. This is the case even though the foreign chefs and owners of these establishments often know little about Belizean food beyond the most ubiquitous dishes. Rice and beans, a cheap and hearty one-pot staple found across the country, epitomizes the mundane and repetitive food that some newcomers believe is all that Belizeans eat. This ignorance is not surprising, given that new immigrants typically have not eaten in many Belizean homes and know little about the cultural and culinary diversity of the country; they are also unable to sample a wide variety of Belizean dishes at area rice-and-beans joints wedded to a restricted menu of "restaurant Kriol" lunch plates. Assuming that what those restaurants serve is all there is to Belizean food, some do not bother to investigate further, missing out on many delicious meals, unique ingredients and appealing flavour combinations. A now closed pricey Austrian restaurant advertised itself on the peninsula by saying "Tired of rice and beans? Try something different." In San Pedro, Ambergris Caye, Belize's premier tourist destination, such signs are relatively common. One foreign chef who has worked all over the world, including in Belize for more than five years, told me: "I don't want to stomp on anyone's toes with Kriol stuff... I want to do dishes that no one else is doing, foods that are available in Belize, locally available foods, but in other ethnic directions." In a later interview, while discussing a menu, he said:

> Truthfully I don't want to the menu to be ... over Krioly, over Caribbeany. ... I want another concept, something people aren't doing. There's no reason to open the twenty-third restaurant in the village if it's what everyone else is doing. So sooner or later people are going to come down; they're gonna want rice and beans, stew chicken, they are gonna want local food. But Americans, Europeans, [they're] always going to go back to a steak or, you know, a burger – the food that they are used to back home!

Here Mintz's (1996) concept of signature foods, dishes or ingredients that have powerful symbolic meaning to a population comes into play as my research participant juxtaposes the Belizean national dish with iconic dishes from North America.

I was given two main reasons for the chef wanting to avoid "Belizean food". The first was not to step on anyone's toes, because the Belizean-owned places could do rice and beans and Belizean dishes better. The second was to distinguish the restaurant from other places that did offer the typical Belizean restaurant menu, to have "something different". For both foreign- and Belizean-owned venues, "something different" usually means non-Belizean food, although there are a few exceptions. One popular higher-end foreign-owned restaurant does not serve rice and beans but does have coconut rice. It also serves a "seafood chowder" described as "our version of hudut", the well-known Garifuna dish of coconut milk–based broth with fried fish and pounded boiled green and ripe plantain. The restaurant introduced this dish after hosting a student from an Indiana University field school on food ethnography in the summer of 2011.[5]

The influence of the field school, which placed student interns in a range of restaurants and cool spots across the peninsula, is impossible to quantify, but it did raise questions and initiate dialogue about Belizean food, cultural representation and cuisine at participating venues. This particular restaurant's chowder distinguishes itself from Garifuna home cooking by including butter and a combination of every available fish and shellfish, some of which would be difficult for a home cook to obtain. The fish is boned fillets, a stark departure from traditional hudut, which is typically made with whole fish. These exceptions only prove the rule that in Belize, French professional cooking and fine dining are associated with foreign food and foreign-owned and/or foreign-operated restaurants.

The resorts that do serve Belizean Kriol and Garifuna food often segregate such offerings by opening an on-site "Belizean restaurant". Up the road from Placencia Village, rice and beans was banned from the menu at the flagship restaurant of a high-end resort, the reason given being that the dish clashed with the non-Belizean theme of the restaurant (though at that time there were other food items on the lunch menu, such as burritos, that were also outside the theme). This same resort has a separate high-priced "Belizean" restaurant headed by a Kriol female chef from Placencia. There one can find rice and beans, coconut curry shrimp and other dishes offered at resort rates. The chef serves many of the same dishes to a mainly Belizean clientele at her own restaurant in the village, for half the price.

The best example of reductionism in Belizean restaurant food is at resort-owned "Belizean" restaurants like Aunt Linda's,[6] a venue at another foreign-owned resort that advertises authentic Belizean food at "Belizean prices". Despite claims of authenticity, the menu also features American fast food such as burgers, hot dogs and fries alongside the daily Belizean special. The special of the day is the same as the staff lunch prepared to feed all the resort employees, except now the cooks prepare extra to sell to guests at the restaurant. The goal is cheap food to feed the staff plus extra income for the resort, not cuisine based on the foodways, history and cultures of the peninsula. This phenomenon of staff lunch becoming tourist lunch at resorts was also noted by Wilk (2006) in his book on globalization in Belize. Several other resorts serve rice and beans as a side dish in their buffet line-ups, but most stand-alone foreign-owned restaurants avoid this iconic staple dish.

Why do most restaurants that serve Belizean home cooking offer only a limited selection of common staple dishes, compared to the wide variety of meals actually prepared in Belizean homes? Even at Belizean Kriol–owned venues on the peninsula, popular home-cooked dishes that have a long history in Placencia, such as stew fish, fish hash and serre, make only an occasional appearance on the specials board, if they appear at all. There are several reasons for this reductionism and the most obvious is economic. Access to Placencia staples such as seafood and coconuts, which used to be readily available, has declined because of hurricanes, overfishing and high demand from restaurants, a result of the growing tourism industry. Their prices have increased dramatically. A big coconut – used for making the coconut milk essential to much Kriol and Garifuna cookery – may cost up to BZ$1.50, when prior to Hurricane Iris most people could simply harvest their own. The lack of a reliable supply of seafood and coconuts and their cost are one reason why dishes like serre and stew fish appear only sporadically as specials on the menus of Belizean-owned restaurants. Ironically, on Placencia Peninsula these dishes are associated with a cash-poor economy, with meals that can be put together using products gathered from the immediate environment. Today they are most commonly prepared at home, far from the gaze of hungry tourists.

The problem of ingredient cost and accessibility is not insurmountable. In wealthier areas like Placencia, the higher cost of ingredients could easily be offset by higher prices. However, the moral obligation of home cooking restricts this possible avenue for Belizean restaurateurs. Blackened boneless fillet of snapper, a touristy seafood entrée, can legitimately be sold for BZ$25 or even BZ$35. To retail a bowl of serre or stew fish – dishes that many Placencia natives call "fisherman food" and which have been prepared in Belizean homes for generations – for BZ$20 might be acceptable to tourists and First World immigrants, but that would lead to ridicule and rejection from Belizean consumers. This may not concern immigrant restaurant owners from other countries if they can survive on a foreigner/tourist customer base, but Belizean-owned restaurants feel the pressure of the moral code. They choose to serve these dishes as occasional lunch specials at a locally acceptable price of BZ$10 to BZ$12 or do not offer them at all.

WHY NOT INNOVATE?

Despite these constraints, I would argue that there is room for Belizean innovation and expansion of local menus without challenging the moral code. So why isn't that happening? Sourcing ingredients, while frustrating at times, is not an unsurmountable challenge. While coconuts may no longer be as plentiful on the peninsula, restaurant owners could find a reliable supply inland or grow their own. Local fruits, vegetables and some seafood may be in season only at certain periods of the year, but restaurants can capitalize on tourist interest in eating local by celebrating the seasons with Placencia delicacies such as stewed cashew or cocoplum. Venues with the space could freeze popular items like mangoes for later. The several reasons that restaurateurs do not offer a broader range of traditional foods or experiment with creating new Belizean dishes are examined in the following pages.

ECONOMIC CONCERNS

There is little room for error in small businesses where the owners do not have much capital to keep the venue afloat if profits should decline. There seems to be an understandable fear of risk-taking on a narrow profit margin when there is no guaranteed payoff. Entrepreneurs who are focused on the bottom line are reluctant to rock the boat if the standard menu seems to be working. For very small businesses, such as cool spots run out of someone's home, the success or failure of new menu items may determine whether the business survives at all. In this context, selling tried and true standards seems the smartest route to earning a sustainable income in the food industry.

Taking precious time and money to experiment with new dishes or acquire different ingredients requires at least some minimal surplus of capital, a strong desire to innovate, and a firm belief that food can be an avenue for creative and, most important, profitable expression. As Cancian (1979) argues in *The Innovator's Situation*, a classic text on innovation, poorer entrepreneurs with a tight bottom line are less likely to take that risk.

LACK OF CREATIVE INVENTION AND IMPLEMENTATION

Creative innovation can be hard to find in Belize, where the educational and social atmosphere tends to reward conformity, repetition and imitation.

Apart from economic reasons for risk avoidance, some entrepreneurs will not try something new if public failure is a possibility. Creative Belizean entrepreneurs often complain that once they come up with a good idea and prove its profitability, everyone copies it instead of developing their own innovative products. Few culinary training opportunities exist to encourage creative thinking in the kitchen. Even in the tourism industry until very recently there has been little government support of creative culinary endeavours, although this seems to have been slowly changing over the last several years.

Professionally trained foreign chefs who do make an effort to train the Belizeans working with them often have little to no knowledge of Belizean foodways, so they end up teaching with an emphasis on foreign techniques, flavour combinations and ingredients. This only reinforces the idea that elevated cuisine equals foreign food. Trainees emulating their teachers end up replicating dishes that may be, to use Sammells's (2017) typology, local/domestic with maybe even a touch of local/native, but that are rarely if ever local/evocative. Shining stars like chefs Jeannie Staines and Sean Kuylen do develop creative Belizean dishes, but they remain the exception.

DEVALUATION OF BELIZEAN DISHES AND INGREDIENTS

An important reason why traditional meals like serre or even innovative new Belizean dishes are not often found in restaurants is the belief that tourists and foreigners will not like them. Eating serre and stew fish, which are typically prepared using whole or steaked bone-in fish, is not a dainty business. Both are best eaten with one's fingers, with a plate on the side to put the bones on as they are picked out of the broth. Fish heads are sucked, cartilage is chewed and succulent pieces of flesh are pulled out by hand.

Belizean and foreign restaurant owners, operators and chefs all told me that tourists do not want to deal with bones in their meal, particularly in their fish. The conclusion drawn by the collective host gaze is that visitors want grilled or seared boneless fish fillets, not rich, heavy, coconut roux–based, bone-in seafood stews. My interviews with visitors seemed to support that conclusion, although a few well-travelled neophilic adventurers would have been happy to find a fish head in their soup. Any Belizean will tell you that bones give flavour. Despite a general reluctance to serve these soups on a regular basis, the owner of a well-known restaurant in Seine Bight offers hudut (the original Garifuna serre with mashed boiled plantain) every Saturday, unless she cannot find fish. The bulk of her clientele, however, are Belizean. Most recently a woman from Placencia opened a new cool spot serving hudut on some weekends. She is not marketing the dish to tourists, but locals are buying all she can make.

The tour guide who shared his tour-cooking experiences with me had some comments with regards to serre and stew fish:

> **Respondent:** A few places used to have it, before tourism really –
>
> **Researcher:** Right.
>
> **Respondent:** Well, it's just dey figure tourists no wan eat dat, but tourists come yah fi eat fi we food, man! [Well, it's just that they figure tourists don't want to eat that, but tourists come here to eat our food, man!]
>
> **Researcher:** So why do you think dat dis stuff no end up in a restaurant?
>
> **Respondent:** Because dey don't tink dat tourists are gonna eat it.

Serre and stew fish, conch soup, wilik (whelk) soup and stew lobster have a deep history in Placencia and symbolize the seafaring and fishing lifestyle of this Kriol community. More than any plate of rice and beans, these are the meals that my research participants labelled as being Placencia food. But despite the importance of these rich seafood stews based on coconut milk roux and ground foods, only conch soup is regularly found on restaurant menus. Why is this? Conch is cheaper than lobster, and it is boneless, unlike fish.

However, bones and the cost of ingredients cannot explain the absence of some home cooking. Fish hash is a delicious dish of boneless shredded fish cooked with garlic, onion and sweet pepper in coconut oil and served with hot pepper sauce. Fresh corned barracuda is rinsed and boiled after being salted overnight in the fridge, then served with coconut oil and pepper sauce drizzled over it. I only once encountered fish hash on a restaurant menu on the peninsula, the first time I had seen it in more than two years of research, and the restaurant folded soon after. Why are these dishes so hard to find when barracuda is cheap and still plentiful?

One thing these meals have in common is that they are strongly associated with a locally focused, cash-poor history, when you ate what you caught, combined with a few things that grew in the yard and some cheap ground foods. Dishes such as serre, conch soup, corned barracuda, fish hash and stew fish require no imported elements apart from a small spoonful of flour. They are the most "local" homemade foods on the peninsula, what many Placencians call "fisherman food" or "Belizean ital". Because they are associated with a lack of cash and because they are made from locally produced foodstuffs, "Belizean ital" dishes are very local, even individual, in their provenance, preparation and consumption. Some Belizeans seem to think they are not fancy enough to serve in commercial venues, especially ones that cater to tourists. Their value lies in the private sphere, where history, family, tradition and individual experimentation meet. When they do appear for sale, it is often at a cool spot or a restaurant in someone's yard, closer to the domestic setting.

These dishes are at the very heart of Kriol home cooking and historic foodways in Placencia. Mentioning their names leads to reminiscence and debate over the best way to make them. Yet while "fisherman food" is symbolically of great importance to Placencia people, it is devalued in the commercial arena in comparison with imported ingredients such as rice and beans and new imported dishes like spaghetti and pizza. Fisherman food has very low visibility and "collectivity" when compared to a rice-and-beans plate. The dishes are mostly hidden from the public view, so tourists and immigrants have trouble learning about them unless they get to know a Belizean and enter the friendship networks of that person's private sphere.

Most Belizean menus reflect a commercial, import-oriented cash economy. The Belizean dishes that are most commonly found on restaurant menus and specials boards are rice and beans, beans and rice plus chicken or some other type of meat side, coleslaw or potato salad and, if you are lucky, fried plantain. Rice and beans and stew chicken with potato salad, the unofficial national dish of Belize, was historically the Kriol Sunday dinner, a special meal requiring the slaughter of a chicken and the use of two once-imported staples, rice and red kidney beans (Wilk 2006). Rice and kidney beans were not grown in any quantity in Belize until the very end of the nineteenth century; for the most part they were imported and distributed to shops as part of the cash economy. In Placencia rice and beans have always been a cash commodity, something you traded for or bought along with flour and sugar. Into the mid-twentieth century Placencians regularly bartered salted dried fish for rice in Monkey River, Dangriga, Guatemala, Honduras or Belize City. Even today the distribution of some types of rice is limited. Belizean-grown brown rice is sometimes available in Cayo District, where rice is cultivated, but it is impossible to find in Placencia. Rice and beans were part of the Sunday dinner because they were special, something different, a treat after the weekday meals of locally available seafood, coconut and bread kind (starchy vegetables such as ground foods, plantain, green banana and breadfruit).

Today in Placencia and across much of Belize, Belizean Kriol dishes featuring these historically imported staples, and variations on what was once a special meal, the Sunday dinner, dominate restaurant menus. While no doubt there was once value and novelty in rice and beans, today even Belizeans get tired of it at times and want something different. But in Placencia, looking for something different when dining out is likely to result not in stew fish or fried barracuda swim bladder but rather American food: spaghetti with meatballs, a burger or some type of pizza, nachos or fajitas. In the restaurants of modern Placencia even a green salad is easier to find than a plate of fish hash. This absence of classic Placencia dishes is a direct result of the assumption, based on Belizean restaurateurs' host-gaze evaluation of our tourists, that visitors will find fisherman food unappealing.

The valuing of imported ingredients and dishes over local food has a long history in Belize (for a thorough analysis, see Wilk [1999, 2006, 2008]). As discussed in chapter 5, Wilk (2008) argues that in Belize, thanks to the lingering effects of an imposed British colonial value system, the more locally rooted food is, the lower its value. Applying linguistic terminology, he claims that foreign or "international" food represents the acrolect, or high-register/high-status choice; locally rooted food represents the basilect, or low-register/low-status option; and a range of blended, "creolized" mesolects create a continuum in between. According to this model, many Belizeans believe that the more foreign a dish is, the higher its value on the open market, while the extremely local fisherman food of Placencia is a low-status basilect, not worthy of commercialization. My research suggests that, despite the rising tide of gastronationalism, imported culinary imaginaries that highly value the exotic local, and many Belizeans' deep love of these dishes, those sentiments have not completely disappeared.

LACK OF KNOWLEDGE

Another reason for the low visibility of many classic Belizean dishes and ingredients in the public sphere is a general lack of knowledge among Belizean cooks of the foodways of other cultures and regions in the country. This restricts the palette of possible ingredients and flavour combinations that creative cooks might utilize to create new and innovative Belizean dishes. Apart from the ignorance of most foreign chefs working in Belize when it comes to the array of dishes and ingredients available, few Belizeans are aware of the full breadth, depth and diversity of ingredients, cooking techniques and dishes found in our culturally and geographically diverse country. Most Belizeans know their own culture and region best, and cross-culinary knowledge is often limited to a few signature dishes. There is a great need for a more profound domestic culinary cosmopolitanism.

Given the widespread ignorance of many foreign and Belizean cooks about the richness of our nation's foodways and the relegation of Belizean food to second-class status behind foreign professional cooking, it is not surprising at all that many foreign- and Belizean-owned restaurants' menus are not particularly creative. Is there any hope that a truly representative national cuisine will arise in Belize? Will we develop Belizean food that has categorical equality with other globally recognized cuisines? Or will Belizean food remain, as Wilk (2006, 187) has suggested, "second-class dining in its own country" – a one-trick pony of rice and beans, with at best the occasional bowl of conch soup or black dinna to liven things up?

NEW AND INSPIRED BELIZEAN CUISINE

The picture may look bleak, but the restaurant scene in Belize has been changing in the past few years. A well-known, long-time Placencia-area immigrant, originally from the United States, who works as a restaurant consultant opined that there are two important things needed to make a real chef. Those are a foundation in the "proper" (i.e., French professional) techniques and an inborn creativity and talent that no amount of training can produce. This reflects the objectives of haute cuisine, which are to push creative expression and turn cooking into an art form. As with painting and drawing, a strong foundation in basic skills and exposure to the work of other artists, combined with natural talent, can result in outstanding, innovative cuisine. To make a chef who can creatively represent and inspire Belizean cuisine, I would argue that these two points must be joined by domestic culinary cosmopolitanism – thorough, in-depth knowledge of the ingredients and flavour combinations of all the cultures and regions of the country. My informant argued that there are few chefs in Belize with that kind of talent and training. He pointed to only one Belizean who he felt made the cut as a truly talented, creative and properly trained chef: Sean Kuylen.

Chef Kuylen is part of a small but visible and growing movement in Belize to develop and market dishes reflecting what he calls "inspired Belizean cuisine". "New Belizean cuisine" is an earlier term for "inspired Belizean cuisine" that my informant claims was first coined in Placencia, by an American chef who worked at a now-defunct resort. This chef ate at Belizean-owned venues and talked with the consultant in an effort to learn about and elevate Belizean food, although Wilk (2006) feels that the results were generic and not really reflective of Belizean cooking. Now younger Belizeans such as Kuylen are getting involved, drawing on childhood memories of home cooking, using their personal *hexis* and culinary capital to create a deeper professional interpretation of Belizean food. His approach draws explicitly on his home-cooking roots. Kuylen stated in an interview with the BTB (2012), "No matter where I work, I still call and email [my mom] for tips, suggestions and cooking techniques that have been in our family for generations. Then I try to put my spin on them."

By transforming well-known dishes and combining familiar flavours with professional techniques and presentation, new/inspired Belizean cuisine offers visitors a safely domesticated culinary other and simultaneously appeals to Belize's educated and patriotic middle and upper class, as well as Belizean Americans visiting home. Kuylen connects local home cooking with cosmopolitan professional technique, an approach that Sammells (2014, 2017) calls "local-politan" or "haute-traditional". According to Sammells (2014, 143), "Haute-traditional cuisines . . . explicitly move between the two extremes of [an] idealized division – local/native/ancestral/feminine vs. cosmopolitan/transnational/ innovative/masculine – in order to claim legitimacy both as heritage cuisines and as global elite commodities."

Hungry sophisticated tourists, well-off and well-travelled Belizeans, and growing numbers of foodie immigrants from wealthy countries help make it feasible for higher-end restaurants experimenting with Belizean food to make a name for themselves. New/inspired Belizean cuisine explores and elevates the rich diversity of Belizean home cooking by creatively combining cultural cuisines with one another and with French-derived professional cooking. The farm-to-table new American cuisine of Alice Waters also influences this rapidly emerging food trend, as locally produced ingredients form the patriotic backbone of new/inspired Belizean cuisine. These innovations reflect processes of creolization, the blending of the old to create something new. In this way some new/innovative Belizean cuisine dishes parallel Medina's synthetic model of nationalism discussed in chapter 5. Kuylen says, "Imagine taking the cacao of Punta Gorda and making a Central American inspired chocolate mole and cooking it with Placencia-harvested shrimp served over Orange Walk Mestizo–inspired corn dukunu. How about pairing Garifuna sere, a rich traditional coconut seafood broth, with Toledo's East Indian curry spices, creating a curried coconut seafood explosion with hints of yard-grown wild basil and habanero?" (BTB 2012; see also the afterword to this book).

Other new Belizean cuisine dishes are more in line with pluralistic nationalism. Kuylen uses French professional techniques to elevate recipes like dukunu, pibil and boil-up – each associated with a particular cultural group – and create a culturally diverse table. His "Boil-Up Bite" is an *amuse bouche* interpretation of the well-known Kriol dish (a midday meal of boiled fish, pigtail and ground foods served with a tomato sauce) and a perfect example of a haute-traditional dish. The Boil-Up Bite contains all the culinary heritage, ingredients and flavour combinations of a hearty plate of boil-up, but with tiny pieces of deboned pigtail and fish in an elegant French-inspired bite-sized cabbage-leaf packet, served on a white plate with an artfully drizzled tomato-based sauce.

For several years the Fuego restaurant, located in San Ignacio Town, Cayo District, had a similar approach. There rice and beans and coconut rice joined smashed potatoes, garden salad and baked plantains as sides, while dishes such as pigtail pie and the dukunu platter rubbed shoulders with braised short ribs and triple-pepper nachos. The bartenders used fresh fruits, coconut water and local rums to create drinks that reminded Belizean diners of childhood treats like craboo with sweetened condensed milk. Unfortunately, the owner tried to open multiple restaurants before Fuego was well established, the head chef left and the quality of its offerings dropped. The restaurant closed in 2016, a sad end for a promising venue.

The newer chefs trying to elevate Belizean dishes and flavour combinations are young Kriol or Mestizo males like Sean Kuylen and Ian Lizarraga (once head chef at Fuego), but female chefs are also creatively engaging with the idea of Belizean cuisine. Chef Jeannie Staines of Elvi's restaurant in San Pedro is a veteran of the industry; despite having no formal culinary training, she is famous for her creative interpretations of Belizean food. Another female chef, Marcia Nuñez, from a resort in Hopkins Village, won the BTB's national culinary competition Taste of Belize in 2012.

New/inspired Belizean cuisine is not the rootless international tropical food found in all-inclusive resorts from Hawaii to Bali, from Mexico to Brazil. It is not a matter of simply mixing French culinary technique with tropical ingredients (Spang 2011). New/inspired Belizean cuisine at its best goes far beyond what Wilk (2006, 184) describes as "generic 'tropical' tourist cuisine" by rooting itself in the home cooking and culinary heritage of a specific place and its peoples. Ideally in this new arena of elevated cuisine, all cultural groups are given a chance to contribute. The foodways of Belize's three Maya groups, especially the Kekchi and Mopan Maya, tend to be greatly underrepresented in restaurants, which focus more on Garifuna, Kriol and Mestizo contributions. Staines's restaurant in San Pedro, Ambergris Caye, which offers elevated Yucatec Maya dishes and seafood, is a notable exception. A truly representative Belizean cuisine would require Kriol home cooking to join the rank and file of all Belizean foodways, losing its privileged role as culinary gatekeeper and making room for all Belizean cultural cuisines great and small. Now, that's inspired!

THE ROLE OF GOVERNMENT

This process of creative experimentation with the culinary riches of the country is not limited to Belize. A number of scholars have examined the emergence of national cuisines in the post-/neo-colonial context since Appadurai's (1988) seminal piece on the topic. Anthropologist Jane Fajans (2012) has chronicled similar processes of national cuisine development in Brazil, where chef Alex Atala is one of a new wave of foreign-trained Brazilian professionals engaged in creating a fine cuisine rooted in the country's culinary heritage. Cusack's (2004) exploration of national cuisine and tourism in Equatorial Guinea illustrates the sometimes clumsy role of the state in cobbling together a national culinary tradition. Clare Sammells's (2014, 2017) explorations of "haute-traditional" and "local-politan" cuisine in Bolivia and Peru are powerful contributions to the discourse about postcolonial culinary developments in the Americas. In Belize, thirty-eight years after independence, new/inspired Belizean cuisine is a response to the increasing number of foreign-owned resorts and high-end restaurants while simultaneously imported frozen pizzas, mac 'n' cheese and marshmallow-encrusted cereals have begun to appear in grocery stores and homes across the country.

The Government of Belize has taken a role in providing some limited opportunities for professional training of Belizean chefs. These include Culinary Institute of America programmes in Belizean technical high schools funded by the BTB and the Organization of American States ("Belizean Chefs Improving Their Skills", *Guardian* [Belize], 6 October 2011). The state plays a part in cuisine development through the BTB, a branch of the Ministry of Tourism, which organizes not only culinary training but also public events promoting experimentation and elevation of Belizean dishes, flavours and ingredients. Kuylen, Staines, Nuñez and Lizarraga have all participated in BTB-funded culinary events, including the annual Taste of Belize, a festival of chef and bartending competitions, with most participants coming from resorts and restaurants in Belize's tourism zones, including Placencia Peninsula. The BTB uses Taste of Belize, along with one-off events such as Chef Staines's cooking demonstration with *Saveur* magazine, to promote cuisine as part of the Belizean tourism package.

While cuisine is still not a major segment in government marketing of Belize as a tourism destination, it is gaining more advertising space every year. *Destination Belize*, the BTB's glossy tourism magazine, has for the past four years included short articles on the diversity of Belizean food, as well as listing things to eat in each district. Meanwhile the private-sector glossy *Flavours of Belize* promotes food from restaurants and resorts in the tourism industry. Notably, the BTB chose for its 2017 annual industry conference the theme "Culinary Tourism: An Emerging Trend". This exciting decision will hopefully pave the way for increased government support of culinary training and creative culinary expression in Belize.

SO, IS THERE A BELIZEAN CUISINE?

In Belize imported foodways have served as a default "haute cuisine" for centuries. British and European continental foodways represented the fine dining of the elite classes in colonial Belize. Local ingredients and flavours were disdained while imported canned, salted and otherwise preserved products from the mother country were lovingly reconstructed into a proper high tea or Sunday dinner (Wilk 2006). Imported foods and foreign foodways were valued over local ingredients and cooking well into the twentieth century, and to some extent those self-defeating attitudes persist to this day. Upwardly mobile Belizeans strove to imitate the tin-opening culture of the early British elites. It was not until substantial emigration occurred that Belizeans began to see more of the world, to open nostalgic "Belizean restaurants" in places such as Los Angeles, New York and Chicago, and to value their own home-cooked dishes that used Belizean ingredients (Wilk 1999, 2006).

Despite this shift in attitudes, Belizean cooking has still been relegated to the sidelines when it comes to fine dining. And imported processed, canned and frozen foods, from ramen and hot dogs to frozen pizza and french fries, have become common in the daily diet of many Belizeans, competing with long-time staples such as root crops, rice, beans, corn and homemade wheat bread. In the post-/neo-colonial tourism zones and cities of Belize, where wealth is concentrated and people are willing to spend money on eating out, the closest thing to haute cuisine has until very recently been limited to imported foreign foods and foodways, including (in Belize City) higher-priced Indian and Chinese restaurants. Squeezed on both sides, when will Belizean food, in all its multicultural glory, be able to spread its wings?

Food historian Michael Freeman (1977, 145) states that "a cuisine is the product of attitudes which give first place to the real pleasure of consuming food rather than to its purely ritualistic significance" (see also Mintz 1989). In order for a cuisine to arise, food has to be a priority in the society and a source of acknowledged pleasure and interest. Mintz (1989, 187) argues that a real cuisine cannot arise in a homogeneous society, a claim which offers much hope for the culinary future of diverse nations like Belize: "the appearance of a cuisine as opposed to 'cooking' seems to hinge in part upon cultural heterogeneity, which the emerging cuisine capitalizes upon, then surmounts".

To develop a national cuisine, there must be a body of "adventuresome eaters" who are interested in trying foods from other cultures and regions in their country. This group must be sufficiently educated and financially secure to have time for food-related travel and leisure activities. Accumulation of cultural capital may drive these neophiliac culinary interests as a way for this group to express their education and upwardly mobile class status (Wilk 1997, 1999). Undergirding these social factors, Freeman (1977) argues, must be an abundance and diversity of foodstuffs, potential ingredients and flavour combinations with which to work. And finally, Wilk (1999) argues that without an awareness of difference between "my food" and "yours", there will be little appreciation for or development of cultural or national food categories and cuisines.

In sum, for a national cuisine to arise there must be

- a belief that cuisine is important;
- a culturally heterogeneous society with a sense of nationalism and national pride;
- a social attitude which prioritizes the pleasure of food consumption;
- awareness and appreciation of the diversity of foods already available within the country/culture;
- a diversity and abundance of potential ingredients; and
- a sufficiently large body of adventurous eaters who have the time and means to explore food.

Today Belize is close to fulfilling these requirements. The processes of immigration, emigration and tourism discussed in previous chapters have encouraged a growing awareness among Belizeans (especially those living in tourism zones) not only of the diversity of foods within our own country but also of the differences between foods found at home and abroad. This awareness has turned into national and cultural pride as increasing exposure to other groups, countries and ways of life leads nostalgic Belizeans to value their home cooking (Wilk 1999).

Helping with this development of gastronationalism has been the tremendous growth of the tourism industry over the past twenty years. Tourists are enjoying local dishes, flavour combinations and ingredients on their vacations to Belize. Belizeans who have not travelled abroad are beginning to realize that what they eat *has* value in the international market and with visitors, even those from wealthy parts of the world. Bit by bit, the colonial hangover is being shed as Belizeans decide that their food is just as good as any European or North American cuisine. Culinary pride is high in tourism areas such as Hopkins and Placencia. There the food of the dominant cultural groups is being marketed,[7] but it still has to fight against the assumptions that guests will not be interested in the more esoteric local dishes and that Belizean food is limited to home cooking. Wilk's requirement of consciousness of difference has been fulfilled, however, and the value of at least some Belizean food has been established in the minds of Belizeans and visitors alike.

The agricultural sector in Belize has grown and diversified tremendously since the 1990s. Mennonite communities, Taiwanese farmers and North American immigrants building their dream farms are experimenting with new crops and growing techniques. Agricultural exchange projects, new cooperatives and non-governmental organizations are facilitating farm diversification across the country and with different farming groups. Restaurants and resorts are constantly seeking a more diverse array and consistent supply of fresh greens, vegetables, fruits, meats and dairy products, and some farmers and distributors are responding.[8] This movement parallels the growth of some relatively new agricultural export crops, such as cacao beans in southern Belize and the ongoing monocropping of citrus, bananas and shrimp in the Stann Creek District near Placencia and of sugar cane in the north and west.

Locally produced vanilla, black pepper, coffee, gourmet chocolate and high-quality cheeses can be found within a two-hour drive of Placencia Peninsula. Marie Sharp's hot sauce, jams and jellies continue to be Belize's most famous processed food export, and the factory is only ninety minutes away. New chocolate, hot sauce and spice companies, cheesemakers and even wineries are popping up around the country. Dried fruits, local fruit wines, chocolate, coffee, rum cake and other food souvenirs can now be found in gift shops across the nation in response to tourist expectations. Even treats such as *Gracillaria* species of seaweed, traditionally used in making seaweed porridge and punch, are now more consistently obtainable, thanks to the Placencia Fishing Cooperative's seaweed-farming project. Can the cultivation of other foods be far behind?

The food-import retail sector, once the fount of British colonial food culture, has also greatly expanded. A diversity of frozen, packaged and processed food products, many imported from China and the United States, are now available in Placencia Village grocery stores. While appreciation and development of elevated Belizean cuisine is growing along with its customer base, so is the presence of processed imported foods. An advertisement for a Kraft culinary demonstration by Sean Kuylen at a Dangriga supermarket seems to contradict the whole "eat local" mission of new/inspired Belizean cuisine, but in a small country like Belize a consultant chef cannot afford to be too picky, and he may be able to use such a demonstration to Belizeanize these imported processed foodstuffs.

The expanding array of processed foods in Belizean grocery stores, homes and restaurant lunch specials (where mac 'n' cheese sometimes appears as a side with stewed chicken) parallels and even outpaces the slow, uneven growth of restaurants that offer high-end, innovative Belizean dishes. This diversification of the Belizean foodscape reflects the growing class divisions between rich and poor, a demand for quick-to-prepare foods as more women work outside the home, and the desires of First World immigrants and tourists. Despite the influx of these convenience foods, and even within its current limitations – a lack of refrigerated trucks for produce transport, the extreme seasonality of popular items like avocados and mangoes, the limited stock of some wild meats and plants – Belize today realizes Freeman's requirement of having an abundance of diverse foodstuffs available for culinary experimentation. As a culturally diverse nation, we also fulfil the demand for heterogeneity.

Belize possesses a growing number of people with the time and means to explore and experiment with the foods of their country. The BTB, along with a handful of Belizean and non-Belizean chefs, finally believes in the importance of Belizean cuisine. This brings us to the final and perhaps most important question: Is there the interest? Is there a social attitude which prioritizes the pleasure of food consumption? After speaking with hundreds of people, it is clear to me that Belizeans have a deep love for their food. We are happy to speak about the topic at length, have strong opinions about how certain dishes should be prepared, and make many and subtle distinctions among different methods of food preparation, flavour combinations, and good and bad renditions of a particular dish. The subtleties of and arguments over what makes a good plate of rice and beans would astound most visitors, and food appreciation goes far beyond the staples.

Food brings great pleasure to many Belizeans, and exposure to food shows via American cable television (available almost countrywide) only reinforces local interest. Most Belizeans today, especially in tourism zones like Placencia Peninsula, have a strong appreciation for local dishes, ingredients and preparation techniques. They will wax nostalgic over the flavours of fire-hearth cooking (even organizing fire-hearth cooking competitions) or the delicious sweets of their childhood, while many, especially younger Belizean cooks, are also excited to experiment with new dishes and ingredients that they have seen on television or read about on the Internet. New cooking shows featuring Chef Kuylen bring Belizean flavour to local television networks, helping to reinforce the legitimacy of Belizean cuisine by placing it side by side with foreign channels such as the Food Network, which is watched by many Belizean food lovers.

With all the basic requirements fulfilled or in process, and with the gradual emergence of well-trained Belizean chefs and new/inspired Belizean cuisine, a national cuisine in Belize is in its exciting first stage of development. With time and more professional training of creative Belizean chefs, haute cuisine in Belize may become more indigenously rooted instead of imported and Belizean fine dining will become a reality. For new/inspired Belizean cuisine to thrive, Belizean chefs not only have to learn and apply some form of professional culinary training, they also have to expand their horizons at home by learning about the wide variety of ingredients, dishes and flavour combinations found across the country and within its different cultural groups. Chefs in tourism zones are culinary ambassadors to the world and have great power to shape a country's culinary imaginaries, both at home and abroad. Without in-depth knowledge of the foodways of each region and cultural group, they will not be able to do justice to Belize's diversity and new/inspired Belizean cuisine will run the risk of becoming cultural tokenism. Belizean individuals from certain regions or cultural backgrounds may feel left out, and chefs will lose the unique opportunity to use their host gaze to educate, expand and direct tourist and local appreciation of innovative Belizean cuisine.

8
THE QUEST FOR CUISINE

EUROPEAN COLONIZERS INVADED OR OUTRIGHT INVENTED ROUGHLY A hundred colonies and territories that are now independent nations.[1] How many of these have a well-developed and internationally recognized national cuisine? Of the fifty-four countries on the African continent, Ethiopian and Moroccan food seem to be the most well known outside of Africa. However, Ethiopia was never colonized (despite attempts by Italy) and Morocco is a special case. Having been long established as an independent state since AD 700, the latter was controlled by the French and Spanish for a mere forty-four years. There was plenty of time over the centuries – helped along by elite nobles with demanding palates – to allow national foodways to evolve into a recognizable and coherent cuisine that European rule could not destroy in such a short span of time.

In the Americas, Peru and Brazil are beginning to develop some international culinary standing, in part through recognition of their heritage cuisines by UNESCO, but their presence is still slight compared to Chinese, Japanese and Thai food, which all developed in countries that were never colonized by European powers (Sammells 2014). India and Vietnam, which have also gained international attention for their cuisines (globally in the case of Indian food), have had millennia of wealthy elites and royal chefs to drive culinary creativity. These greatly elaborated and long-established foodways easily survived a relatively short period of European colonialism. Much less often do we hear about the food of countries that were created by European colonial rule and suffered centuries of domination, such as Guyana, Chile, Guinea and Belize.

Most world-famous cuisines come from countries that either were not colonized or endured a relatively short period of European domination.

Mexico is the exception that proves the rule. Of the scores of countries created by European powers, Mexico has a truly world-famous national cuisine. Its large size, the great diversity of its cultural and regional cuisines, the survival of millions of indigenous Mexicans despite the genocidal acts of the Spanish, and early attempts to seek autonomy from its colonizer may all have contributed to the development of a national Mexican cuisine as part of independence movements to assert a national identity and distinguish the country from Spain (Pilcher 1996). Today Mexican, Italian and Indian cuisines have "gone viral" and are found in tourism destinations across the planet, often in forms that their originators might barely recognize (Sammells 2014).

Most countries with a long history of European colonialism have less culinary visibility internationally. Many have impressive diasporas, spanning continents, that could introduce their food to the societies of their destination countries, yet their impact tends to be quite localized. Rarely in North America does one overhear a person ordering some Gambian food, making a reservation at their favourite Guatemalan restaurant or picking up Chilean takeout. How do culture and nation intersect and cuisines form in an ethnically diverse post-colonial country? Do most post-colonial nations simply not possess well-elaborated cuisines? Or have they just not received the necessary attention, discussion and distribution to bring them onto the world stage? Like the proverbial tree falling in the forest, can a cuisine exist without recognition?

According to Wilk, it cannot. Without awareness of difference and cross-cultural comparison, the boundaries necessary for the formation of culinary categories cannot be formed. Food is simply food and a bounded cuisine cannot exist in a vacuum. Belize was controlled for centuries by a British colonial elite who actively discouraged farming, rejected indigenous dishes and were hell-bent on maintaining British traditions and foodways in the new land. Many visitors today are looking for "local food" with little idea of what that might mean in Belize. The increased focus on food in tourist-origin countries means increased focus on food in tourism destinations across Belize, as host populations begin to realize that some visitors want and are willing to pay for more than "restaurant Kriol" rice and beans. Tourism plays a key role in increasing recognition of culinary possibilities through international cross-cultural exposure that encourages culinary awareness and marketing at both the cultural and national levels. Internal comparisons between cultures create the concepts of Maya, Garifuna, Kriol, Spanish (Mestizo) and East Indian food. This gives knowledgeable restaurateurs plenty of room to experiment and to use their culinary cosmopolitanism and code-switching talents to market as Belizean food a wide range of ingredients and dishes from across the country. Yet because of the historical dominance of "restaurant Kriol" cooking, superficial domestic cosmopolitanism, the valuing of foreign foods over local dishes, economic factors and the fear of failure if tourists do not like the food, the variety and richness of ingredients and dishes have been neglected.

Further complicating culinary evolution, different models of national identity shape the face of Belizean gastronationalism, directing the culinary interactions between our many cultures and the nation. How do cultural identities relate to national identity in a heterogeneous, highly globalized, transnational,[2] post-colonial society like Belize? How does their interaction affect the creation of a national cuisine? National and cultural cuisines are influenced by external factors like tourism and Belizean expectations and desires as well as by internal cultural politics. In Belize the latter reflect a long history of dominance by the Kriol cultural group and, more recently, of historically marginalized groups like the Garifuna and Maya building consciousness; organizing themselves through cultural councils; fighting for recognition, legal rights and resources; and entering the tourism industry both collectively and individually. As we have discovered, in Belize some cultural groups and their food are considered more Belizean than others. Complex processes determine what dishes and which cultural groups are first choices to represent the nation as "Belizean food".

Hegemonic nationalism insidiously undermines the harmony espoused by the national policy of pluralistic nationalism and prevents delicious Maya, Garifuna, East Indian and Mestizo dishes from fully participating in the national culinary category. Hopefully this will change as Belizeans with disposable income and access to the Food Network seek out creative food that tastes like *all* of Belize, supporting the success of chefs such as Jennie Staines and Sean Kuylen and the concept of inspired/new Belizean cuisine. If developed in an inclusive way, new/inspired Belizean cuisine has the potential to address the problems of hegemonic nationalism and reduce unequal representation of Belize's various cultural groups at the national level.

The pressure of a growing tourism industry and the food-obsessed tourist gaze adds a powerful angle to the forces shaping the development of cuisines in Belize today. We asked at the beginning of this inquiry whether tourism pushes Belize towards one simple homogenized cuisine or a diversity of culinary categories. Aside from "restaurant Kriol", visitor attention for the most part seems focused on examples of "traditional" dishes from different Belizean cultural groups or more pricey tropical resort fare from (typically foreign-owned) restaurants. Few guidebooks direct tourists to a unified Belizean cuisine except to describe rice and beans as a national dish. This focus on rice and beans, the backbone of restaurant Kriol food, tends to gloss over the Belizeanness of many other meals, which are often listed by cultural instead of national affiliation.

The tourist gaze plays an important role in making visible the diversity of Belizean food by encouraging cultural food marketing as part of nascent cultural tourism activities in the country. Visitors are generally unaware of what might comprise each culinary category, which puts the onus on Belizeans to decide which aspects of their culture's foodways would appeal to them. Foreign interest in the diversity of Belize has contributed to the growing cultural awareness, pride and organization of Belizeans since the early 1990s. Instead of pushing to be better represented in the Kriol-dominated national culinary category, less powerful Belizean ethnic groups are capitalizing on the idea of the "exotic other" and engaging with culinary tourism through the marketing of cultural cuisines. Cultural food marketing in Belize centres on "tradition" and home cooking; it does not tend to promote a level of elaboration, innovation and experimentation that might substantially alter classic dishes, techniques and flavour combinations.

Cultural tourism is a logical step for Maya and Garifuna groups already involved in cultural preservation activities, with "cultural food" as an important component. Visitors to the Garifuna community of Hopkins Village find signs advertising "cultural dishes" at many locally owned restaurants. Some Maya women's groups and tourism entrepreneurs are beginning to offer dishes reflecting Maya culinary heritage as part of cultural tourism in Toledo District. A good example of Maya food marketing as part of a tourism experience is the Ixcacao Chocolate Company, a Kekchi Maya–owned chocolatier in Toledo District, where guests are shown how to make their own chocolate, using heirloom stone tools. For lunch, visitors are served food from the family farm and surrounding jungle. Depending on the day, they might encounter two types of wild palm heart, jippy jappa and cohune, as well as callaloo or chaya greens, culantro-rich dishes of local pumpkin or okra, chicken or pig from the yard and handmade corn tortillas. Making corn tortillas and learning about Maya food has been a part of overnight family stays in the district since the 1980s, but now day-trippers can also get a taste of Maya culture in the form of palm hearts and even chu'u kwa, a sweet corn wafer hand-stamped with a seed pod to make a lacy design.

Even the dominant Kriol communities are beginning to engage in cultural marketing. In Placencia, more and more dishes and menu descriptions use the word *creole* to advertise local Kriol food as something special. Omar's Creole Grub sells guava jelly and food by the plateful on the strength of its pan-creole cultural marketing.

But does the development of cuisine have to be a blind response to tourist demands? Tourists are not the only ones who affect culinary developments in Belize. Immigration, from both tourist-origin countries (mainly North America) and surrounding Central American nations, has changed the demographics of Belize, complicated questions of national identity and belonging, and altered the foodscape of the country. Emigration from Belize to the United States, Canada, Europe and other regions has transformed Belizean society into a transnational one. Returned Belizeans, shaped by their experiences abroad, often bring with them a different vision of their country, new skills and useful cross-cultural knowledge. The Belizean chefs and restaurateurs at the forefront of the nascent culinary movement have lived for at least a few months outside their country, gaining perspective and appreciation for home. Belizeans in the tourism and restaurant industries have the power and, I would argue, the responsibility to use their host gaze to educate visitors about the diversity of Belizean cuisine instead of merely reflecting back what they believe tourists want.

Both Freeman and Appadurai posit that a true national cuisine should draw from the foodways and dishes of different cultural groups and regions. For this reason, Appadurai (1988, 13) claims that Mughlai food, "a royal cuisine that emerged from the interaction of the Turko-Afghan culinary traditions of the Mughal rulers with the peasant foods of the North Indian plains", is not truly national cuisine, even though it is called "Indian food" in restaurants across India and the world. In Belize, what I call "restaurant Kriol" occupies a similar position to that of Mughlai food in Appadurai's India. National cuisines may emerge from royal courts inspired by culinary traditions gathered from across the country, as in the cases of China and France, but the food of the elite that spreads across a nation reflects an unequal division of power among different regions and cultural groups and ignores many locally rooted culinary practices. This is certainly the case in some post-colonial culinary contexts, as Cusack (2004) documents for Equatorial Guinea, where imported Spanish food still reflects the status and power of that European colonizer. By examining the way that food reflects the internal inequalities and hierarchies of a country, this book answers important questions about the power dynamics that shape cuisine formation. Widespread adherence to the discriminatory model of hegemonic nationalism plays a key role in structuring selection and categorization processes for Belizean food.

Gastronationalism is not a simple concept once we begin to ask whose food, and why? In a heterogeneous post-colonial society, not everyone gets the same level of representation on the national culinary stage. The model of hegemonic nationalism that informs many Belizeans' beliefs about Belizean identity has limited tourist exposure to the full array of foodways and dishes found in the different regions and cultures of Belize. The "national" food category in Belize reflects Kriol socio-economic and cultural dominance as inheritors of British colonial power. Given the Kriol domination of politics, the national anthem and national creation stories, it is not surprising that Kriol people should also be on top in Belizean food hierarchies (for more on the anthem and creation stories, see Shoman 2010). The end result of hegemonic nationalism, combined with visitor curiosity about "exotic" cultures they may have never heard of before (such as the Garifuna people) and international marketing of the "Maya mystique", is that many non-Kriol dishes are not admitted to the "Belizean food" category. The foodways of historically marginalized groups are more likely to be relegated to "cultural" culinary categories before they are considered part of a national Belizean cuisine. Until this changes, "Belizean food" remains an impoverished and pale reflection of the rainbow of flavours making up our nation.

In this book I use Moufakkir and Reisinger's (2013) concept of the host gaze as a challenge to the homogenizing tourist gaze introduced by Urry

(2002) in his seminal publication. The host gaze allows individuals from the host country to exercise agency in the context of a fluid and heterogeneous international tourism zone. Directed at tourists, it allows hosts to categorize, evaluate and interact with visitors on the basis of cross-cultural knowledge. Frontline personnel present themselves, via self-commodification and code-switching, in ways that challenge and correct some visitor perceptions and stereotypes while creatively elaborating on others. This active host gaze leaves room for creative culinary expression that does not always cater to tourist expectations and desires.

Belizean cooks, restaurant owners and even tour guides have a great opportunity and responsibility to help the world learn about the breadth and depth of our foodways. Belizeans who engage in cultural and national food marketing can use their powerful host gaze to educate visitors and locals about the diversity of ingredients and dishes to be found in our country. The effectiveness of cultural marketing in Belize will increase if more entrepreneurs take risks and offer a wider array of ingredients and dishes to visitors. The same applies to the national culinary category. Visitors look to frontline personnel to tell them about Belizean food. Belizean chefs can use their host gaze and culinary experimentation with Belizean dishes, cooking techniques and flavour combinations to direct visitors towards a new innovative, pluralistic Belizean cuisine that embraces all our cultures.[3]

Thus a national cuisine emerges in dialogue with – and in spite of – the tourist gaze and prevalent touristic culinary imaginaries (Salazar 2010; Salazar and Graburn 2014). Frontline personnel and chefs working in the tourism industry have great power to mould visitor perceptions of Belizean cuisine, and those perceptions and experiences feed back into Belizean society, shaping our evaluation of our own food. Our job as industry professionals is to encourage creative expression of Belizean identity and introduce our guests to delicious dishes and flavour combinations that they did not even know to ask for.

The uneasy codependent relationship between home cooking and professional cooking is another piece of this culinary puzzle. Is a national cuisine built on the back of home cooking or does it require the intercession of professional chefs? After all, it was chefs working for powerful elite families who elevated French, Indian and Chinese cookery to the heights of culinary artistry and international fame. It appears that both are necessary in today's cosmopolitan global marketplace. To gain international legitimacy a cuisine "must be simultaneously grounded in local food ways and appeal to global communities of elite diners" (Sammells 2014, 144). My conclusions support Sammells's (2017, 2014) observations in Bolivia and Peru that the "haute-traditional" national cuisines being created today combine local home-cooking traditions with a cosmopolitan international, French-derived professional cooking framework.

The flexible way in which home cooking has entered commercial and semi-commercial spaces while remaining symbolic to Belizeans of home, family and community challenges the simplistic binary of public and private spheres and the idea of purely commercial transactions. The sale of home-cooked food, even in a sit-down restaurant context, does not necessarily render it a neutral commodity in a commercial market. In a small, sparsely populated country like Belize, the purchase of home-cooked food provides a personal connection between the cook and the customer. This is exemplified in the moral imperative, discussed in chapter 7, which leads many Belizean restaurateurs to offer some dishes at Belizean-friendly prices even in tourism zones that cater to wealthier visitors. However, these delicious, filling yet economical meals do not reach the heights of haute cuisine.

To develop an elevated and elaborated culinary genre, home and professionalized cooking play off one another, with wealthy diners (tourists, immigrants and Belizeans) driving culinary innovation in the public sphere and revealing contradictions about commercialization, cultural appropriation and promotion in the tourism industry. There is a growing demand by educated white-collar Belizeans for creative gourmet interpretations of Belizean home cooking which also appeal to sophisticated tourists. The flavour combinations, ingredients and classic dishes of home cooking inspire professional culinary experimentation in the form of inspired/new Belizean cuisine that may spell the way forward.

Most Belizean chefs gained some or all of their culinary training and experience in the restaurants and resorts of Belize's international tourism sector. According to one informant, even the idea of new Belizean cuisine was initially devised by an American restaurant manager at a resort on Placencia Peninsula. It is clear that the tourism industry provides spaces and opportunities for Belizeans to hone their skills and increase their culinary capital. The initial impetus for an elevated dining experience came from the tourism industry, the context in which Belize's first fine-dining restaurants were created (Sluder 2010).

Tourism plays a key role in the creation of these restaurants (see Sammells 2017), but inspired/new Belizean cuisine restaurants are not just for tourists. A coterie of educated, well-travelled white-collar Belizeans are excited to see their home flavours receiving professional treatment. Without the training, financial resources and demand generated by the international tourism industry, local chefs would likely be further behind in the development of innovative Belizean cuisine. More comparative work between countries with different colonial histories is needed to establish how common this is in other emergent post-colonial nations. It will be especially important to investigate other countries where there is little industrialization and tourism is the main economic sector responsible for the professionalization and expansion of the restaurant industry.

THE REST OF THE WORLD

What does this case study of cultural and national culinary development in Belize say about the rest of the world? Dozens of culturally diverse colonial creations have become independent nations in the past hundred years. They do not have the culinary fame of Mexico, Italy, China or France, but that does not mean they do not have amazing food worthy of exploration, food that the rest of the planet may be missing out on. Many may already have recognized cultural cuisines within their own borders. These are important, but they often cross international borders and thus cannot be called national cuisines. For example, the Yucatec Maya and their dishes are found in both Belize and southern Mexico.

An inclusive national cuisine unites a country across cultural, geographic and religious lines. Developing a national cuisine to share with the rest of the world is an act of patriotism, an important part of nation-building exercises meant to unify diverse groups under one flag. It is also a valuable tourism "product" to offer visitors who are seeking out new tastes. Having a national cuisine is a way to assert one's identity as a country through gastronationalism, to develop and export a locally rooted yet cosmopolitan brand, and to stake out a place in a world of flavour that still values European (particularly French) and Chinese culture over that of the rest of the planet.

RECOMMENDATIONS FOR THE TOURISM INDUSTRY IN BELIZE

What is the future of Belizean food? Belize has a strong agricultural sector, a diverse population and an appealing identity as both Caribbean and Central American. It is uniquely positioned to capture part of the revived interest in food among the middle and upper classes in North America. Food-focused tourism provides a wonderful opportunity to link our two biggest industries, tourism and agriculture. We have long capitalized on our cultural diversity in marketing Belize as a travel destination, but we still do not do justice to the wide array of foods in our country, in part because many of us are unaware of exactly how varied a food environment we have. As a result, we tend to undervalue our culinary diversity. We need to educate our tourism professionals at all levels and think outside the hegemonic nationalism model that leads many people to market a limited version of Kriol cuisine as "Belizean food".

Will the increasing segmentation and specialization of the international tourism industry and the new culinary focus of the tourist gaze have divisive effects on Belizean food? The current growth of food tourism as a sector of the industry may cause guests to demand a wide array of novel offerings and hosts to provide them by segmenting and marketing Belizean foodways as a series of "exotic" ethnic cuisines, resulting in the divided-plate scenario described by Wilk. We already see this effect in the growing presence of cultural food marketing in Belize. Five years ago it was almost impossible to find cooking classes or food tours in Belize. Today a number of resorts offer on-site cooking classes and a growing number of companies offer food-focused tours. At the same time, some young Belizean chefs rising in the ranks are applying professional culinary training to local foodways to create a new Belizean cuisine, rooted in the home cooking of Belize's diverse population (Wilk 2006). Both of these culinary developments are occurring as processes of differentiation and blending arise simultaneously in the face of a diverse tourist gaze and an increasingly educated class of upwardly mobile Belizeans with money to spend.

Cultural food marketing and inspired/new Belizean cuisine both provide broad avenues of opportunity to escape the restrictive grasp of hegemonic nationalism and "restaurant Kriol" food. By implementing culinary code-switching on a large scale, we can promote a cosmopolitan Belizean food category based on traditional home cooking that includes all the different cultural groups in Belize, while also taking care to remain accessible to Belizeans on a budget. We can encourage higher-end innovation and experimentation in the genre of new/inspired Belizean cuisine using the techniques of international professional cooking to showcase Belizean ingredients, flavour combinations and traditional dishes in new and exciting ways.

New/inspired Belizean cuisine is slowly beginning to emerge as professionally trained chefs break away from the pan-tropical and "international" hotel cuisine common at many resorts. Belizean chef Sean Kuylen's Boil-Up Bite is a great example of fusing traditional Belizean flavours with high-end restaurant technique. And we do not want to ignore innovation elsewhere – it does not have to be five-star. The Maya sandwich, a burger between two corn tortillas sold at a takeaway restaurant in Cayo District, is a budget-friendly version of fusion cuisine, in this case bringing together staple food elements from two different cultures.

Advertising traditional foodways should be part and parcel of the whole "cultural package" marketed to visitors. Revival of "traditional" (historic) food practices within the tourism industry is not yet commonplace, but some individuals and businesses are leading the charge. In San Pedro, Ambergris Caye, the popular restaurant El Fogon markets fire-hearth cooking, a nostalgic treat for Belizeans and an "authentic" experience for tourists. In Placencia the local fishing co-op is selling seaweed to Belizeans, area restaurants and interested visitors. In Punta Gorda visitors can book a cultural tour to learn Kriol or Garifuna drumming and how to make serre, all in one evening.

Placencia, like many other communities across Belize, has many aspects of local foodways that could be marketed to tourists. These include Kriol-style fire-hearth cooking, traditional fishing skills and "fisherman cooking", as well as homemade fruit jellies and jams, coconut oil and sweets. Further up the peninsula in Seine Bight, cassava-bread making and Garifuna food could be a big draw, forming part of cultural tourism to the community along with the village's well-known musical talent. Locally produced value-added products such as stewed fruits, jellies and jams, cashew nuts, oils and sweets can cater to visitors looking for souvenirs that are locally rooted, tell a story, support cottage-industry production and move beyond the ever-present bottle of Marie Sharp's hot sauce.

Belizean cooks and tour operators should take the opportunity to promote cooking demonstrations and lessons to their clientele. Even seeing a coconut grated to produce fresh coconut milk is an exotic experience for many of our visitors, one that they rarely have the opportunity to enjoy. Food experiences can be the centrepiece or an important complementary component to many tours and activities and can bring much-needed tourist dollars to struggling rural areas. The growth of the Toledo Chocolate Trail and associated tours and activities is a great example of how rural food tourism can create intersectoral linkages and spread the economic benefits of tourism beyond the beaches and archaeological sites of our country.

The idea of Belizean food should be a pluralistic one that embraces all Belizeans and the diversity of our nation. We need to capitalize on the "eat local" and "eat seasonal" movements in North America to offer our guests (and ourselves) dishes that reflect the full range of ingredients, techniques and flavours found in Belize. Moving beyond the narrow hegemonic nationalist approach will reinforce our self-image of "all ah wi da one" and bring our food marketing in line with the pluralistic model of multiculturalism that has been so successfully used in tourism campaigns to date. Promoting both culturally rooted Belizean home cooking and innovative new Belizean cuisine – a cuisine that combines local culinary practices in exciting new ways – will bring a wide and attractive range of food experiences into the market, not only for international tourists but for Belizean diners as well. Perhaps, for the good of the nation and our palates, it is time we laid hegemonic nationalism to rest. Let us put our national pride on our plates with a Belizean cuisine that truly represents our unique identity: as a jewel of multiculturalism on the shores of the Caribbean in the heart of Central America.

AFTERWORD
BY CHEF SEAN KUYLEN

In 2012 I asked Chef Sean Kuylen, one of the best-known professional chefs in Belize (along with Jennie Staines and Rob Pronk),[1] to tell me how he defines what he calls "inspired Belizean cuisine". His answer serves as an evocative afterword and hints at the ideas, flavours and techniques that Belize offers its dedicated cooks and chefs.

This is a great question, and it's like asking if Christopher Columbus discovered the New World. In my opinion, Belize has always had a cuisine; however, we were just a bit timid in showcasing her. I am Belizean and studied culinary arts in the United States, where I was taught classical French techniques and the way of Escoffier. To the culinary world, his way and techniques are like the Bible! I was taught to choose wild catch over farmed; to look for organic and avoid processed and genetically modified; and that monosodium glutamate and corn syrup were bad. I observed that everything came with bar codes, including apples! But who am I to argue? This was the way of the New World!

    Back home in Belize I grew up eating fresh fish that we caught in the Caribbean Sea, drank coconut water from the tree, savoured the ripest mangoes as they fell to the ground and enjoyed the sweetest orange juice by picking it off the tree myself – without that annoying little sticker! We fished for grouper, yellowtail snapper and barracuda, then scaled, gutted, cleaned and fried them in coconut oil. We had traditions of eating different food at different times and seasons which every culture in Belize celebrates. This was just our way of life that we took for granted and never once had to question if there was another way. So, back to culinary school. I was taught how to fillet that strange-looking fish called salmon but quickly realized that it was only different in appearance and colour from our own Spanish mackerel: the anatomy was the same. And to be honest, I did not like the sterile meat lab. I much preferred standing barefoot in ankle-deep warm reef water removing gills on a wooden butcher's block, where I could use an old paint can to quickly clean up.

Over the semesters I progressed in acquiring cooking techniques and terminology. I learned how to make fancy sauces such as demi-glace, where we roasted veal bones and added tomato paste and red wine for acidity, added herbs, bay leaves, onions, celery and carrots (known as *mirepoix*) and water, and reduced it for hours until nicely thick and silky. Then I remembered my Granny Manuela Young making cowfoot soup and always cursing if we did not put in tomato paste, because the water would look and taste unappealing, like "stinking Choro or Kinel water". Eureka! She was right! I learned that the acid of the tomato paste and red wine helped break down the tough fibres in her cowfoot. Interesting!

Later on I began to understand the power of roux, which is a combination of flour and fat to thicken soups and sauces. Immediately I started to think of Old Pa Charles Kuylen making the wickedest brown-flour stew, where he mixed coconut oil and flour to thicken the fish soup, or tikini. Imagine that rich, thick goodness, with whole roasted habanero peppers, conch, whole snapper, coco and okra! No wonder he called it "Married Man Go Home"! I went on to learn how to make a French velouté: any stock thickened by roux, which we added to fish or meats as a sauce. Really? Wait a minute. . . . My mom used to make a Yucatecan dish called *pebre*, where she took leftover escabeche liquid, thickened it with fat and flour (roux!), added peppercorns and oregano, and ladled that over smoked turkey meat. She was making velouté!

You mean to say I'm learning all kinds of fancy French words and techniques and right at home the Maya, Garifuna, creole and Mestizo have cooked with these highly complex methods for years and I never even knew it? So escabeche is literally a chicken stock flavoured with acid, and Garifuna serre is a fumet blanc (fish stock) flavoured with coconut milk. Good old creole stewed local fowl and stewed gibnut are nothing more than our chef instructor's suggested technique of braising, for when meats are naturally tough. And even the barbecue technique came from the Caribbean's Taino people, who called it *barbacoa*. Maddas! You mean to say Belize has a cuisine?

Fast-forward to current day and take a minute in my brain. I have worked in Belize, the United States, Dominica, and St Vincent and the Grenadines.

I have cooked in Taiwan, Barbados, Mexico and El Salvador and left behind my interpretation of new Belizean cuisine everywhere. How is this possible, when if I were to ask you "What is Belizean cuisine", more than likely your answer would be rice and beans, stew chicken, potato salad, red Kool-Aid and ripe plantain. In Dominica and St Vincent we faced similar challenges identifying Caribbean cuisine. The resorts in many of these islands, along with Central American countries like El Salvador, are riddled with North American fast-food chains. Their resorts import chefs to serve lasagne, basil pesto, pasta, shepherd's pie, strawberry cheesecake and piña coladas. I guess they figure it's safe to give visiting tourists something they are accustomed to, therefore not running the risk of complaints – that is the safest way.

Now back to Sean Kuylen's mind. Remember, I am an adrenaline junkie and cannot be ordinary. Because I understood the science behind the food and what makes it work and not work, creating a slightly different take on familiar cuisine became my chosen avenue. Later I would coin the term *inspired Belizean cuisine* to describe what I do. Sure, there are critics; many of them are appalled by my interpretation, some accept it and others are like, "You crazy!" Nevertheless I continued on my culinary path, beginning with basic techniques. And as an absolute must, I started simply by cooking *only* local foods. Yes, I was trained in French cuisine, but if I can make a roux from butter and flour, I can now use cohune oil from San Ignacio or coconut oil from Mr Kwame Reynolds in Sittee River Village for that familiar and exotic flavour and aroma. I throw away the Idaho potato when making a croquette and now substitute it with coco, which is also called taro root or tannia in the Caribbean.

Remember that imported cheesecake with strawberries? Last I checked, they do not grow too well here in our climate. So why not take some blackberry wine from the Belize River Valley and reduce it with thick, rich burgundy guava jelly and make a sauce to pour over that cheesecake or, even better yet, fried jacks. If that is not good enough, let us use mango, passion fruit, stewed green papaya or mammee, with her rich and eye-appealing terracotta colour. Let us forget regular crème anglaise, a rich English sauce made of heavy cream and egg yolks. Let's make a chocolate cake with Toledo cacao, add some Maya smoked habanero powder and flavour this "crème anglaise" with Toledo's yellow ginger and curry powder to marry them together. Trust me, it works.

How about Italian gnocchi, where they take potato, egg yolks and flour to make little dumplings? Let us now use this technique with our very own sweet potatoes or yams and add that to our hearty split-pea and pigtail soup. The elements of shepherd's pie can be substituted by layering roasted breadfruit and ground deer or gibnut meat, baked in a casserole dish for a local spin.

Similarly, have you heard of a French delicacy called escargots? What is it? It is snails cooked with butter, garlic and parsley and eaten only in fancy restaurants with a fancy price tag. Now, have you heard of jute? What is it? It is a river snail found in our clear, fresh rivers and eaten by the Maya in Succotz Village, San Ignacio, all the way down to Indian Creek, Toledo. Is this a new cuisine? No, because it has been eaten by the Maya for hundreds of years. So now let us add culantro, butter and tons of garlic, pair it with some achiote (called *recado* or *roucou* in the Caribbean) and some steamed chocho (also called *wiskil*, *chayote* or *christophene*), put it in a Maya clay pot, cover it with a buttery pastry crust, egg-wash and bake. *Boom!* Inspired Belizean cuisine.

The way I see it, I become the matchmaker, like eharmony.com, and my local ingredients and cultures are the subjects awaiting introduction, to be flirted with and intermarry. I am not a genius, just the person making the introduction, and the rest of the flavour compilation is up to them. With this thought process, the creations are endless.

Our food can be showcased among the world's finest, as our rainforest is naturally organic and our barrier-reef system is very much alive and healthy. Cooking fresh is not a choice but a way of life for us Belizeans. In school we earned points for cooking with what was in season. That meant we had to go to the library and find the chart with the current month and foods that were in season at the moment. In Belize I cook seasonally not by choice but simply because if avocado and mango are not in season, you had best believe they will not be at the market. Why is that? Like, duh, it is not in season, so cannot be found! Do not be afraid to substitute and use our local peppers, produce and seafood or drink our local beer and rums. To paraphrase something Mrs Kim Barrow once said: Don't you find it bizarre that perfumes, lotions and shampoo boast being made with "all-natural herbal essences" yet we ingest food and beverages containing artificial colours and flavourings?

Belizean families living abroad always ask for red recado, Marie Sharp's, local rums and Belikin beer when family members visit, yet we at home actively (and illegally) smuggle Mexican beer, strawberry jelly, tabasco peppers, vegetables, fruit and even granulated sugar because it is "whiter in Chetumal"! We go to the local grocery store and quickly choose the imported Cadbury's chocolate over the local chocolate bar because it is perceived as better. Here is food for thought: Beneath that hypnotizing coveted foreign label is chocolate that was grown and harvested in your very own Toledo District, bought and exported by Kraft, packaged in the United Kingdom and sweetened with your very own exported Orange Walk sugar. It got wrapped in eye-appealing gold foil and purple paper, slapped with a bar code, then put on a ship back to Belize. When it arrives "home" again, it pays import duty and taxes and then proudly sits on your grocery shelf with a "born-on" date of *seven months ago*.

Now do you see that other chocolate bar beside it? It was handmade using only local ingredients at a small artisanal factory named Ixcacao (the Maya goddess of chocolate), not by fictional orange Oompa Loompas but by a Maya couple named Juan and Abelina Cho in San Felipe Village, Toledo. The bean was picked seven days before, left to ferment on crocus sacks on the rainforest floor, shelled by hand and later roasted with a regular hairdryer. The cacao bean was then conched (a process of agitating and distributing cocoa fat through friction) with a traditional corn mill whose handle still has yellow spots from making dukunu the day before. Those beans are then tempered, also by hand, using a stone mortar and pestle called a pilon, which has been passed down as a wedding present for generations. After the chocolate is made and moulded, it gets wrapped in foil and labelled with Scotch tape and a square of regular typing paper printed with a non-electric ribbon typewriter. These bars are packed in paper bags and sent to your grocery store via a half-day journey on the James Bus Line. Its handwritten "born-on" date reads: *last Saturday*.

Now which do you choose? By buying the purple-wrapped chocolate you will be contributing to a megacorporate brand whose net worth was a mere BZ$37.8 billion at the time of their merger in 2009. The choice is yours. I don't know about you, but I am Chef Sean Kuylen and I embrace our local foods. You should too, and continue to be inspired by Belizean cuisine.

A SHORT CULINARY GLOSSARY

boil-up: A hearty midday meal associated with the Kriol people. This dish is made with boiled ground foods such as sweet potato, cassava and yampi (purple taro) and served with a homemade tomato sauce to pour over it. Pigtail boil-up contains only pigtail, but most boil-up includes both pigtail and a piece of fish (fried in coconut oil) on the plate.

bread kind: A Kriol term that describes all starchy vegetables, including but not limited to root crops. Coco yam, yampi, cassava, soup yams, green bananas and plantains, and breadfruit are all considered bread kind.

brown flour: A Kriol term that refers to all soups made with a roux of fat and flour. Historically, coconut oil or lard was typically used. Conch soup and stew fish are "brown flour" stews.

bundiga: Called *Matilda foot* in Kriol and *bundiga* in Garifuna, this dumpling made of finely grated raw green banana or plantain is served as large dumplings with a coconut gravy (lasus) and fish for bundiga. For Matilda foot it is rolled into small balls, seasoned with a little salt and pepper and dropped into a soup.

caan lab (corn lab, atole de maiz): This porridge is a seasonal treat made from fresh harvested green corn that is ground into a paste and cooked with spices and sugar or sweetened condensed milk to taste. This is eaten as a breakfast dish or a sweet treat.

caldo: A spicy soup with a red broth – dyed with annatto (achiote) paste – that is associated with the Maya culture. Made with chicken or wild game and flavoured with smoked dried bird peppers and lots of culantro (called *samat* in Kekchi Maya), it may include jippy jappa or cohune palm heart or other wild vegetable additions. The soup is usually served with corn tortillas.

chimole: Called *chimole* (or *chirmole*) by the Spanish, whom most Belizeans believe originated the dish, and *black dinna* by the Kriol, this soup contains chicken, hard-boiled eggs, onion and other vegetables. The broth is black thanks to the hearty application of black recado (achiote paste). It is typically served with corn tortillas.

chu'uk kwa: Also called *sweet corn biscuit* in English, this paper-thin wafer is shaped like a corn tortilla and made out of corn masa and brown sugar ground together. When baked on the comal each wafer is hand stamped with the lacy star shaped seed pod of the chu'uk plant, hence the name.

coconut oil: The cooking oil of choice for Kriol and Garifuna people, but now often replaced by much cheaper imported soy-based 123 brand vegetable oil. Valued for its nutty flavour, coconut oil is an essential ingredient in dishes from boil-up to serre to fried fish. Making the oil was once a significant cottage industry on Placencia Peninsula, but today I know of only two older women in Placencia Village who still make it on a semi-regular basis.

cohune cabbage (curried): Cohune cabbage is a Belizean English and Kriol name for the heart of the cohune palm, which in East Indian–descent communities in Toledo District is often curried. Cohune cabbage is also put into tamales and soups in Maya communities across southern Belize.

cohune oil: The original cooking oil of Maya peoples in Belize, made from nuts of the wild cohune palm, which also provides thatching material. The taste is very similar to coconut oil. The nuts are small and have a very hard, thick shell, so the oil has been supplanted in some places by coconut oil and imported oils, but it can still be found in some Maya villages.

comal: A cast-iron griddle on which corn and flour tortillas are baked over a fire. Ceramic griddles are still used in some parts of Mexico, but ceramic comals are rarely found in Belize.

conch soup: A thick, roux-based soup made with ground or finely chopped conch, ground foods and vegetables (okra is a popular choice). Pigtail is often added. Occasionally conch soup is made with coconut milk. Like cowfoot soup, it is supposed to improve sexual stamina and performance. It is a popular dish on restaurant specials boards during conch season.

cowfoot soup: A thick, gelatinous soup made from the cleaned ankle and hoof of a cow. Usually made with root vegetables, this soup is famed for curing hangovers (goma) and is supposed to be good for the back and for sexual stamina and performance.

craboo: The strongly scented and flavoured yellow fruit of a small tree, *Byrsonima crassifolia*. Also known as *nance*, it grows abundantly in the littoral forest and pine savannah on and near the Placencia Peninsula. In Belize we love craboo: it is preserved in water, bottled in rum, mixed into frozen treats called milky ways, or mashed and eaten with condensed milk, as well as being consumed right under the tree it falls from.

culantro: A relative of cilantro, with the same strong flavour but with leaves shaped like a dandelion. Also known as *samat* in Kekchi Maya, this herb is an essential component in Maya cooking.

darasa: Pounded green plantain wrapped in a banana leaf and steamed, served as a starchy accompaniment to seafood stews and coconut gravies. It is strongly associated with the Garifuna culture.

dukunu: Dukunu is a Belizean Kriol name for tamales made with green corn and coconut milk, often with no filling. The word comes from the West African Fanti language group.

escabeche: A spicy chicken soup with a clear broth, made with onions, jalapeños and allspice seed. Although associated with the Spanish, it is cooked by the Kriol as well. The soup is typically served with corn tortillas.

fish hash: Leftover cooked fish is pulled into small pieces and fried up in coconut oil with onions, sweet pepper, garlic, oregano and cilantro to make a delicious breakfast meal. This may also be served for lunch with rice.

fry jacks: Fry jacks are a popular breakfast item of Belizean Kriol derivation made by rolling out the dough for a flour tortilla and then deep-frying it. Almost identical in form to a sopapilla, the fry jack will puff up while frying and is typically served with beans, eggs and cheese for a classic and hearty Belizean breakfast.

gacho: Typically a flour tortilla filled with refried beans and cheese and toasted. There is a variation in which a hot dog is included. Both typically include a touch of habanero hot sauce.

garnaches: A crispy fried corn tortilla topped with a smear of refried beans, grated cheese, a squirt of ketchup and a shredded cabbage slaw. A popular street food sold from food stalls and cool spots along the roadside in Placencia and many other villages and towns across Belize. If made with shredded meat instead of beans these are called tostadas.

gibnut: A large, tailless member of the rodent family, known to natural scientists as *Cuniculus paca*. It is called *paca* in Spanish-speaking countries. Nicknamed "royal rat" by the British tabloids after Queen Elizabeth the II ate it while visiting Belize, it is a Belizean delicacy and highly sought after

Great Dog: A flour tortilla wrapped around a hot dog with coleslaw and hot sauce.

ground food: A Kriol term referring to all root crops.

hudut: A Garifuna dish, hudut is made from green and ripe plantains, boiled, peeled and then pounded together in a large wooden mortar called *mata* in Kriol. The mash is formed into balls and served with serre and other soups as a starchy accompaniment. The dish is called *fufu* in Kriol.

jippy jappa: Also spelled *jippi jappa*, a small wild palm (*Carludovica palmate*) that grows in clumps in disturbed areas of the tropical broadleaf forests of southern Belize. Maya women use the leaves to make the now-famous jippy jappa baskets found in this region. The palm heart can easily be pulled out along with the young leaf without killing the palm. It is a favourite vegetable among the Maya, who put it in caldo or sauté it. The flower stamens are also edible and are added to soups.

johnnycakes: Biscuit-like quick breads made with coconut milk and white wheat flour, pricked with a fork so they do not rise. A popular morning and evening meal, often sold as street food, they are typically split in half and filled with refried beans, cheese, ham, pulled chicken or (rarely) fish. They were originally associated with the Kriol culture but are popular with and made by many different groups in Belize today.

Kriol bread: A coconut milk–based yeast bread associated with the Kriol people but baked today by the Garifuna as well. It is traditionally baked in a fire-hearth oven over coconut-husk coals.

lancha: A cooking technique prized in Maya communities. Multiple layers of waha leaf are wrapped around well-seasoned fish or game meat and vegetables to form a package, which is cooked on a comal over a fire hearth, steaming the contents.

long-water beans: Beans that are simmered in plain water for a long time until they break apart. They are associated in Belize with Spanish people. Some of my Kriol informants considered them to be not as tasty as Kriol-prepared beans because they lack seasoning and flavour.

panades: Derived from the Spanish word empanades which means wrapped in bread or breaded, panades are half-moons of corn masa dough that has been seasoned with recado and then filled with fish, beans or chicken and deep-fried. Typically served with a vinegary onion/cabbage slaw spiced with habanero.

pibil: Cochinita Pibil is traditionally made by seasoning a whole young pig with recado paste and other spices and herbs, then wrapping it in banana leaves and burying it in the ground with with hot stones that cook the pig within its leaf blanket. The leaf wrapping causes the pig to steam and when ready it falls off the bone. Many people today across northern Belize make a version of pibil on their stove top. The pulled pork meat is served with hot corn tortillas and pickled onions and habanero.

pigtail: Imported (from Canada and the United States) pigtails brined in salt. Pigtail is a key flavour component of stewed beans and split peas, boil-up and conch soup, and is also cooked on its own as stewed pigtail. Pigtail can be found in greasy five-gallon buckets (pigtail buckets) in most Belizean grocery stores.

poch: Corn masa steamed in waha leaf until cooked through. This heavy accompaniment to caldo is often prepared in Maya communities for parties and events where many people will be fed. It is guaranteed to fill up the hungry masses.

recado: A thick, dough-like red or black paste made from the seeds of *Bixa orellana*, the achiote or annatto shrub. The seeds are ground together with salt, vinegar, onion, garlic, cloves or allspice and black peppercorns. The paste is used by all cultural groups in Belize to season meat for stewing as well as to colour the filling for tamales. Black recado is typically made with burnt corn tortillas to provide the colour. Pure annatto paste is made by washing the colourful paste off the seeds and boiling down the water to a paste consistency. It is used in cooking by Kekchi and Mopan Maya villagers in southern Belize.

sea meat: A Kriol term referring to turtle meat and also, historically, the flesh of manatees.

serre: A fish stew with a coconut milk–based broth associated with the Garifuna people but also prepared by the Kriol, East Indians and even Maya. Garifuna typically serve it with hudut, while the Kriol often cook ground foods right in the broth.

stew fish: A brown-flour stew made with a roux of flour and coconut oil, ground foods and fresh fish, often served over rice. It is strongly associated with the fisherman culture along the coast of Belize.

tacari chicken: A dish prepared chiefly in the East Indian–descent communities of Toledo District, tacari (which can be made with chicken or other meats) is made by cooking the protein with turmeric and other spices. Often served with cohune cabbage.

tamalitos: The Spanish word for green corn tamales. Typically if they are called tamalitos and not dukunu, they are *not* made with coconut milk. May be plain or filled with a meat filling (often chicken or pork). These are wrapped in corn husks instead of waha leaf, which is preferred in Belize for tamales made from mature corn.

waha leaf: The leaf of *Calathea lutea*, a member of the arrowroot family that grows in the tropical lowland forests of Belize. The large leaves are used to wrap fish, game meat and vegetables into a package that is cooked over the Maya fire hearth in the technique called lancha. They are also used as wrappers for tamales and like wax paper to wrap up leftovers and hot corn tortillas.

wiliks/whilks/whelks: The edible marine snail *Cittarium pica* or West Indian top shell is not related to the whelks of Europe and the United States, but rather is a native of the Caribbean where it can grow to the size of a tennis ball. It has been heavily overcollected both in Belize and other parts of the Caribbean (in some regions it has disappeared entirely due to overfishing). In Belize it is ground in a meat grinder and used to make the prized and increasingly rare wiliks soup. Its black and white shell is also polished and used by jewellery makers in Placencia and across Belize.

NOTES

CHAPTER 1

1. I use the Kriol orthography recommended by the Kriol Language Project and the National Kriol Council of Belize when referring to the Belizean Kriol language and people. All other references to *creole* and *creolization* as generic terms and processes are spelled with English orthography. Here Kriol refers specifically to the Belizean Kriol people and is pronounced like the more general term *creole*.
2. All scientists, including those in the "hard" sciences, should critically examine the way in which their personal experiences and backgrounds may shape their research, data analyses and conclusions.
3. A rich fried patty made of meat scraps and cornmeal, a typical part of a Pennsylvania "Dutch" (i.e., Deutsch, or German) farm breakfast.
4. A rich, savoury coconut milk–based fish soup. See the glossary for more detailed definitions of Belizean food.
5. The one group I did not interview as extensively as I would have liked was immigrants from the surrounding countries of Mexico, Guatemala, Honduras and El Salvador, many of whom work in the food industry and other service sectors on the peninsula.
6. According to DeSoucey (2010, 433), gastronationalism "signals the use of food production, distribution, and consumption to demarcate and sustain the emotive power of national attachment, as well as the use of nationalist sentiments to produce and market food".

CHAPTER 2

1. More than sixty-six restaurants, grocery stores, food carts and established street vendors as of July 2013.
2. The Garifuna people, one of Belize's cultural groups, arose in the early 1600s on the island of St Vincent, in the Lesser Antilles, through mixing of the native Carib population with West Africans. Garifuna communities today are found

along the coasts of Nicaragua, Honduras, Guatemala and Belize; significant populations also live in New York, Chicago, Los Angeles and Miami. To learn more about the Garifuna people of Belize, please read the work of renowned scholar Dr Joseph Palacio.
3. A cool spot is a small building open to the street or beach, typically with rudimentary seating, that serves food and/or drinks. See chapter 4 for more on these venues.
4. Dr Anne Pyburn, personal communication, 2017.
5. The names in this historical section are real unless noted.
6. United Fruit Company boats and tenders picked up bananas from Monkey River and coastal plantations farther south. The industry had collapsed by the early twentieth century after disease ravaged the farms.
7. The fruit of the small native tree *Byrsonima crassifolia*. See the glossary for more details about craboo.
8. A large and delicious member of the rodent family, *Cuniculus paca*. Much prized in Belize, it is called *paca* in Spanish-speaking countries.
9. White-lipped and collared peccaries are pig-like members of the New World family *Tayassuidae*; they are popular game meats in Belize.
10. A pseudonym.
11. Today Mango Creek is a poorer village that is economically dependent on a deepwater port, export-oriented agriculture and small industry.
12. Hard candies also known as "boil sweets".
13. The first bus was a van driven by a Belizean who had returned after years of living in Los Angeles.
14. Personal communication.
15. A washed-up bale of cocaine is also called "square grouper" in the Caye Caulker area.
16. "September Celebrations" is a catch-all phrase used to refer to the festivities and celebrations leading up to and surrounding the national holidays of the Battle of St. George's Caye on 10 September and Belizean Independence Day on 21 September.
17. Along with Venezuela and Palau.

CHAPTER 3

1. One notable attempt is Joshua Samuel Brown's 2013 edition of the *Lonely Planet Guide to Belize*, which has a well-written section on the diversity of Belizean food, aptly titled "Beyond Rice and Beans".

2. I want to note that most of this research focuses on the imaginaries and expectations of "Western" tourists from North America and Europe who are typically visiting countries outside their homelands. There is a great need for more work like Yuk Wah Chan's article on Chinese tourist experiences in Vietnam which investigates the nature of tourist imaginaries and master narratives outside of the "Western" tourist experience.
3. The recent explosion of interest in the history and practice of mead-making in the United States is a good example of the application of culinary cosmopolitanism to the history of food and foodstuffs.
4. In North America it was initiated by Valene Smith and a 1974 conference on the anthropology of tourism held in Mexico City.
5. Cosmopolitanism was not something that I discussed with all the visitors I interviewed; it emerged as a theme later on during data analysis. For this reason I cannot give any percentage estimates or fully unpack a definition of cosmopolitanism here. This remains an intriguing area for future research.
6. Consider, for example, the American phenomenon of the "stay-cation" or the idea of a "mini-vacation" that may last only an afternoon.
7. A pseudonym.
8. Pseudonyms.
9. The gacho is usually just refried beans and cheese in a toasted flour tortilla but some venues in Belize City serve the hot dog in a tortilla with beans while others include coleslaw in the mix.
10. In other words, it is mentioned in guidebooks or online as being Belizean, it is on lots of menus and it is considered Belizean by Belizeans.
11. A pseudonym.
12. Local fisheries continue to be strained by overfishing, poaching, the use of gillnets and illegal fishing in Belizean waters by Honduran and Guatemalan nationals. A lack of resources makes enforcement of fishing laws difficult for the understaffed rangers and non-governmental organizations in charge of monitoring marine protected areas. The latest expression of concern regarding Belize's fishing future is a push from tour guides and boat captains in Placencia and other coastal tourism zones, such as Caye Caulker and Ambergris Caye, to ban gillnets in an attempt to preserve declining fisheries and fishing heritage for future generations.
13. See the glossary for definitions and descriptions of these dishes.
14. A pseudonym.
15. The real name of the restaurant, as requested by the owner.

CHAPTER 4

1. This is a problematic term but so is "Western". In this case, by "First World" I refer to countries with a high level of technological and infrastructural and service development. In the Belizean context, these are usually people coming from countries whose societies are dominated by European-descent persons.
2. Most Belizeans who were either born in Belize or who grew up here do not consider the word *local* to include those who immigrated to Belize as adults. People born and raised in Placencia Village use an even more restrictive criterion, limiting *local* to the Belizean-born with families who have lived for at least a couple of generations in the community. On the other side of this debate, many new arrivals from North America to Placencia Peninsula use a very loose definition of *local* to refer to any individual who was in Placencia or Belize before their arrival, including immigrants from other countries who moved to Belize as adults. This debate over the word's meaning reflects many of the cultural and socio-economic tensions between new North American immigrants and those from Placencia Peninsula and Belize more broadly.
3. The title alone provides sufficient fodder for a whole other book on tourism imaginaries, expectations and migration.
4. With more popping up every day.
5. Which I define here as Placencia-born Belizeans.
6. These figures date to mid-2017. Restaurants, cool spots and bars open and close constantly on Placencia Peninsula, so the numbers may have changed slightly by time of publication.
7. It is now difficult to find a one-bedroom apartment on Placencia Peninsula for less than US$500 a month.
8. Belizeans often say "across" to refer to Guatemala. Honduras is also a source of illegal human trafficking.
9. This number is an educated guess based on observed regular bus and pickup truck traffic between these communities and the peninsula.
10. As of 2018 multiple buses run from Bella Vista, with stops in Santa Rosa, San Roman and Santa Cruz, all mainland villages on the way to Placencia Peninsula, and back. In the busy winter season, hundreds of people commute daily.
11. Panades are delicious deep-fried half-moons made of seasoned corn masa dough filled with pulled and seasoned fish, chicken or beans. A common street food across Belize, they are served with an onion, cabbage, habanero and vinegar salsa.
12. "Cool spot" is a Belizean term referring to a small shed or shack, typically by the roadside, that serves food and beverages. There is often a picnic table or a

couple of stools in the shade of a tree where customers can eat their purchase. Some cool spots serve only snacks such as tacos and garnaches, while others may offer full "rice and beans plates". A cool spot may be built in a private yard, on public land or in a commercially rented space.

13. Much (though not all) of this research in the Caribbean focuses on the phenomenon of female tourists seeking out sexual/romantic encounters with male sex workers while on vacation. Among many others, see Brennan (2004); De Albuquerque (1998); Frohlick (2007); Kempadoo (2003 , 2004); Phillips (1999); and Taylor (2001).
14. A public page that the same immigrant had created for restaurants to post their daily specials on.
15. Special American holidays are the exception here. Thanksgiving dinners are widely advertised.
16. Oftentimes Americans or Canadians selling property in Belize refuse to sell to Belizeans unless the transaction can be completed in US or Canadian dollars, as they seek to acquire home currency when divesting themselves of Belizean real estate. This makes it difficult and costly for Belizeans to use a local mortgage to finance their purchase of foreign-owned property, rendering inaccessible the majority of the real estate for sale on Placencia Peninsula and across the country.

CHAPTER 5

1. Mark died suddenly in November 2017. He was a key informant in the early stages of my research.
2. Anthropologist Peter Wilson introduced the idea of reputation and respectability in 1969 as gendered twin models of behaviour and value that individuals in the anglophone Caribbean could use to build status. His model has been critiqued for gender bias (both men and women engage in reputation-building activities) but remains popular in a more nuanced form with many Caribbean scholars. See Wilson (1969).
3. There is no doubt that the Caribbean's colonial history was long and brutal. What is not certain is whether it was more brutal than every other colonized area on the planet.
4. Common non-food-related catch-and-kill activities include raking and otherwise cleaning yards and properties, doing handyman jobs, selling tours for a commission, selling clothing and housewares, and (illegally) selling drugs or arranging their sale for visitors.

5. "Mash" refers to providing sexual satisfaction to her husband. While considered old fashioned by some, this phrase still circulates through Belizean society, even on twenty-first-century social media.
6. Selling clothing, housewares and jewellery are other areas where Placencia women have established a notable business presence on the street.
7. Ms Brenda passed away in October 2018. Her legendary character and spirit will be missed by many residents and visitors to Placencia.
8. The Coconut Man disappeared in 2016, perhaps returning to Belize City. In the meantime another man has established a totally informal coconut-water business with the aid of a machete, a long pole for knocking down green coconuts, reused gallon water bottles to hold his product, and a wheelbarrow as his mobile sales station.
9. "'Creole' will ring a bell because the southern United States is creole. Some tourists think its Cajun creole from Louisiana. We say, 'No, it's our own creole, the real creole, not French creole . . . No patois business here!' They say, 'Okay, we'll try it,' and they say, 'Oh, it's good!'"
10. "Mirna" is a pseudonym.
11. Marie Sharp's is a well-known Belizean brand exported to twenty-two different countries.

CHAPTER 6

1. For more on signature foods, see Mintz (1996).
2. At one point immediately after the Mexican Caste War in the 1850s, a large influx of Mexican refugees into the northern half of the country tipped the balance in favour of the "Hispanic" or "Spanish" population, but in the later years of the nineteenth century the Kriol regained numerical dominance.
3. Both these terms refer to a highly heterogeneous group comprising not only more recent immigrants from four different neighbouring countries but also Belizeans descended from nineteenth-century Mexican Caste War refugees. The problematic homogenization of such a diverse group is based on a presumed cultural unity and linguistic difference from other Belizeans. The term *Hispanic* is used in some public political discourse and by the national census, but most Belizeans use *Spanish* to refer to the same populations.
4. Where Spanish-speaking immigrants with some African ancestry fit into these beliefs is unclear.
5. Except for Mennonites, none of whom live in Placencia Village, to my knowledge.
6. "In Honduras we make that, because you find that in Honduras but in a different

way. In Honduras they do not put coconut milk in it and then it is served with corn tortillas. Here they put coconut milk in it and serve it with rice."
7. "Because Belizean-style – the Garifuna, real Belizeans, always have coconut oil. [Researcher: So who cooks with coconut oil?] The ones who cook real Belizean style, Kriol people."
8. "But if we Kriol people make them, they will be tastier than the Spanish-made. [Researcher: Why is that?] Because we take more care with the taste; we might add more seasoning or some herbs or something. Even though it's someone else's dish, we master it better."
9. "[Chimole/black dinna] is what the . . . borderline Belizeans – it comes from them, you know. And you know, the borderline Belizeans, who we call the Mestizos – a mix of Kriol and Spanish – most of their ancestors originated from somewhere across the border. Now and then they mix with the Kriol, but they *are* Belizean, you know? You've probably heard the poem that says, 'I think I see a new Belize.' We can't separate them, because we are all Belizean, you know?"
10. Belize's first Corn, Coconut and Barbecue Festival was held in Corozal Town in 2017, perhaps a sign of the increasing multiculturalism registered in the 2010 census. I optimistically hope this signals a new era for Belize, where hegemonic nationalism is left behind once and for all.
11. A Belize-specific creolization process.
12. "Same with the corn tortilla. Corn tortillas started, came from the Latin countries. Long-water beans and corn tortillas are Spanish delicacies."
13. "Black dinner is what Belizeans make, and this cowfoot dish is what Belizeans make. The Spanish make it sometimes, but they don't make it the way we Belizeans make it, so we would call it a Belizean dish."
14. "We make them too, but they are more Spanish dishes. The Kriol really ended up copying them afterwards and making them our food, but that's more from the Spanish side. If it's Belizean Spanish or Spanish from Honduras – I don't know where these dishes are from. But if we Kriol make them, they must be tastier than the Spanish."
15. Called "Matilda foot" in Kriol and "bundiga" in Garifuna, this dish is a dumpling made of grated raw green banana formed into small balls and dropped into a soup.
16. Pounded green plantain wrapped in a banana leaf and steamed, served as a starchy accompaniment to seafood stews and coconut gravies.
17. A chicken dish made with freshly grated turmeric.
18. Green and ripe plantains boiled, peeled and then pounded together in a large

wooden mortar (called a *mata* in Kriol), then formed into a ball by hand and served with serre and other soups as a starchy accompaniment.

19. The Hong Kongers who came to Belize were fleeing the 1999 handover of the island to mainland China. Many returned to Hong Kong or moved on to the United States after several years in Belize.

20. "And then this again [chow mein], this is a Chinese food, but this [picture] looks more Kriol-style. [Researcher: What makes it Kriol-style?] Well, the Chinese one wouldn't have all these vegetables, all these colours – just fast... When we make a chow mein, we would put everything in it that would build up the taste and the looks, you know... more our style of food. Even this fried rice here, that's more a Chinese food, but you could see no Chinese person made it. That is more Belizean-style. [Researcher: What makes it more Belizean-style? Tell me what makes you think that.] Because, well, the way it looks. The Chinese have a way of using more cabbage and celery and plain stuff, that if you see a green pepper in it or carrots, you could pick out the colour. This one just has a little more... I don't know. If I made a fried rice I'd have a lot more veggies in it than what this has, but it still doesn't look like a Chinese fried rice."

21. "This is American... Belizeans like them too, so... Well, then that could go in any one of the three [categories], because it's not only Belizean people who make pancakes. Because we usually make them. I make them a lot, because that one over there [girlfriend] likes it when I make pancakes. But when I make pancakes, I make them from scratch. Pancakes with eggs and bacon."

22. "Because the burger didn't originate in Belize and it's a worldwide meal [hot dog]. Same with the hot dog and pancakes. It's here, we eat it a lot, but it's not something – it's not a main Belizean staple. [cornflakes] Mainly a breakfast thing. A lot of Belizeans eat them, but it's not a Belizean food. Because it's not a Belizean staple. They're not going to eat that every day."

23. "It's *the* cereal that people eat for breakfast all over."

24. "I hate the idea of cornflakes, seriously. I mean, when you're on a diet, it works, but I mean, again it's the same thing. I guess we grew up with *breakfast*. You don't eat cornflakes for breakfast.... With six children you can't give them cornflakes to eat! It falls under the American idea of breakfast: cereal."

25. "These come off to me mostly as, I would even say as indigenous food. Corn – the corn in most of these foods and the guacamole and the black dinner come off as Mayan, Indian-ish, Spanish-ish.... Ah, how to put it to you – it's like ... Maya-type foods they really have. And when I say Maya, I really think about Mexicans as well, because of the guacamole you find in Mexico. All those things come from those people. We know they eat a lot of corn, although we may take it and make our own things like panades here. Guacamole, now,

again the avocados and stuff, those are again like food that Mexicans eat a lot, Maya eat a lot. The only reason why I was thinking all those things – everybody eats them but one set of people definitely deal with them: the Maya Spanish people. I threw in the cornflakes simply because they're corn. Tamalitos and such, definitely Maya foods."

26. "That sounds Maya, and the Maya were the first settlers in Belize. I mean the first people here, so."
27. "Because caldo with corn tortillas is only Maya people's food, and Spanish people's. Real Belizean people don't really like to eat that. They don't make that. They eat it, but they don't make it. [Researcher: Who are the real Belizean people?] The people who say they are born Belizean. Some Maya people come from Guatemala. It's not really Belizean food because you have Guatemala Maya people, because you can find these dishes in Guatemala. [poch] That's like – I don't know how to say it. Because it's mostly Maya people who like that."
28. This dumpling made of finely grated raw green banana or plantain is served as large dumplings with a coconut gravy (lasus) and fish for bundiga. For Matilda foot it is rolled into small balls, seasoned with a little salt and pepper and dropped into a soup.
29. Also known as *fufu* in Belizean Kriol.
30. Which may be for the best in terms of snapper roe. Higher demand would cause a crisis in Belizean fisheries.

CHAPTER 7

1. The nostalgia around fire-hearth cooking and the loss of knowledge about how to cook on a fire hearth led Willows Bank Village, in the Kriol-dominated Belize River Valley near Belize City, to start an annual fire-hearth cooking competition in 2011.
2. Her real name, used with permission.
3. In much of Asia, Chinese (and Japanese) *haute cuisine* and chef codes of conduct still dominate the world of professional cooking, although in recent years there has been increased mingling of "Eastern" and "Western" professional culinary systems and exchanges between respected chefs from both traditions.
4. "That's our *local* food family . . . I could understand if it was a piece of fillet [fish] or lobster or something, but it was our local food!"
5. Which I helped direct along with Dr Richard Wilk of Indiana University.
6. A pseudonym.
7. In less touristy communities this is not yet the case. Maya food in particular has not received much attention from the tourism market to date (except at

a few restaurants in San Pedro), despite its use of more vegetables and wild "bush foods" than the cuisine of most other Belizean cultural groups. I believe this will change as more and more visitors make their way to villages in Toledo District and as villagers, through education, travel and work in the tourism sector in places like Placencia, gain the awareness necessary to see business opportunities in marketing their food.

8. See Lauren Miller Griffith work on organic agriculture and tourism in Belize. Dr Miller Griffith is an assistant professor at Texas Tech University in Lubbock, Texas.

CHAPTER 8

1. Scattered around the planet, outposts of colonialism linger on, but most former colonies have become independent countries.
2. The Belizean diaspora and travel and communication between those at home and abroad form an important part of social and economic life and identity work for many Belizeans.
3. Culinary cosmopolitanism and the ability to code-switch are also necessary skills for Belizean entrepreneurs who want to successfully market food to tourists.

AFTERWORD

1. As time goes by, more rising stars are appearing in the Belizean chef scene. This book is not the place to give all of them the attention they deserve, but it should be said that more culinary innovators are appearing in our little country.

REFERENCES

AAA (Association of American Anthropologists). 2018. "Association of Indigenous Anthropologists". http://aia.americananthro.org/.

Adams, K.M. 1997. "Ethnic Tourism and the Renegotiation of Tradition in Tana Toraja". *Ethnology* 36 (4): 309–20.

Appadurai, A. 1988. "How to Make a National Cuisine: Cookbooks in Contemporary India". *Comparative Studies in Society and History* 30 (1): 3–24.

Ardren, T. 2004. "Where Are the Maya in Ancient Maya Archeological Tourism? Advertising and the Appropriation of Culture". In *Marketing Heritage: Archeology and the Consumption of the Past*, edited by Y. Rowan and U. Baram, 103–13. Lanham, MD: AltaMira.

Avakian, Arlene, and Barbara Haber. 2005. *From Betty Crocker to Feminist Food Studies: Critical Perspectives on Women and Food*. Amherst: University of Massachusetts Press.

Beck, Ulrich. 2006. *Cosmopolitan Vision*. Cambridge: Polity Press.

belizeinfocenter.org. 2012. "History: 1871–1950". http://belizeinfocenter.org/history/1871-1950/.

Belize Specialists. 2013. "About Placencia". http://www.belizespecialists.com/Placencia.htm.

Besson, J. 1993. "Reputation and Respectability Reconsidered: A New Perspective on Afro-Caribbean Women". In *Women and Change in the Caribbean: A Pan-Caribbean Perspective*, edited by Janet Momsen, 15–37. Bloomington: Indiana University Press.

Bilgrami, Sana, dir. 2004. *Tree Fellers*. Denholm, Scotland: Asylum Pictures.

Bolland, O. Nigel. 1987. "Race, Ethnicity and National Integration in Belize" In *Belize, Ethnicity and Development*, eited by SPEAR. Belize City: SPEAR Press.

———. 1998. "Creolisation and Creole Societies: A Cultural Nationalist View of Caribbean Social History". *Caribbean Quarterly* 44 (1–2): 1–32.

Bourdieu, P. 1977. *Outline of a Theory of Practice*. Cambridge: Cambridge University Press.

———. 1979. *Distinction: A Social Critique of the Judgement of Taste*. Cambridge, MA: Harvard University Press.

Brennan, Dennis. 2004. *What's Love Got to Do with It? Transnational Desires and Sex Tourism in the Dominican Republic*. Durham, NC: Duke University Press.

Bromley, Rosemary D.F., and Peter K. Mackie. 2009. "Displacement and the New Spaces for Informal Trade in the Latin American City Centre". *Urban Studies* 46 (7): 1485–506.

Brown, Joshua Samuel, and Mara Vorhees. 2013. *Belize*. 5th ed. London: Lonely Planet.

Browne, K.E. 2002. "Creole Economics and the Débrouillard: From Slave-Based Adaptations to the Informal Economy in Martinique". *Ethnohistory* 49 (2): 373–403.

———. 2004. *Creole Economics: Caribbean Cunning under the French Flag*. Austin: University of Texas Press.

Brulotte, R.L., and M.A. Di Giovine, eds. 2014. *Edible Identities: Food as Cultural Heritage*. Farnham, UK: Ashgate.

Bruner, Edward M. 2004. *Culture on Tour: Ethnographies of Travel*. Chicago: University of Chicago Press.

BTB (Belize Tourism Board). 2011. "Savor Belize". http://travelbelize.org/savor belize/ [webpage removed in 2014].

———. 2012. "From Punta Rock Star to Celebrated Chef". *Destination Belize*.

———. 2018. "Qualified Retired Persons Incentive Program". http://belizetourismboard.org/wp-content/uploads/2016/10/Belize-Retired-Persons-Incentives-Program-Official-2016-1.pdf.

Bunten, A.C. 2008. "Sharing Culture or Selling Out? Developing the Commodified Persona in the Heritage Industry". *American Ethnologist* 35 (3): 380–95.

Butler, R.W. 1980. "The Concept of a Tourist Area Cycle of Evolution: Implications for Management of Resources". *Canadian Geographer/Géographe canadien* 24 (1): 5–12.

Calhoun, Craig. 2003. "'Belonging' in the Cosmopolitan Imaginary". *Ethnicities* 3 (4): 531–53.

Cancian, Frank. 1979. *The Innovator's Situation: Upper-Middle-Class Conservatism in Agricultural Communities*. Palo Alto, CA: Stanford University Press.

Carne, Lisa, ed. 2010. *Way Bak Den: Preserving and Celebrating Creole and Garifuna Culture on the Placencia Peninsula, Belize*. Placencia: Inter-American Development Bank Cultural Development Program.

CDRA (Caribbean Disaster Relief Agency). 2001. "Report: First Evaluation of Effects of Hurricane Iris". https://reliefweb.int/report/belize/first-evaluation-effects-hurricane-iris.

Chan, Y.W. 2006. "Coming of Age of the Chinese Tourists: The Emergence of Non-Western Tourism and Host–Guest Interactions in Vietnam's Border Tourism". *Tourist Studies* 6 (3): 187–213.

Chen, De-Jung. 2017. "Couchsurfing: Performing the Travel Style Through Hospitality Exchange". *Tourist Studies* 18 (1): 105–22.
Cohen, Erik. 1972. "Towards a Sociology of International Tourism". *Social Research* 39 (1): 164–68.
———. 1988. "Authenticity and Commoditization in Tourism". *Annals of Tourism Research* 15 (3): 371–86.
Connolly, Sean. 2013. *British Army on the Rampage (B.A.O.R.). Bk 2, Muck 'n' Bullets.* www.armynovels.com.
Culinary Institute of America. 2014. http://www2.ciachef.edu/ldg_adm/fil_google_b.html?gclid=CMiX9MyX2b0CFaMcOgod1GUAPw.
Cusack, I. 2004. "'Equatorial Guinea's National Cuisine Is Simple and Tasty': Cuisine and the Making of National Culture". *Arizona Journal of Hispanic Cultural Studies* 8:131–48.
Davidson, Alan, ed. 1983. *Food in Motion: The Migration of Foodstuffs and Cookery Techniques.* Proceedings of the Oxford Symposium, 1983. Oxford: Prospect Books.
De Albuquerque, K. 1998. "Sex, Beach Boys, and Female Tourists in the Caribbean". *Sexuality and Culture* 2:87–112.
DeSoucey, M. 2010. "Gastronationalism: Food Traditions and Authenticity Politics in the European Union". *American Sociological Review* 75 (3): 432–55.
Di Giovine, Michael A. 2010. "La Vigilia Italo-Americana: Revitalizing the Italian-American Family Through the Christmas Eve 'Feast of the Seven Fishes'". *Food and Foodways* 18 (4): 181–208.
Diner, Hasia. 2001. *Hungering for America: Italian, Irish, and Jewish Foodways in the Age of Migration.* Cambridge, MA: Harvard University Press.
Douglas, Mary. 1972. "Deciphering a Meal". *Daedalus* 101 (1): 61–81.
Duffy, Rosaleen. 2002. *A Trip Too Far: Ecotourism, Politics and Exploitation.* New York: Taylor and Francis.
Fahim, H., and K. Helmer. 1980. "Indigenous Anthropology in Non-Western Countries: A Further Elaboration". *Current Anthropology* 21 (5): 644–63.
Fajans, J. 2012. *Brazilian Food: Race, Class and Identity in Regional Cuisines.* London: Bloomsbury Academic.
Farb, P., and G. Armelagos. 1980. *Consuming Passions: The Anthropology of Eating.* Boston: Houghton Mifflin.
Feifer, W. 1985. *Going Places.* London: Macmillan
Ferguson, P.P. 2004. *Accounting for Taste: The Triumph of French Cuisine.* Chicago: University of Chicago Press.
Freeman, C. 2007. *Neoliberalism and the Marriage of Reputation and Respectability: Entrepreneurship and the Barbadian Middle Class.* Nashville, TN: Vanderbilt University Press.

Freeman, M. 1977. *Food in Chinese Culture*. New Haven, CT: Yale University Press.
Frohlick, S. 2007. "Fluid Exchanges: The Negotiation of Intimacy between Tourist Women and Local Men in a Transnational Town in Caribbean Costa Rica". *City and Society* 19 (1): 139–68.
Gille, Zsuzsa, and Seán Ó. Riain. 2002. "Global Ethnography". *Annual Review of Sociology* 28 (1): 271–95.
Goetze, Tara C. 2009. "Protecting Our Resources: (Re)negotiating the Balance of Governance and Local Autonomy in Cooperative Natural Resource Management in Belize". In *Unsettled Legitimacy: Political Community, Power and Authority in a Global Era*, edited by Steven Bernstein and William D. Coleman, 129–48. Vancouver: University of British Columbia Press.
Goffman, E. 1956. *The Presentation of Self in Everyday Life*. New York: Doubleday.
———. 1967. *Interaction Ritual: Essays on Face-to-Face Behaviour*. London: Penguin.
Goody, J. 1982. *Cooking, Cuisine and Class: A Study in Comparative Sociology*. Cambridge: Cambridge University Press.
Graburn, Nelson H.H. 1985. "The Anthropology of Tourism". *Man* 20 (1): 189.
———. 1989. "Tourism: The Sacred Journey". In *Hosts and Guests: The Anthropology of Tourism*, 2nd ed., edited by Valene Smith, 21–36. Philadelphia: University of Pennsylvania Press.
Guttentag, Daniel. 2015. "Airbnb: Disruptive Innovation and the Rise of an Informal Tourism Accommodation Sector". *Current Issues in Tourism* 18 (12): 1192–217.
Hall, C. Michael. 2014. "Second Home Tourism: An International Review". *Tourism Review International* 18 (3): 115–35.
Hall, Colin Michael, Liz Sharples, Richard Mitchell, Niki Macionis and Brock Cambourne. 2003. *Food Tourism Around the World: Development, Management and Markets*. Oxford: Elsevier.
Halloran, Vivian Nun. 2016. *The Immigrant Kitchen: Food, Ethnicity and Disapora*. Cleveland: Ohio State University Press.
Harris, Deborah A., and Pattie Giuffre. 2015. *Taking the Heat: Women Chefs and Gender Inequality in the Professional Kitchen*. New Jersey: Rutgers University Press.
Hayes, M. 1975. "In Belize with Palm and Pothole". *New York Times*, 9 February, 317.
Heldke, L. 2008. "Let's Cook Thai: Recipes for Colonialism". In *Food and Culture: A Reader*, edited by C. Counihan and P. Van Esterik, 175–93. New York: Routledge.
Henderson, Joan C., Ong Si Yun, Priscilla Poon and Xu Biwei. 2012. "Hawker Centres as Tourist Attractions: The Case of Singapore". *International Journal of Hospitality Management* 31 (3): 849–55.
Hobsbawm, E.J., and T. Ranger, eds. 1983. *The Invention of Tradition*. Cambridge: Cambridge University Press.

Hom, Stephanie. 2004. "The Tourist Moment". *Annals of Tourism Research* 31 (1): 61–77.
Horwitz, Morton J. 1982. "The History of the Public/Private Distinction". *University of Pennsylvania Law Review* 130 (6): 1423–28.
Houston, Lynn Marie. 2005. *Food Culture in the Caribbean*. Westport, CT: Greenwood Press.
Hsieh, An-Tien, and Janet Chang. 2006. "Shopping and Tourist Night Markets in Taiwan". *Tourism Management* 27 (1): 138–45.
Hughes, George. 1995. "Authenticity in Tourism". *Annals of Tourism Research* 22 (4): 781–803.
Huitric, M. 2005. "Lobster and Conch Fisheries of Belize: a History of Sequential Exploitation". *Ecology and Society* 10 (1): 21.
Hyde, E.X. 2017. "From the Publisher". *Amandala* [Belize].
Hymes, Dell. 1972. "On Communicative Competence". In *Sociolinguistics: Selected Readings*, edited by J.B. Pride and J. Holmes, 269–93. Harmondsworth, UK: Penguin.
IDB (International Development Bank). 2007. "BL-L1003: Sustainable Tourism Program" [Placencia pier project]. https://www.iadb.org/en/project/BL-L1003.
International Living. 2018. Belize. https://internationalliving.com/countries/belize/.
Iyora-Diaz, S.I. 2012. *Foodscapes, Foodfields and Identities in the Yucatan*. New York: Berghan.
Judd, K. 1989a. "Cultural Synthesis or Ethnic Struggle? Creolization in Belize". *Cimarron* 2 (1–2): 103–18.
———. 1989b. "Who Will Define Us? Creole History and Identity in Belize". Paper presented at the American Anthropological Association annual meeting, Chicago.
Kempadoo, Kamala. 2003. "Theorizing Sexual Relations in the Caribbean". In *Confronting Power, Theorizing Gender: Interdisciplinary Perspectives in the Caribbean*, edited by Eudine Barriteau, 159–85. Kingston: University of the West Indies Press.
———. 2004. *Sexing the Caribbean: Gender, Race, and Sexual Labor*. London: Routledge.
Kempton, Wayne, comp. 2014. "Silver Jubilee of the Most Reverand Edward Arthur Dunn, D.D.". http://anglicanhistory.org/wi/dunn1942.html.
Key, C.J. 2002. "The Political Economy of the Transition from Fishing to Tourism in Placencia, Belize". *International Review of Modern Sociology* 30 (1–2): 1–18.
Khan, A. 2001. "Journey to the Center of the Earth: The Caribbean as Master Symbol". *Cultural Anthropology* 16 (3): 271–302.
Koc, Mustafa, and Jennifer Welsh. 2001. "Food, Foodways and Immigrant

Experience". Paper presented at the Canadian Ethnic Studies Association conference, Halifax, Nova Scotia.

Landes, Joan B. 1998. "The Public and the Private Sphere: A Feminist Reconsideration". In *Feminism, the Public and the Private*, edited by Joan B. Landes, 135–64. Oxford: Oxford University Press.

Leslie, Norman. 2007. Sea Spray Hotel. http://www.seasprayhotel.com/seaspray.html.

Little, Kenneth. 2014. "Belize Ephemera, Affect, Emergent Imaginaries". In *Tourism Imaginaries: Anthropological Approaches*, edited by Noel B. Salazar and Nelson H.H. Graburn, 220–41. New York: Berghahn.

Loewe, R. 2010. *Maya or Mestizo? Nationalism, Modernity and Its Discontents*. Toronto: University of Toronto Press.

Long, L.M., ed. 2004. *Culinary Tourism*. Lexington: University Press of Kentucky.

MacCannell, D. 1973. "Staged Authenticity: Arrangements of Social Space in Tourist Settings". *American Journal of Sociology* 79 (3): 589–603.

MacKinnon, J.J. 1989. "Coastal Maya Trade Routes in Southern Belize". In *Coastal Maya Trade*, edited by H. McKillop and P.F. Healy, 111–22. Occasional Papers in Anthropology 8. Peterborough, ON: Trent University.

Mauss, M. 1950. *The Gift: The Form and Reason for Exchange in Archaic Societies*. Paris: Presses universitaires de France.

Medina, L.K. 1997. "Defining Difference, Foraging Unity: The Co-construction of Race, Ethnicity and Nation in Belize". *Ethnic and Racial Studies* 20 (4): 757–80.

———. 2003. "Commoditizing Culture: Tourism and Maya Identity". *Annals of Tourism Research* 30 (2): 353–68.

Mintz, S.W. 1989. "Cuisine and Haute Cuisine: How Are They Linked?" *Food and Foodways* 3:185–90.

———. 1996. *Tasting Food, Tasting Freedom: Excursions into Eating, Culture and the Past*. Boston: Beacon.

Mintz, S., and Richard Price. 1992 [1976]. *The Birth of African-American Culture: An Anthropological Perspective*. Boston: Beacon.

Mitchell, R., and C.M. Hall. 2003. "Consuming Tourists: Food Tourism Consumer Behaviour". In *Food Tourism Around the World: Development, Management and Markets*, edited by C.M. Hall, L. Sharples, R. Mitchell, N. Macionis and B. Cambourne, 60–80. Oxford: Elsevier.

Moisio, Risto, Eric J. Arnould and Linda L. Price. 2004. "Between Mothers and Markets: Constructing Family Identity Through Homemade Food". *Journal of Consumer Culture* 4:361–84.

Moufakkir, O., and Y. Reisinger, eds. 2013. *The Host Gaze in Global Tourism*. Wallingford, UK: CABI.

Musa, Said. 2001. "Prime Minster's Statement Following Hurricane Iris". https://reliefweb.int/report/belize/prime-ministers-statement-following-recent-world-events-and-hurricane-iris.
Naccarato, P., and K. Lebesco. 2012. *Culinary Capital*. London: Bloomsbury Academic.
Neuhaus, Jessamyn. 2003. *Manly Meals and Mom's Home Cooking: Cookbooks and Gender in Modern America*. Baltimore: Johns Hopkins University Press.
News 5. 2002. "Iris Remembered One Year After". http://edition.channel5belize.com/archives/16397.
———. 2009. "Placencia Residents Assess Damages after Tremor". http://edition.channel5belize.com/archives/1603.
———. 2017. "Placencia Peninsula Readies for Harvest Caye Tourists". http://edition.channel5belize.com/archives/147019.
Oceana. 2010. "Belize Bans Bottom Trawling in Exclusive Economic Zone". Press release. http://oceana.org/press-center/press-releases/belize-bans-bottom-trawling-exclusive-economic-zone.
Palacio, J. 1988. "May the New Belize Creole Please Rise". Paper presented at the SPEAR National Cross-Cultural Awareness Conference, Belize City, 26–27 March.
Palacio, Myrtle. 2018. "Redefining Ethnicity in Post-independent Belize: A Case of the Garifuna and Creole". Paper presented at the Cultural Syncretism in the Caribbean conference, Belmopan, Belize, 4–11 March.
Peddicord, Kathleen. 2014. "Four Countries That Welcome American Retirees". *US News and World Report*, 17 June. https://money.usnews.com/money/blogs/on-retirement/2014/06/17/4-countries-that-welcome-american-retirees.
Perez, A.A. 2003. "Assessment of Socioeconomic Conditions at Placencia, Hopkins and Monkey River in Belize". Report prepared for Coastal Resources Comanagement Project, Centre for Resource Management and Environmental Studies, University of the West Indies.
Peters, Tom. 1997. "The Brand Called You". *Fast Company*, 31 August. https://www.fastcompany.com/28905/brand-called-you.
Phillips, Joan L. 1999. "Tourist-Oriented Prostitution in Barbados". In *Sun, Sex and Gold: Tourism and Sex Work in the Caribbean*, edited by Kamala Kempadoo, 183–200. Lanham, MD: Rowman and Littlefield.
Picard, David, and Sonja Buchberger. 2013. *Couchsurfing Cosmopolitanisms: Can Tourism Make a Better World?* Bielefeld: Transcript.
Picard, David, and Michael A. Di Giovine. 2014. *Tourism and the Power of Otherness: Seductions of Difference*. Bristol, UK: Channel View.
Pilcher, J.M. 1996. "Tamales or Timbales: Cuisine and the Formation of Mexican National Identity, 1821–1911". *The Americas* 53 (2): 193–216.
PPC (Placencia Producers Cooperative). 1987. Annual Report.

Quan, Shuai, and Ning Wang. 2004. "Towards a Structural Model of the Tourist Experience: An Illustration from Food Experiences in Tourism". *Tourism Management* 25 (3): 297–305.

Ramos, Adele. 2010. "Belize Totally Bans Bottom Trawling". *Amandala* [Belize], 10 December. http://amandala.com.bz/news/belize-totally-bans-bottom-trawling/.

———. 2013. "Norwegian Gets Green Light for Harvest Caye Port". *Amandala* [Belize], 23 July. http://amandala.com.bz/news/norwegian-green-light-harvest-caye-port/.

Ray, Krishendu. 2016. *The Ethnic Restaurateur*. New York: Bloomsbury.

Red Cross (International Federation of Red Cross and Red Crescent Societies). 2001. "Belize: Hurricane Iris Appeal No. 33/01, Operations Update No. 1". https://reliefweb.int/report/belize/belize-hurricane-iris-appeal-no-3301-operations-update-no-1.

Reeser, D. 2012. "Food and Buckets: Mobile Treats and Identity in Belize". *Views from the ANThill* [blog], 20 July. http://www.recycledminds.com/2012/07/views-from-anthill-of-food-and-buckets.html.

Roudometof, Victor. 2016. *Glocalization: A Critical Introduction*. New York: Routledge.

Salazar, N.B. 2010. *Envisioning Eden: Mobilizing Imaginaries in Tourism and Beyond*. New York: Berghahn.

Salazar, N.B., and N.H.H. Graburn, eds. 2014. *Tourism Imaginaries: Anthropological Approaches*. New York: Berghahn.

Sammells, Clare A. 2014. "Haute Traditional Cuisines: How UNESCO's List of Intangible Heritage Links the Cosmopolitan to the Local". In *Edible Identities: Food as Cultural Heritage*, edited by Ronda L. Brulotte and Michael A. Di Giovine, 141–58. Farnham, UK: Ashgate.

———. 2017. "'Local-politan' Gastronomy and Bolivian Cuisine: How the Cosmopolitan Is Forged from the Local". In *Cosmopolitanism and Tourism: Rethinking Theory and Practice*, edited by Robert Shepherd, 163–77. Minneapolis, MN: Lexington.

San Pedro Sun. 2001. "Placencia Post-Hurricane Report". *San Pedro Sun* [Ambergris Caye, Belize], 11 October. https://www.sanpedrosun.com/old/01-421.html.

———. 2009. "Powerful 7.1 Quake Shakes Belize, Honduras and Mexico". *San Pedro Sun* [Ambergris Caye, Belize], 4 June. https://www.sanpedrosun.com/old/09-213.html.

Shepherd, Robert. 2017. *Cosmopolitanism and Tourism: Rethinking Theory and Practice*. Lanham, MD: Lexington.

Shoman, Assad. 2010. "Reflections on Ethnicity and Nation in Belize". Working document 9. Mexico: Proyecto AFRODESC/EURESCL.

Shoman, Lisa. 2018. "Avocados, Cops and Stupidity". Breaking Belize News, 17 March. https://www.breakingbelizenews.com/2018/03/17/on-avocados-cops-and-stupidity/.

SIB (Statistical Institute of Belize). 2013. *Belize Population and Housing Census 2010: Country Report*. Belmopan, Belize: SIB.

Sidali, Katia Laura, Elisabeth Kastenholz and Rossella Bianchi. 2015. "Food Tourism, Niche Markets and Products in Rural Tourism: Combining the Intimacy Model and the Experience Economy as a Rural Development Strategy". *Journal of Sustainable Tourism* 23 (8–9): 1179–97.

Simmons, D.C., Jr. 2001. *Confederate Settlements in British Honduras*. Jefferson, NC: McFarland.

Skinner, J., and D. Theodossopoulos, eds. 2011. *Great Expectations: Imagination and Anticipation in Tourism*. New York: Berghahn.

Sluder, L. 2010. "Key Dates in Development of Tourism in Belize". http://www.belizefirst.com/documents/BelizeHistoryofTourism.pdf.

———. 2016. *Easy Belize: How to Live, Retire, Work and Buy Property in Belize, the English-Speaking, Frost-Free Paradise on the Caribbean Coast*. 2nd ed. Asheville, NC: Equator.

Spang, Lyra. 2011. "Paradise in a Bun". *Indiana Food Review* 1 (1). http://www.indianafoodreview.com/archives/issue-1/paradise-in-a-bun.

———, comp. 2013. "Oral Histories: Data from Transcribed Interviews Conducted with More Than Twenty Members of Placencia Village from 2012 to 2013, Including Village Elders". Typescript.

———. 2014. "A Real Belizean: Food, Identity and Tourism in Belize". PhD diss., University of Indiana.

Spang, R.L. 2000. *The Invention of the Restaurant: Paris and Modern Gastronomic Culture*. Cambridge, MA: Harvard University Press.

Strong, R.C. 2002. *Feast: A History of Grand Eating*. London: Jonathan Cape.

Sutherland, A. 1998. *The Making of Belize: Globalization in the Margins*. Westport, CT: Bergin and Garvey.

Swenson, Rebecca. 2013. "Domestic Divo? Televised Treatments of Masculinity, Femininity and Food". In *Food and Culture: A Reader*, 3rd ed., edited by Carole Counihan and Penny Van Esterik, 36–53. New York: Routledge.

Taylor, John P. 2001. "Authenticity and Sincerity in Tourism". *Annals of Tourism Research* 28 (1): 7–26.

Tinker, Irene. 2003. "Street Foods: Traditional Microenterprise in a Modernizing World". *International Journal of Politics, Culture, and Society* 16 (3): 331–49.

Trubek, A.B. 2000. *Haute Cuisine: How the French Invented the Culinary Profession.* Philadelphia: University of Pennsylvania Press.

Truong, V. Dao. 2018. "Tourism, Poverty Alleviation, and the Informal Economy: The Street Vendors of Hanoi, Vietnam". *Tourism Recreation Research* 43 (1): 52–67.

Turner, Victor. 1969. *The Ritual Process: Structure and Anti-Structure.* Chicago: Aldine.

UNESCO. 2018. *Belize Barrier Reef Reserve System.* https://whc.unesco.org/en/list/764.

United States. 2010. *American Community Survey.* Washington, DC: US Census Bureau.

UNWTO (United Nations World Trade Organization). 2012. *Global Report on Food Tourism.* Madrid: UNWTO.

Urry, J. 1990. *The Tourist Gaze: Leisure and Travel in Contemporary Societies.* London: Sage.

———. 2002. *The Tourist Gaze: Leisure and Travel in Contemporary Societies.* 2nd ed. London: Sage.

Volkman, T.A. 1990. "Visions and Revisions: Toraja Culture and the Tourist Gaze". *American Ethnologist* 17 (1): 91–110.

Weintraub, J., and Krishan Kuma, eds. 1997. *Public and Private in Thought and Practice: Perspectives on a Grand Dichotomy.* Chicago: University of Chicago Press.

Whitaker, Jan. 2005. "Domesticating the Restaurant: Marketing the Anglo-American Home". In *From Betty Crocker to Feminist Food Studies: Critical Perspectives on Women and Food*, edited by Arlene Avakian and Barbara Haber, 89–106. Amherst: University of Massachussetts Press.

Wilk, Richard. 1995. "Learning to Be Local in Belize: Global Systems of Common Difference". In *Worlds Apart: Modernity Through the Prism of the Local*, edited by D. Miller, 110–33. New York: Routledge.

———. 1997. "A Critique of Desire: Distaste and Dislike in Consumer Behavior". *Consumption, Markets and Culture* 1 (2): 175–96.

———. 1999. "'Real Belizean Food': Building Local Identity in the Transnational Caribbean". *American Anthropologist* 101 (2): 244–55.

———. 2006. *Home Cooking in the Global Village: Caribbean Food from Buccaneers to Ecotourists.* New York: Berg.

———. 2008. "A Taste of Home: The Cultural and Economic Significance of European Food Exports to the Colonies". In *Food and Globalization: Consumption, Markets and Politics in the Modern World*, edited by A. Nützenadel and F. Trentmann, 93–108. Oxford: Berg.

———. 2012. "Nationalizing the Ordinary Dish: Rice and Beans in Belize". In *Rice and Beans: A Unique Dish in a Hundred Places*, edited by Richard Wilk and Livia Barbosa, 203–19. London: Berg.

Wilk, Richard, and M. Chapin. 1988. "Ethnic Minorities in Belize: Mopan, Kekchi and Garifuna". *Cultural Survival International Working Papers*, Cambridge, MA.

Williams-Forson, Psyche A. 2006. *Building Houses Out of Chicken Legs: Black Women, Food and Power*. Chapel Hill: University of North Carolina Press.

Wilson, P.J. 1969. "Reputation and Respectability: A Suggestion for Caribbean Ethnology". *Man* 4 (1): 70–84.

Yoder, Don. 1972. "Folk Cookery". In *Folklore and Folklife: An Introduction*, edited by R.M. Dorson, 325–50. Chicago: University of Chicago Press.

Zhu, Yujie. 2012. "Performing Heritage: Rethinking Authenticity in Tourism". *Annals of Tourism Research* 39 (3): 1495–513.

INDEX

Page numbers in italics indicate figures.

achiote shrub (*Bixa orellana*), 229, 235. *See also* recado
African ancestry: of Garifuna, 141; of Kriol, 139
African diaspora and Kriol people, 140
African heritage food, 154
agency in identity work, 123
aliens as inhabitants of Placencia, 89, 94–97
all-inclusive resorts and Belizean cuisine, 167. *See also* foreign-owned resorts
Ambergris Caye, 44, 93
amenities at tourist destinations, 93
"America" as food category, 155
American migration to Belize, history of, 157
angelfish, mislabelling of, 43
annatto shrub (*Bixa orellana*), 235
anthropology, practice of, 2
Appadurai, Arjun, 6, 9–10, 162, 207, 218–19
armadillo as bush meat, 134
Armelagos, George, 6
Association of Indigenous Anthropologists, 3
Atala, Alex (Brazilian chef), 207
atole de maiz. *See* caan lab, definition of
Aunt Linda's (restaurant), 197

authenticity: and cultural marketing, 84–88; and cosmopolitanism, 59–60; on guided tours, 183–84; novelty and, 57–58; and postmodernity, 60; as staged, 121–23; and subjective definitions of local cuisine, 69; of tourist experience, 53–54, 56, 105; as viewed through socio-economic class, 60–61
avocado suppression unit, 105–8

baby boomers as retirees, 91
baleadas, 96
barracuda, 169, 201
barrier reef. *See* Belize Barrier Reef Reserve (World Heritage Site)
Barrow, Mrs Kim, 229
barter system, 178
Battle of St George's Caye, 140
Beck, Ulrich, 55
Belize: agricultural sector, 211; economy of, 3, 106; Caribbean identity of, 141; cultural diversity of, 5, 9; map of, 2; nationalism and cuisine, 10–11; promotion as expat site, 91
Belizean cuisine, 171, 204–7, 209–13, 226; development of, 216–22. *See also* Belizean food
Belizean East Indian food, 143
Belizean food: categories displayed as Venn diagram, *163;* as a culin

259

Belizean food (*continued*)
ary category, 167, 168; dominated by Kriol cuisine, 162, 170; foreign origins of, 161; future of, 223–25; gastronationalism and, 141–42; lack of innovation in restaurants, 199–204; local perceptions of, 86; marginalization of, 153–55; national cuisine, 170; and national identity, 136–37; as second-class cuisine, 195–98; tourist experience with in public sphere, 174; visitor perceptions of, 78–80. *See also* Belizean cuisine

Belizean foodscape, diversification of, 212

Belizean identity, 44–46, 134; and code-switching, 115; conflating Kriol identity with, 140; and ethnicity, 139; models of, 137; participation in multiple cultures, 120; racialization of, 137–38; tour guides and, 125

Belizeanized "turkey dinner", 108

Belizean Kriol heritage, 131, 138–39

Belizean Maya, 97

Belizean restaurant in the US, 167

Belize Barrier Reef Reserve (World Heritage Site), 43, 229

Belize-continuum pile sort, 149–50

Belize Tourism Board (BTB), 1, 93; establishment of, 27; marketing of food tourism, 49–50; and pluralistic nationalism, 137, 162; promotion of retirement programme, 34, 89, 94; support for development of national cuisine, 208

Bella Vista, 95

"Beyond Rice and Beans" (Brown), 238n1

Bixa orellana, 235

Bizarre Foods (television programme), 56, 78, 174

black corn porridge with allspice, 169

black dinna. *See* chimole

black pepper locally produced, 211

boil-up, 78; definition of, 231

Bolland, Nigel O., 136–37

Booze Traveler (television programme), 174

born Belizean (emic label), 81

Bourdieu, Pierre, 64–65, 123

Brazilian cuisine, 214

bread kind, definition of, 231

British colonialism in Belize, 139, 140

Brown, Joshua Samuel, 238n1

Browne, K.E., 126

brown flour, definition of, 231

Brulotte, Ronda, 9, 11

Bruner, Edward, 5, 51

bucket food, 80

bundiga, 154, 169, 243n15; definition of, 231

Bunten, A.C., 114, 116, 120, 122, 123, 125

Burg Wartenstein conference (1978), 2

Butler, R.W., 92

Byrsonima crassifolia, 233, 238n7

caan lab, 146; definition of, 231

Cabral family, 16

cacao from Toledo, 228, 230

Cadbury's chocolate, 230

caldo, 165, 169; definition of, 231

Calhoun, Craig, 59

callaloo, 218

Canadians: development in Belize, 14; tourists, 120

Cancian, Frank, 199

INDEX

Carib ancestry of Garifuna, 141
Caribbean colonial history, food representative of, 154
Caribbean Creole history, 126
Caribbean cuisine, 162, 228
Caribbean identity of Belizean food, 79–80
Carludovica palmate, 234
Carnival Cruise Lines, 47
cart vendors, 98–100. *See also* taco stands
catch and kill, 126, 241n4
Caye Caulker, 44, 93
Cayo District, 100
ceviche, 80
Chan, Yuk Wah, 9
chaya greens, 218
cheeses locally produced, 211
chefs: avoidance of Belizean dishes by, 196–98; and gendered nature of profession, 171; males predominate in Belize, 192–93
Chicago Belizean Garifuna restaurant, 168
chickens, raising of, 18, 19
chicken: in Belizean diet, 80; served on tours, 181–82; stewed, and visitor perception of Belizean food, 78
chimole, 78, 145–46, 151, 243n9; definition of, 231
Chinese cuisine, 214
Chinese: food as culinary other, 143, 155–57; history of immigration to Belize, 155–56
Chinese-owned grocery stores, 89, 105, 109, 156; selling tortillas, 100
Chinese restaurants, 209; in Placencia, 110

chocho (chayote squash), 229
Cho, Juan and Abelina, 230
chocolate locally produced, 211, 230
chow mein, 156
chu'uk kwa, 169, 218; definition of, 232
Cittarium pica. *See* wiliks/whilks/whelks, definition of
Cochinita Pibil. *See* pibil, definition of
coco (taro root), 228
coconut as marker of Belizean identity, 145
coconut macaroons, 128
Coconut Man (craftsman), 128
coconut milk, 143
coconut oil: associated with Kriol and Garifuna, 143; definition of, 232; economic use of, 19; grating coconuts for, 177
coconut rice, 79
coconut trees, 199; and lethal yellowing disease, 170
code-switching, 117, 132; in Creole economics, 126; definition of, 115. *See also* culinary code-switching
coffee locally produced, 211
Cohen, Erik, 53, 55, 57, 59, 122
cohune cabbage (curried), 155, 169, 218; definition of, 232
cohune oil, definition of, 232
coleslaw Belizean style, 184
colonial-era food staples, 100
comal, definition of, 232
commodification. *See* self-commodification
commodified persona, 114; definition of, 116. *See also* self-commodification

common difference, 136
communicative competence, code-switching as, 115
conch fishing, 24, 43
conch soup, 201; definition of, 232
cool spot, 14, 238n3, 240n12; Kriol-owned, 99; Ms Radiance's, 178–81; in Placencia Village, 80; private into public space, 177; Spanish-owned, 99
cornflakes, 158–59, 160, 164
corn foods, 98, 100. *See also* taco stands
corn lab. *See* caan lab, definition of
corn tacos, 151–52
corn tortillas, 169, 218; food served with, 231, 232, 233; pibil, 235
cosmopolitanism, 48, 116–17, 119, 125, 129, 239n5: and common difference, 136; definition of, 55, 116; and search for authenticity, 59; *See also* culinary cosmopolitanism
Costa Rican cuisine, comparison of Belizean cuisine to, 67
The Cove (resort), 24
cowfoot soup, 78; definition of, 232
craboo, definition of, 233
creole foods, 169
Creole economics, 126
Creole Gial Guava Jelly, 130–31
cross-cultural comparison of foodways, 90
cross-cultural experiences through food, 105–6
cross-cultural foods, 152
cruise ships: Carnival Cruise Lines, 47; Norwegian Cruise Lines, 47; tourism port (Harvest Caye), 31, 47
cuisine, 11; definition of, 6–8

cuisine development: affected by culinary cosmopolitanism, 65; immigrants influence on, 112–13; influenced by hegemonic nationalism, 219; in the post-colonial world, 3; tourist influence on, 48, 58
culantro, definition of, 233
culinary capital, 63–64; related to cultural capital, 65
culinary classification of Belizean food, 141–47
culinary code-switching, 5, 8, 9, 54, 65, 132, 135, 183; definition of, 117; examples of, 118–20, 128
culinary cosmopolitanism, 8, 48, 55–63, 65, 205, 246n3; and culinary capital, 63–64; degrees of, 129–30; and mead making, 239n3. *See also* cosmopolitanism
culinary heritage, 11, 97
culinary identities of Belize, 1
Culinary Institute of America: graduates of, 186–87, 193–94; programmes offered in Belize, 208
"culinary other" in Belizean cuisine, 142–47
culinary tour company, 4–5
culinary tourism, 8, 54, 135
Culinary Tourism: An Emerging Trend (BTB 2017 conference theme), 208
cultural affiliation of immigrants, 96–97. *See also* identity practices
cultural capital, 65
cultural marketing of Belizean cuisine, 84–86, 185, 220, 223–24; of Kriol cuisine, 218
Culture on Tour: Ethnographies of Travel (Bruner), 5

culture tourism, 47, 49
Cuniculus paca (lowland paca), 234, 238n8
curry cohune cabbage, 78
Cusack, I., 208, 219
cuttobrutte, 128

darasa, definition of, 233
DeSoucey, Michael, 10, 161
dessert foods. *See* sweets
Destination Belize (magazine), 174, 208
Di Giovine, Michael, 9, 11, 57, 59, 105
Diner, Hasia, 104
Diners, Drive-Ins and Dives (Food Network programme), 77–78
Driscoll's strawberries, 107
drug trade, effects of, 40–41
dukunu, 145–46; definition of, 233
Dunn, Bishop Edward Arthur, 20–21
Durkheim, Émile, 57

earthquake (2009), damage from, 31
East Indian-descent communities, 236
East Indian foods, 153–55
ecotourism, 47, 49
Edible Identities (Brulotte and DiGiovine), 9
education opportunities, 36
Eiley, John, 15
E-Lee Hotel, 24
El Salvador, immigrants from, 14, 94–95, 143
Elvi's restaurant, 207
emigration: for education, 36; from First World countries, 92; Kriol and Garifuna families, 35; and tourism, 92

entrepreneurship and identity work, 125–33
Equitorial Guinea, emergence of national cuisine in, 208, 219
escabeche, 145, 147–48; definition of, 233
Esquivel, Manuel, 26
Ethiopian cuisine, 214
ethnicity in Belize, 139
Ethnic Restaurateur (Ray), 110
ethnography of tourism development, 1, 5
exotic/authentic/novelty, conception of, 58, 60
exotic other, 51, 56
expats: influence on foodscape, 109–13. *See also* First World immigrants and retirees; North America: immigrants from
expat service businesses, 91–92; websites, 101
exploration stage of the tourism-area life cycle, 92
Euro-American comfort food, 192
Eurocentrism: in culinary heritage, 11
European colonialism, influence on national cuisines, 214
European heritage in Belize, 139

Facebook survey, 109
face work, 115
Fajans, Jane, 6, 207
familiar foods category of food tourist, 54, 64, 67, 85
Fanti language, 233
Farb, P., 6
farm animals, 18
farm innovation in Belize, 211
fast-food: tourist expectations of

chain restaurants, 73; served at resorts, 228; tropicalization of, 85
Faux family, 16
Feifer, W., 60
female chefs, 207
Fieri, Guy, 77–78
fine dining in Belize, 192
fire-hearth cooking, 176, 245n1
First World immigrants and retirees, 91, 104–5, 110–13, 240n1
fisheries in decline, 27, 28, 43, 239n12
fishermen: male identity of, 44–45; as tour guides, 27. *See also* fishing
fishermen dishes, 169
fish hash, 201; definition of, 233
fishing cooperative. *See* Placencia Producers Cooperative
fishing: in Placencia, 16, 17, 21, 22–24, 27; by women, 17, 22, 44; on tours, 183
Flamboyant Tree (restaurant), 25
Flavours of Belize (magazine), 208
fly fishing, 27; home-cooked meals when, 182
food and nationalism, 139
food categories and cultural context, 135
food experiences, and comparison of cuisines, 65–69
food-focused travel, 80
food marketing in tourism industry, 166
Food Network, 168, 195, 213
foodscapes in tourism zones, 69
food shopping in Belize, 105; informal channels for, 106–8
food systems, 36–40
food tourism: experiences, 54–55; marketing of, 49–50; popularity of food-focused travel, 80. *See also* tourism typologies
food venues in Placencia Village and on Placencia Peninsula, *81*
foodways, 3, 4, 9; immigrant influence on, 89–90, 97–98, 109–13; tourist experiences of, 135–36
foreigner: definition of, 90; as immigrants, 101; as residents of Placencia, 89, 90–91
foreign-owned resorts: employing foreign chefs, 192; unimpressive food served at, 182
founding families of Placencia, 16
Freeman, Michael, 209–10, 212, 218
French cuisine, 172, 185–87
fried doughnuts, 99
Friends of Nature. *See* Southern Environmental Association
frontline personnel in tourism industry, 117, 220; and creole economics, 126; tour guides as, 120; use of host gaze by, 123
fruits: abundance of in Placencia diet, 18; seasonal availability of, 199; tourist expectations of, 76, 78. *See also* vegetables
fry jacks, 79; definition of, 233
fry rice, 156
fufu. *See* hudut

gacho, 239n9; definition of, 233
Galley (restaurant), 30
Garbutt family, 15
Garifuna, 12–13, 96, 139, 237–38n2; food associated with, 233, 234, 236, 153–55, 163, 207; and hegemonic nationalism, 137; heritage of, 141

Garifuna restaurant featured on TV programme, 78
garnaches, definition of, 233
gastronationalism, 8, 135, 161, 167, 170, 216, 237n6; definition of, 10–11; research on, 141–42
gastronome category of food tourist, 54, 56; linked to culinary cosmopolitanism, 64
gastro-touristic cuisines, 69
gender inequality in restaurant industry, 171–72
generic "tropical" tourist cuisine, contrasted with inspired Belizean cuisine, 207
Georgetown and ties with Seine Bight, 28
Ghana, dukunu eaten in, 146
gibnut: 134; definition of, 234
gift exchange, 178–79
Giuffre, Pattie, 171
global citizens, locals as, 114
Goffman, Erving, 115, 121
Golden Corral Buffet (Mennonite restaurant), 154
Goody, Jack, 162, 186
government support: of national cuisine, 207–8; of tourism, 27
Graburn, Nelson, 51, 57, 67, 69
Gracillaria species of seaweed, 211
Gravari-Barbas, Maria, 51
Great Dog, definition of, 234
Great Expectations: Imagination and Expectation in Tourism (Skinner and Theodossopoulos), 69
green corn tamales. *See* dukunu, definition of; tamalitos, definition of
Griffith, Lauren Miller, 246n8
grocery stores: Chinese-owned, 89, 105, 100, 109; requests for special items, 109–113
ground food, definition of, 234
Guatemala, immigrants from, 13, 14, 94–95, 143; Kekchi-speaking Maya, 96
Guatemalan food in Belize, 80
guidebooks, information on Belizean cuisine in, 71

habitus: and culinary cosmopolitanism, 65; informing imagination, 69
Hall, C. Michael, 54–55, 57, 64, 67, 91
hamburgers, 157, 159
hand-wash-hand (Belizean expression), 178
Harley's department store (Brodies), 19
Harris, Deborah, 171
Harvest Caye, 31, 47
hegemonic nationalism category, 137, 161, 169; and marginalization of Maya foods, 166; undermines inclusiveness of national cuisine, 216
Heldke, L., 58, 105, 124
Hispanic culture. *See* Spanish-speaking immigrants in Belize
Hokey Pokey Water Taxi, 32
home cooking, 211; as commodity, 178; as criteria for Belize-continuum pile sort, 148–49; associated with women, 171; importance of, 147–52, 162; influence of on "inspired Belizean cuisine", 205–6; and Kriol gastronationalism, 147; and national cuisine, 220; personal connections formed with, 183; practices of, 11; in the public sphere,

172, 173–77; tour guides serving, 181–85
home shops, 20
Honduran immigrants: baleadas, 96; cool spot run by, 100; immigrants from, 13, 14, 94–95, 143
Hopkins Village (Garifuna community), 168; Chef Rob Pronk, 193
host gaze, 5, 9, 48, 51, 54; as challenge to tourist gaze, 219; cosmopolitanism and, 119; and lack of Belizean dishes, 200–201; self-commodification and, 116. *See also* tourist gaze
hot dogs, 157, 159
housing markets, effect of tourism on, 105
Houston, Lynn Marie, 162
hudut, 154, 169, 201; definition of, 234
Huitric, M., 27
hunting in Placencia, 17
Hurricane Hattie (1961), 28, 29
Hurricane Iris (2001), 28–30; long-term effects of, 30–31; new development after, 94
Hyde, Evan X, 140
Hymes, Dell, 115

identity politics, 161
identity practices, 9, 96–97, 114; and code-switching, 115; through cuisine, 10, 134; tour guides involved in, 120–25. *See also* Belizean identity
identity work, 115, 118; and entrepreneurship, 125–33; power and agency in, 123–24
imagination, role of in tourist expectations, 69

immigrants: as entrepreneurs, 96; from China and Taiwan, 37; from El Salvador, 14; from Guatemala and Honduras, 13, 14; from North America, 13–14; in food business, 89; Spanish-speakers, 89, 95
immigration to Placencia, 89, 102
Independence, 28; high school established in, 36
Indian cuisine, 10, 155, 214; restaurants in Belize, 209
indigenous anthropology, 3
indigenous foodie category of food tourist, 54
informal food businesses and catch and kill, 126
informal markets impacted by tourism, 105
informants: and culinary code-switching, 54; tourist typologies according to, 52
innovation in Belizean restaurants: devaluation of Belizean dishes, 200–203; and economic concerns, 199; lack of creative invention, 199–200; lack of knowledge, 204
The Innovator's Situation (Cancian), 199
insider knowledge and food procurement, 108
inspired Belizean cuisine, 86, 205, 222, 224
international cuisine in Placencia restaurants, 193–95
International Living report for Belize, 91–92
interviews with foreigner immigrants, 103–4
interviews with tourists, 48–50, 56;

according to food tourism typology, 54–55; comparing cuisines, 65–69; concerning expectations, 73–78, 83–84; descriptions of Belizean foods, 78–80, 181–82; and pre-trip research, 71–72; terms employed, 73

introduced food items, 147

involvement, development, consolidation stage of the tourism-area life cycle, 92–93

Italian cuisine, category of, 155, 215

Iyora-Diaz, Steffan Igor, 6

James, Hermina, 20

Japanese cuisine, 214

jerk chicken in Belize, 128

jippy jappa, 165, 218; definition of, 234

johnnycakes, definition of, 234

jute (river snail), 229

Kekchi Maya, 96, 97, 139, 233; use of recado by, 235

King Fisher (hotel), 24

kinship ties and reciprocity exchanges, 178–79, 189; through tour guides serving home-cooking, 183

Kraft culinary demonstration, 212

Kriol (Belizean), 4, 12, 14, 96, 97, 237n1; and hegemonic nationalism, 137–39; home cooking as defining Belizean food, 162

Kriol bread, 175; definition of, 234; and wheat flour-based foods, 100, 143–44

Kriol communities, trading among, 19

Kriol culinary style, 152–53

Kriol food: offered in restaurants, 207; prioritizing of, 141–42

Kriol home in Placencia Village, 175

Kriol-Garifuna cultural dynamics, 14, 141

Kriol identity, 138–41; through food, 143–47

Kriol Language Project, 139

Kriol Sunday dinner: adoption of by Mayan Belizeans, 146; as signature food, 76, 168

Kuylen, Sean, 200, 205, 208, 212, 213; classical training, 226–28; discussion of inspired Belizean cuisine, 226–30

labour-intensive jobs, 95

lancha, definition of, 234

Leach, Edmund, 57

Lebesco, K., 63

Leslie, Doris, 24, 25

Leslie family, 16

Leslie, Mark, 121

Little, Kenneth, 60

livestock, 18; raising of pigs, 19

Lizarraga, Ian, 207, 208

lobster fishing: regulation on, 24, 43; trade with North America, 22

lobster, stewed, 201

local: as a contested term, 89, 240n2; inhabitants, 48

local foods: expense of, 170, 191–92; lack of, 200–203; history of marginalization, 209; tourist expectations for, 74–75; typology of, 85–86; use of, 228–30

local ingredients, 228–30. See also local foods

logging as iconic symbol, 44

long-water beans, definition of, 234–35
Lonely Planet (guidebook), 70, 76
lowland paca (*Cuniculus paca*), 234
lunch specials, importance of, 190

macaroni and cheese, 157; as example of overlap between home cooking and professional cooking, 172; Kraft, 146
MacCannell, Dean, 57, 121–23
manatees, 42. *See also* sea meat, definition of
Mango Creek, 96, 98
mangrove forests, destruction of, 44
Marie Sharp's processed foods, 211, 242n11
Martinique, Creole economics in, 126
master narratives, 51
Matilda foot. *See* bundiga, definition of
Mauss, Marcel, 178
Maya archaeology, 49
Maya Beach, 14
Maya cooking: jippy jappa, 234; lancha cooking technique, 234; use of corn in poch, 235; use of culantro in, 233
Maya food, 163, 164–65, 218, 244–45n25, 245–46n7
Maya people, 12, 96–97; as early inhabitants of Placencia Peninsula, 15; Belizean identity contested, 139; foodways incorporated into cuisine, 207; use of cohune oil, 232
Maya Beach, 12, 13
Maya hot-dog stand, 79
McDonald's, 10
mead making, 239n3

Medina, Laura K., 137, 162
Mennonites, 143, 211; food associated with, 153; Golden Corral Buffet restaurant, 154
Mestizo Belizean food, 163
Mestizo food culture: perceptions of, 144; in Placencia, 98–99; in restaurant cuisine, 207
Mestizo people, 12, 14, 96
Mexican cuisine, 215
Mexican food in Belize, 80, 155
Mexico, comparison of Belizean cuisine to cuisine of, 67–68
migration: on Placencia Peninsula, 32, 34; business of, 92
Ministry of Tourism, establishment of, 27
Mintz, Sidney, 76, 186, 196, 209
Mirna's Guava Jelly, 130
Mitchell, R., 54–55, 57, 64, 67
modernist mode of thinking, 60
Monkey River, 79
Mopan Maya, 139, 235
moral economy of food, 189–95
Moroccan cuisine, 214
Moufakkir, Omar, 51, 219
Mr Earl (food vendor), 19
Ms B. (food entrepreneur), 176
Ms Brenda (cool spot proprietor), 128, 242n7
Ms Radiance's cool spot, 189–90. *See also* Williams, Radiance
Mughlai food, 218–19

Naccarato, P., 63
nance. *See* craboo, definition of
national cuisine, 9–10, 222; emergence in post-colonial times, 207–8, 214–16; influenced by dominant

culture group, 161; influenced by home cooking and professional, 220–22; requirements for emergence of, 209–11; tourist gaze influencing, 220
National Garifuna Council, 139
national identity models, 136–37
National Kriol Council, 139, 140
National Maya Council, 139
nature tourism, 47, 49
Nautical Inn, 29
New Belizean cuisine, 205. *See also* inspired Belizean cuisine
North America: as food category, 143, 155; immigrants from 13–14, 89, 90–92, 104–5, 211; tourists from, 49, 118, 120. *See also* expats
North Americanized restaurants, 82–83
Northern Cooperative, 22
Norwegian Cruise Lines, 47
novelty and authenticity in the tourist experience, 58, 124
Nuñez, Marcia, 207, 208

Ocean Motion Real Estate, 26
Ocean Spray cranberries, 107
okra, 218; as ingredient in conch soup, 232
Omar's (restaurant), 30
Omar's Creole Grub (restaurant), 85, 130, 218; use of code-switching at, 129
Organization of American States and support for culinary training, 208
otherness concept, 57
overfishing, 23–24

paca. *See* lowland paca (*Cuniculus paca*)
Palacio, Joseph, 139, 238n2
panades, 151, 240n11; definition of, 235
panades lady, 99
pan-Africanism and Kriol people, 140
pancakes, 157–58, 159, 160
parrotfish, mislabelling of, 43
participant observation, 51, 115
peccaries, 238n9
performance: and staged authenticity, 121–23; and self-commodification, 116
Peruvian cuisine, 214
Peter, Tom, 116
pibil, 78; definition of, 235
Picard, David, 57, 59, 105
pigtail, definition of, 235
pig raising, 18, 19
Pilcher, Jeffrey, 6
pirates, 15
Placencia Kriol identity, 143
Placencia Peninsula: businesses catering to locals, 131–32; catch and kill strategies, 126; census of 2010, 94; coconut population in decline, 170; contemporary community on, 41–42; development and consolidation phase on, 93; dining establishments on, *81*, 93; drug trade effects on, 40–41; emigration, 35–36; environment of, 42–44, 46; First World residents on, 94; history of, 15–16; international ties, 41–42; investment in, 93–94; Main Street shift post-hurricane, 30; map of, *13*; migration to, 32, 34; new appreciation for local dishes, 213;

Placencia Peninsula (*continued*)
population by cultural group, 33, 95; as postmodern ethnoscape, 97; restaurant industry impacted by foreigners, 110–13; Spanish-speaking immigrants to, 95; tourism-area life cycle of, 92–93; tourism impact on food scene, 80–84; trade systems, 19; transportation improvements on, 27

Placencia Producers Cooperative, 21–24, 27

Placencia restaurants: foreign-owned compared to locally owned, 187–89; high-end international cuisine, 193–95; limited Belizean dishes offered, 196–98; limited menu in, 172; specials board, 194

Placencia tourism: early years, 24–25; self-commodification and, 116

Placencia Village, 1, 5, 9, 168; Belizean food in, 167, 174; class division in, 17, 19; creole foods served in restaurants, 169–70; dining establishments in, 80, 81, 82, 93; earthquake damage in, 31; economic development in, 21–24; food-services industry in, 14–15; food systems in, 16–20, 36–40; gardens in, 17; home-cook entrepreneurs in, 178; history of, 15–25; Hurricane Iris long-term effects, 30–31; hurricane damage, 28; impact of foreigners on foodscape, 89–94, 109–13; as an international tourism destination, 82, 166; tension with Garifuna, 154; ties with Silk Grass, 28; tourism-area life cycle in, 92–93; tourism in post-independence, 26–28; tourism in pre-independence, 25; as tourism site, 12–15; trade systems, 19; transnational nature of, 42; street food in, 174

pluralistic nationalism, 137, 146, 164–65

poch, 78, 165, 169; definition of, 235

positionality, 2, 3; of the author, 3–5

post-colonialism and national cuisine, 9–10, 207–8, 214–15

post-modern "post tourist", 59–60

potato salad as authentic food, 124

power in identity work, 123

Price, George Cadle, 26

price increases due to foreigners, 90, 190–92

produce vendors, 100; procurement strategies of, 106–8

professional chefs and national cuisine, 220

professional cuisine, 11, 171; building on home cooking, 172; and haute cuisine in France, 185–87; in Placencia, 193–95

projection of self, concept of, 57–58

Pronk, Rob, 193

public-private dichotomy of cooking, 171–73

public-private divide, 178; female cooks bridging the, 174–77; tour operators and guides bridging through home-cooked foods, 183

public sphere as site of tourist food experience, 174–77

pumpkin, 218

racialization: of foreigners, 90; and hegemonic nationalism, 137–39, 163

INDEX 271

racism against Seine Bight Garifuna people, 14, 154
rainforest of Belize, 229
Ran's Travel Lodge, 24
Ray, Krishendu, 110
real estate industry, 31
recado, 151, 229, 232; definition of, 235
reductionism in Belizean restaurant food, 195–98
Reeser, Douglas, 80
refried beans as Belizean food, 79–80
Reisinger, Yvette, 51, 219
ReMax (real-estate company), 26
representation of self, 115
reputation-building activities and Creole economics, 126, 127
research methods, 5–6, 115. *See also* participant observation
research participants in categorization of Belizean food, 141–47
restaurant, definition of, 93
restaurant Kriol food, 192, 216, 219
restaurants: creole foods served in, 169; immigrants influence on, 110–13; representing different forms of localness, 86–88; tourist expectations of locally owned, 71–76
retirees in Placencia, 89
Reynolds, Kwame, 228
rice and beans, 75–76, 195; guidebooks listing of, 71; as home-cooked food served to tourists, 181–82; tourist expectations of as iconic dish, 78–79
Riversdale, 12, 14
Robert's Grove (all-inclusive resort), 29, 30

Rodriguez, Manuel, 15
root crops. *See* ground food
roucou. *See* recado
royal rat, eating of, 58
Rum Point Inn, 24, 27

Salazar, Noel, 51, 55, 67, 69
Salvadoran food in Belize, 80
samat. *See* culantro, definition of
Sammells, Clare, 6, 48, 56, 69, 85–86, 200, 208, 221
San Pedro Scoop (blog), 92
Santa Cruz, 96
Saveur (culinary magazine), 50, 208
seafood: availability during high tourism season, 28; decline of the industry, 24; importance of in diet, 17; informal channels for purchase of, 106; seasonal availability of, 199; tourist expectations for, 75, 78
Seahorse pier, 31
sea meat, 16; definition of, 236
Sea Spray Hotel, 24, 25, 27
sea turtles, 42
seaweed: as Belizean food, 149, 211; Placencia Fishing Cooperative's farming project, 211
Seine Bight Village, 12, 13, 14; tension with Placencia Village, 154
self-branding, 116, 130–31
self-commodification, 115; in Creole economics, 126, 128–29; definition of, 116; tour guides practicing, 120–25
September Celebrations, 238n16
serre, 78, 154, 201; definition of, 236
sexual stamina and performance, food associated with, 232
Shepard, Robert, 48, 55

signature foods, 76, 196
Silk Grass, 28
Skinner, Jonathan, 48, 51, 69
Slow Food Movement, 11
Sluder, Lan, 91
socio-economic class: and identity work, 129–30; influencing food perceptions, 63
sociological research on tourism development, 92
Sonny's Resort, 24, 27
Sotheby's (real-estate company), 26
Southern Environmental Association, 43
smuggling of foods, 106–7
snorkeling, 27, 50
spaghetti and meatballs, 157
Spang, Lyra, and positionality of, 3–5
Spanish food culture: category of, 163; in Placencia, 98–99
Spanish-speaking immigrants in Belize: as demographic majority, 138; motivations for relocating, 89; role of foodways, 98–100; influencing hegemonic nationalism, 137
special order requests, 109–13
smugglers of foreign foods, 107
staff lunch, 197
"Staged Authenticity: Arrangements of Social Space in Tourist Settings" (MacCannell), 121
stagnation stage of the tourism-area life cycle, 92
Staines, Jeannie, 200, 207, 208
stew fish, 201; definition of, 236
street food in Placencia, 174–77
substitution of food, 146
Sutherland, Anne, 1, 27, 97

sweet corn biscuit. *See* chu'uk kwa, definition of
sweets, 169
synthetic nationalism, 137

tacari chicken, 154, 155, 169; definition of, 236
taco stands, 98–100; competition of, 99
Taiwanese farmers in Belize, 211
tamales, 145, 169, 175; as Belizean food in home cooking, 150
tamalitos, 145–46; definition of, 236
Taste of Belize, 50, 174, 207, 208
Thai cuisine, 214
Thanks Giving (American) dinners in Placencia, 108
Theodossopoulos, Dimitrios, 48, 51, 69
Tlingut tour guides, 120, 123
tortilla factory, 98, 100
tortillas: sold in Chinese-owned grocery stores, 100. *See also* corn tortillas
tour food, 181
tour guides: cooking, 127; professionalization of, 27–28; self-commodification by, 120–25. *See also* tour operators
Tourism and the Power of Otherness (Di Giovine and Picard), 57
tourism-area life cycle, 92–93
tourism areas: culinary pride in, 211; identity work in, 115; life cycle of, 92
tourism, 1, 47; advertising, 49; code-switching and, 115; cuisine development, 58; development of, 14; ethnography of, 1; government

support of, 27; informal markets of, 105; marine tours, 43; repeat customers, 93; role of in post-colonial cuisines, 8–10
tourism imaginaries, 48, 51–52, 57, 239n2; expectations shaped by, 69–76; modernist, 60; seeking authenticity, 121–23
tourism impact: on Belizean cuisine, 217; on cross-cultural consciousness, 8, 119–20; on food prices, 112; on Placencia food scene, 80–84, 166, 221–22
tourism industry, 27, 31, 48; chefs and bartenders in, 50; code-switching in, 115, 132; Creole economics in, 126–33; frontline personnel in, 115, 116, 117, 119, 120, 123–34, 132, 220; host gaze in, 51; self-commodification in, 120–25; staged authenticity in, 121–23
tourism marketing: compared to cultural marketing, 85; Creole Gial Guava Jelly as example of, 130–31; culturally framed strategies, 168; and food promotion, 166–67
tourism policy, 26–28
tourism typologies, 52–55; adventure continuum, 53, 56; authenticity continuum, 53–54; categories of, 54–55; emic perspective on, 52, 54
tourist expectations about food, 69–76. *See also* tourism imaginaries
tourist experiences, 57; home-cooking as insight into Belizean culture, 183
tourist foodie category of food tourist, 54, 64, 85
tourist gaze, 5, 9, 48, 51, 57, 58–59, 62, 67, 68, 101, 112, 122, 123–25, 132, 217, 219, 220, 223; implications for cuisine, 84–88; tour guides and, 122. *See also* host gaze
touristic-cosmopolitan cuisines, 48
Tourist Imaginaries: Anthropological Approaches (Salazar and Graburn), 69
tourist impressions of Belizean cuisine, 61–63
tourists to Belize: contact with Belizeans, 53; interests in food, 47–50, 215; interviews of, 49–50, 56; planning and research by, 70
tour operators, and serving of home-cooked food, 181–85
Traveler's Inn, 24
TripAdvisor reviews, 70, 128
Trubek, A.B., 162, 185–86
Turner, Victor, 57
Turtle Inn, 30
turtle meat. *See* sea meat, definition of

United Black Association for Development (UBAD), 140
United Fruit Company, 238n6
United States, emigration to, 35. *See also* immigrants: from North America
Urry, John, 51, 61, 67, 58, 219–20

vacation as ritual, 57
vanilla locally produced, 211
vegetables: lack of in Placencia diet, 18; seasonal availability of, 199. *See also* fruits
Vietnamese cuisine, 214

waha leaf (*Calathea lutea*): cooking with, 234, 235; definition of, 236
Wendy's (restaurant), 30, 79
Westby, Abner, 15
wheat flour–based Kriol foods, 100
white-flour-eating as a cultural identifier, 98
wild palm heart, 218
wiliks/whilks/whelks, , 201; definition of, 236
Wilk, Richard, 5, 6, 55, 118, 136, 137, 162, 167, 181, 187, 197, 204, 205, 207, 211
Williams, Radiance, 177, 178–81
Williams-Forson, Psyche, 123
Wilson, Peter, 241n2
women: and culinary heritage, 147; and fishing, 44; home-cooked food served on tours by, 181; operating food businesses, 127–28; promoting Belizean cuisine through microenterprises, 174–77; as tour guides, 28; work opportunities in tourism for, 35. *See also* female chefs; public-private divide: female cooks bridging the
World Heritage Site, 43
World War II and effect on Belize, 18–19

Yearwood Properties, 26
Yucatec in Belize, 139

Zimmern, Andrew, 56, 78